MUSIC IN THE MIDDLE AGES

A REFERENCE GUIDE

SUZANNE LORD

GREENWOOD PRESS
Westport, Connecticut • London

Library of Congress Cataloging-in-Publication Data

Lord, Suzanne, 1946-
  Music in the middle ages : a reference guide / Suzanne Lord.
    p. cm.
  Includes bibliographical references and index.
  ISBN 978–0–313–33884–7 (alk. paper)
  1. Music—500-1400—History and criticism I. Title.
  ML172.L67 2008
  780.9'02—dc22   2008020717

British Library Cataloguing in Publication Data is available.

Library of Congress Catalog Card Number: 2008020717
ISBN: 978–0–313–33884–7

First published in 2008

Greenwood Press, 88 Post Road West, Westport, CT 06881
An imprint of Greenwood Publishing Group, Inc.
www.greenwood.com

Printed in the United States of America

The paper used in this book complies with the
Permanent Paper Standard issued by the National
Information Standards Organization (Z39.48–1984).

10 9 8 7 6 5 4 3 2 1

CONTENTS

Contents

PREFACE

This book is intended for the general reader who is curious about music and its development between the years 1000–1450 A.D., and the world in which it was written and performed. It is not intended to be a scholarly tome. Although there were, as in any era, many solutions to questions of notation and performance, this book will deal with the most prevalent of the time. And as a final caution, this book will not be dealing with two systems that were actually the more sophisticated musics of the time: those of Byzantium and Islam.

It is difficult to deal with an area the size of Europe over a span of 450 years. To help the reader, this book first presents a general background of the main events affecting the continent and the effects that they had on music in general. A chapter follows describing the foremost institution within which European music theory and practice were developed—the Church—and the role of music within it. The subsequent chapters delve more deeply into the development of music in various areas of Europe. Because of this format, there is a certain need to move back and forth in time. If a reference is made to something already mentioned, the readers will be referred to the relevant chapter to refresh their memory.

Also, to help the reader, areas of Europe are loosely referred to by their present-day names. However, one must remember that words such as "France," "Italy," "Germany," and even "England" are really misnomers in a medieval context. This is because what the reader now knows as a continent divided neatly into unified countries was, in the Middle Ages, a patchwork of city-states, principalities, fiefdoms, and occasional republics. These were bound in two ways: (1) a system of reciprocal responsibility known as Feudalism and (2) the Christian religion.

One must remember that during the Middle Ages, the European continent was overwhelmingly Roman Catholic. There were Jewish communities and (particularly in Spain) some Islamic areas. But there were no Protestants. So for the most part a person of the time and place of this book would either be a Roman Catholic, a pagan diehard, or a heretic.

A WORD ABOUT COLLECTIONS

There are a few general words to look for when considering collections of music from the Middle Ages. Those words are: chansonniere, codex, liederbuch, and manuscript. These words show up in books about Middle Ages music time and time again, but what do they mean?

CHANSONNIÈRE

Chansonnières are collections of chansons (French secular songs), usually put together as the favorite works of a private patron. These little books (many were the size of postcards) began appearing in the twelfth century and were produced continuously throughout the Middle Ages. Passed down from generation to generation, some chansonnières survived fires, floods, wars, and other catastrophes. Those that are still with us have kept alive many works—poetry, music, or both—and the names of composers whose identity might otherwise have been lost. Although the name implies that only chansons were collected, these books also contain other works such as monophonic songs of troubadours and trouvères, sacred works such as motets, and even occasional dance tunes. Also, because French culture was so pan-European in the Middle Ages, chansonnières can be found in many areas besides France. As a result, lyrics may be in Latin, German, English, Italian, or Dutch as well as French.

LIEDERBUCH

A liederbuch is simply the German word for songbook. These collections of poems, and sometimes polyphonically treated music to go with them, were a bit later than the French chansonnières and go back only to the fifteenth century. The *Lochamer Liederbuch* and *Glogauer Liederbuch* are the most well-known. Scholars believe that, as with the French chansonnières, the occasional pieces of music printed without text were most likely played by an instrument or group of instruments.

CODEX

A codex is something more generic. The word is Latin and simply indicates a bound book with separate pages, such as the one you are reading, as opposed to a scroll or wax tablet, two other writing media used in ancient times. Wax tablets were meant to be reused like a chalkboard; paper (papyrus or parchment in ancient times) was used for writings that needed saving. But imagine having to find something specific by unrolling one side of a scroll and rolling up the other side of a sheet that might be 30 feet long! One can certainly see how turning pages would be an improvement, and it is no mystery why the codex rapidly overtook the scroll. The plural of *codex* is *codices*.

MANUSCRIPT

A manuscript is simply something that was (or is) handwritten, as opposed to being printed. Until the invention of movable type in 1450, almost all writings were manuscripts, whether they were in the form of a scroll, codex, or other medium. In the Middle Ages, manuscripts were likely to be "illuminated"—that is, decorated with some sort of artwork in addition to words and/or music. The art might be anything from a highly decorated first letter on each page, to elaborate edging, scenes of daily life, and even flights of fancy showing imaginary beasts and instruments that never actually existed.

CHAPTER 1

THE MIDDLE AGES: GENERAL BACKGROUND

To understand the Middle Ages and their music, it is necessary to understand the world that preceded them: the late Roman Empire.

THE DECLINE AND FALL OF THE ROMAN EMPIRE

Today, Rome is still one of the world's great cities, but once it was a byword for the entire civilized world. "All roads lead to Rome" was meant literally in an Empire that stretched from Northern Africa in the south to Scotland in the north, the Atlantic Ocean in the west, and Armenia and Syria in the east. To be a "Roman" was to be plugged into its vast network of resources and accepted as a civilized human being—a person of worth.

But to manage an area that size from a relatively small base of native leaders— i.e., Romans born in the vicinity of Rome—required adjustments. Foreign-born people who had shown leadership skills or had proved themselves useful to the Empire became legal Roman citizens without ever having seen the actual city. On the other hand, some Roman soldiers were based at outposts for years on end and either had their Roman wives living with them and raised their families far from Rome or intermarried with locals. As generations passed, loyalty to Rome as a cultural center waned.

Moreover, Roman society was fueled by a large, dissatisfied work force—slave labor. Conquered people were always subject to enslavement, and this created an ever-growing undercurrent of rebellion. Sometimes, as in the famous case of Spartacus, this feeling boiled over into outright rebellion—in his case brutally crushed. But in all times, it meant an underclass waiting for the chance to rid themselves of their overlords.

The end of the Roman Empire did not come as a tidal wave. It was rather a gradual leakage that weakened the forces holding back the non-Roman world. Emperors came and went who were born nowhere near Rome. From what is now France came Emperor Caracalla (211–217), who was born in what is now Lyon, and Carus (282–283), who was born in Narbo, now Narbonne. Emperor Trajan (98–117) was born in Spain, Emperor Decius (249–251) in what is today Hungary, and Aurelian (270–275) and Probus (276–282) in an area then called Sirmium, which is present-day Serbia. Emperor Maximinus (235–238) was from Thrace, which is now Bulgaria. Claudius II (268–270), Diocletian (284–305), and Valentinian I (364–375) came from present-day Croatia. Elagabalus (218–222) was born in Syria, Alexander Severus (222–235) in Phoenicia, Philip the Arab (244–249) near present-day Damascus, Septimius Severus (193–211) in modern-day Libya, and Aemilianus (253) from an area that is now Tunisia.

THE SPLIT INTO EASTERN AND WESTERN EMPIRES

After the death of Claudius II in 270 A.D. Rome underwent a terrible time when the army forced their choice of Emperor. These Emperors, known as the "barracks Emperors," were put up and taken down like laundry. Between the years 275 and 276 A.D., Rome had four Emperors in a row! The last one "ruled" from 284 to 285, but a real ruler took over in 284 and held the post for twenty years. This was Emperor Diocletian.

Diocletian is most famously known for throwing Christians to the lions, but in his day he was known for his imperial reforms. For one thing, he realized that this far-flung empire was too much for a single Emperor to control, so he split the Empire into two parts—Eastern and Western—for which he drew up a complicated system of succession based on appointment. Both the Eastern and the Western Emperors were called *Augusti* and were the administrators of their share of the Empire. Their subcommanders were *Caesares* and handled military matters. In principle, when an *Augustus* died or abdicated, the *Caesar* would become the next *Augustus* and would then choose a *Caesar* of his own. This would ensure a smooth line of succession. Furthermore, every *Augustus* would have already had experience in the field as a military commander (and the support of the army!). Things never went quite so smoothly, however. These posts did not change in a synchronized fashion, and the double line of Emperors is quite complicated.

Adding to the general confusion, after sharing the rule for some years, Constantine I (The Great) took all the power back in 324 A.D. In 328, this same Emperor, most famous for including Christianity as one of Rome's official religions and personally converting to it in 312, took Rome's government offices eastward and set them up in a city he built and named after himself—Constantinople. This city would evolve into the capital of the Byzantine (Eastern) Empire and the head of the Eastern Orthodox Christian Church.

The division of the Roman Empire continued, and power changed hands with dizzying speed and complexity. Sometimes a single strong ruler might take over two or more parts of the Empire, and occasionally one person took it all. Because of this constant changeover, at various times the overall Roman Empire had one Emperor, sometimes two, and other times three or four.

The Eastern Empire retained its Greco-Roman roots and the continuity of its history, government, and cultural institutions. So it grew, while the remnants of the Western Roman Empire were in terrible flux. The Western capital was variously Rome, Milan, and Ravenna. It was considered a substate of the real power, which was now in Constantinople. At one time it was even linked with northern Africa as a single prefecture.

DEATH OF AN EMPIRE

The city of Rome was ultimately left without a government and bereft of its leading citizenry. Much of the power and initiative in the Western Empire during its last years was wielded not by Romans but by Germanic-speaking tribes such as the Goths. In 410 A.D. Rome was sacked by the Visigoth (western Goth) tribe, headed by Alaric. What was left of the life of the Western Roman Empire was a few decades full of in-fighting, assassinations, and puppet rulers. By 476 A.D., the last Western Roman Emperor was a boy named Romulus Augustulus. When he was deposed by Odoacer, a Visigoth, the collapse of the Western Roman Empire was complete.

The year 476 brought to Europe the era often called the Dark Ages today. Although civilized life was not entirely destroyed, it was seriously derailed. One of the reasons that Rome had been able to keep such a large empire running was because of its excellent network of roads. Not only were they well-built and well-maintained, but Romans took such practical measures as cutting back roadside shrubbery to prevent attacks from highway robbers. Now most of those roads were in disrepair and many were impassable. The regrowth of plants broke up smooth passages and slowly made travel harder and harder, while shrubbery regrowth around even the most durable roads provided cover for robbers and made travel a dangerous affair.

But even in its death throes, the West enjoyed a sort of "twilight" before the lights went out. The Ostrogothic (eastern Gothic) king Theodoric (493–526) fought the Visigoths and solidified his power in the Italian peninsula. He set up his capital in Ravenna and kept it as civilized as possible, even though the real power was still in Constantinople.

THEODORIC IN RAVENNA

Actually, Theodoric had acquired his polish in Constantinople, where he had been raised as a child hostage—a common practice with children of rulers to ensure that (a) one's parents would not start a breakaway state, and (b) the next generation would have a thorough education in the ways of Rome-East. Having been raised in a civilized environment, Theodoric was in favor of order, law, and culture. He repaired and rebuilt his area's roads and bridges, and paid attention to city infrastructure. He put Roman law to work and stopped robbers from pillaging travelers in his territory. He also supported the arts. So for a moment—an important one for the later history of the Middle Ages and its music—the downward spiral of the Dark Ages was halted at dusk.

BOETHIUS AND CASSIODORUS

Among the nobles in Theodoric's court was one named Anicius Manlius Torquatus Severinus Boethius. As his long string of names implies, he came from an old and distinguished upper-class Roman family. Following his patrician ancestors' footsteps, Boethius was a politician. He rose to a position of counselor in Theodoric's court and was widely respected for his learning. During his lifetime, Boethius wrote several works. One—*De Institutione Musica*—concerned music.

Boethius wrote that music was one of the "liberal arts," considered worthy to be studied by free men—that is, men who did not have to work for a living. Like the ancient Greeks from whom he learned, Boethius believed that music and numbers were closely connected. For us, mathematics is a tool that helps us perform tasks, from balancing a checkbook to steering a space probe. But to the ancient world, the fact that numbers could represent the orderly rotation of the stars in the heavens and the seasons on earth was profoundly significant. It meant that God was in charge, watching from a higher plane and guarding against universal chaos, and it also meant that humans could understand something of God. Because musical intervals could be expressed in mathematical terms through the study of acoustics, music was honored as "number made audible."[1]

Steeped in Greco-Roman tradition, Boethius had read the music theories of ancient Greece. In his work he wrote both their theories and his own. He believed that there were three kinds of music. In order of increasing value, they were *instrumentalis*, *mundana*, and *caelestis*.

Musica instrumentalis meant music that people can hear. Following the ancient Greek thinker Pythagoras, Boethius used a one-stringed instrument called a monochord to show how musical intervals represented pure number ratios (i.e., ratios of string lengths for Boethius, ratios of sound wave frequencies for us). Boethius showed that a unison represented a 1:1 ratio; a fourth, 4:3; a fifth, 3:2; and an octave, 2:1. These intervals were called "consonant" (sounding together) because they sounded agreeable to the ear, and they were called "perfect" because, using these ratios, they could be repeated every time with scientific accuracy. These names affected which intervals were considered better than others in the Middle Ages. Even today a fourth and a fifth are called "perfect."

Musica mundana went beyond what the ear could hear, to embrace human physical and spiritual beauty. Physical beauty showed in the balance and symmetry of external and internal organs. Spiritual beauty was the relationship between body and soul, shown in such traits as intelligence and love. Boethius taught that these relationships, too, are a form of music. Although this music cannot be heard with the human ear, it is nonetheless felt.

Musica caelestis was the harmony of the world and the heavens. This, too, cannot be heard with the human ear, but it can be seen in the orderly regularity of seasons, months, years, and movements of the heavens. It is a reflection of the ancient Greek idea of Music of the Spheres—the idea that heavenly bodies, moving regularly across the sky, perform a kind of music, although we cannot hear it.

Boethius counted music as a mathematical discipline, but maintained that it was different from others. Pure mathematics, he explained, pursues truth. Music does that too, but it is also related to morality. He agreed with the ancient Greek philosopher Plato that different kinds, or modes, of music could affect the personalities of human beings in different ways.

The modes to which Boethius referred were different relationships of pitches, like our major and minor scales, which were believed to bring out different feelings in human beings. Some modes aroused honest and upstanding sentiments. Others were effeminate or thought to bring out beastly behavior. Although this idea may sound strange, remember that even today, different modes are considered appropriate for different feelings and occasions. A comic song or a march for a parade is likely to be in a major key, whereas music for a funeral procession is more likely to be minor. Arguments have been made in every age about music having good or bad effects on society. For instance, many on both sides of the debate about the considerable changes in American social attitudes and values from the 1950s onward have maintained that rock and roll was a major player in promoting those changes.

Boethius also claimed that there were three classes of musicians. The lowest class were instrumentalists, because they were servants to their instruments. Vocalists were better, but they were still really concerned with their poetry. The third class—and in his opinion, the only *true* musicians—were learned theorists who could judge the work of instruments and songs.

Important as he was in his own time, Boethius became immensely more important to the music of the Middle Ages. During the worst part of the Dark Ages, much knowledge from the past was lost to the Western world. But Boethius's writings— and thus a little of the ancient Greek thought about music—survived. Boethius's writing thus became the main source of reference for musicians of the Middle Ages and provided an underpinning for its musical evolution.

Boethius's life did not end well. Boethius was accused of participating in a plot against King Theodoric and thrown into prison. In 524 he was executed for treason.

Flavius Cassiodorus Magnus Aurelius Senator was another noble in Theodoric's court. Cassiodorus was a contemporary of Boethius's, but a bit younger. He too was from an ancient patrician family that had been in government service for generations. Cassiodorus was a politician for about thirty years. In fact, when Boethius fell out of favor, Cassiodorus was picked to take over his post. Not only was Cassiodorus never executed, but he lived to the remarkable old age of 95! He retired in his fifties and spent his last forty years teaching and writing in a monastery. Between the years 550 and 562, Cassiodorus, like Boethius, wrote a book about music that became a source for music theory in the Middle Ages. In his book, *Institutiones*, he called music the "second part of mathematics."[2]

Cassiodorus also divided music into three parts, but in a different way than Boethius had. For Cassiodorus, music consisted of harmonics, rhythmics, and metrics. Harmonics concerns the relationship between high and low sounds. Rhythmics tells us what words sound well together—or do not. Metrics is the choice of various meters (what is usually meant by "rhythm" today). He also classified instruments into three categories: percussion, wind, and tension. Percussion and wind instruments are those that are struck or blown into, respectively. Tension instruments are stringed instruments, because the sound comes from the tension of the string. Musicologists still use forms of these categories. Cassiodorus named fifteen modes, explained the function of each, and went into an intensive study of their relationships. He also recommended certain ancient Greek and Roman theorists to read, whose names would have otherwise been lost to us.

Cassiodorus's writing was not as influential as Boethius's, but was still an important source of knowledge for the Middle Ages, and helped form opinions about what music was, its purpose, and how it should develop.

THE DARK AGES

After Theodoric, the court in Ravenna began to fall apart. The Byzantine Emperor Justinian I did not want the Western Church or the Ostrogothic kings to have any independent power. He invaded Italy and conquered Ravenna, which became merely an Italian branch of the Byzantine government.

This was the darkest hour for Europe. The breakdown of travel and communication caused areas to be cut off from one another. Instead of agreeing on common laws, customs, and religious practices, people in different individual pockets of territory broke away and lived independently. The Papacy of the Western Church was still in Rome, but the city was in ruins. When Alaric overran Rome in 410, its population had been about 800,000. By 552 that number was about 30,000. The Roman population went up in subsequent years, but only because of refugees from other invasions. In fact, by the late 500s, most of the populace was not even living inside the city walls any more. The old city area within the walls was known as the *disabitato*—the "disinhabited" place. The people instead centered around Tiber Island, the *abitato*—the "inhabited" place.

THE RISE OF THE EARLY CHRISTIAN CHURCH

While the Roman Empire was crumbling—or perhaps, partially, as a result of it—a religious sect had been gathering followers throughout Rome's Near Eastern and Northern African colonies. Initially they were one sect among many within Judaism, claiming that the object of their adoration—Jesus of Nazareth—had been the Messiah, or Anointed One, hoped for by the Jewish community. But by late in the first century A.D. they had evolved into a separate religion, and there were believers throughout the Empire, even in Rome itself.

The Roman Empire incorporated many, many religions. And as long as people obeyed Roman law and served in its armed forces, they could basically worship as they saw fit. In fact, the military's favorite object of worship was Mithras, an import from Persia! The trouble with Christians, as followers of Jesus called themselves (after *Christos*, the Greek translation of Messiah), was that they refused to obey Roman laws and customs that violated their religious boundaries—including military oaths and rituals that involved worshiping the Emperor or the gods. This made the Christians useless to the state, and potentially dangerous. So, for some time, Christians were an object of persecution.

There is very little documentation of music in Christian antiquity. From their Jewish roots, the early Christians had inherited the idea of a religiously based calendar, with one day each week set aside for worship, and certain other days set apart for a variety of religious reasons. Worship services included Biblical readings and the singing of the psalms as instruments of praise. Early Christians had communal meals (called *agape*, "love feast") followed by the Eucharist (Greek for "thanksgiving") or Communion, when they consumed what they believed to be the body and blood of Jesus in the form of consecrated bread and wine. At first the meal was for everyone who wanted to learn about Christianity, but the Eucharist was reserved for believers only. By the third century A.D. these two were melded into one loosely developed service. Apparently, music was sung. An early source from the second century wrote, "the Greeks use Greek . . . , the Romans Latin . . . , and every one prays and sings praises to God as best he can in his mother tongue."[3]

From early times, vocal music was the only kind of music favored in Christian worship. Instrumental music had too many associations with the old, but still smoldering pagan religions. St. Jerome, who translated the Bible into Latin, wrote to one woman who had asked for advice about raising her daughter: "Let her be deaf to the sound of the organ, and not know even the uses of the pipe, the lyre, and the cithara." But the Church Fathers wrestled with the many Biblical references to instruments. Ultimately they decided that these were not real instruments—they were only symbolic! One wrote that the trumpet symbolized "the efficacy of the Word of God," the tympanon (a type of drum) was "the destruction of lust," and cymbals represented "the eager soul enamored of Christ."[4]

When the Emperor Constantine passed the Edict of Milan in 313, recognizing Christianity as a state religion (and later made it *the* state religion), the Church came out of hiding. Instead of holding services in private homes or in catacombs underground, they began building houses of worship. The state of music in the church began to mature as well. Singing began to be transferred from the congregation to the priest and to trained singers who learned more difficult and complex music in *scholae cantorum*, or schools of singers.

After Constantine took the Roman government eastward, church music's evolution took a giant leap forward. The use of psalm singing was especially popular there. St. John Chrysostom (345–407), the Bishop of Constantinople, wrote: "When God saw that many men were lazy, and gave themselves only with difficulty to spiritual reading, He wished to make it easy for them, and added the melody to the Prophet's words, that all being rejoiced by the charm of the music, should sing hymns to Him with gladness."[5]

But the East-West division of government made religious unity a big problem. While the East added to its culture, the West lost a lot—including the everyday use of Greek and the knowledge gathered by ancient Greece. What was left was an often imperfect Latin translation of Greek learning. Because of barbarian invasions, knowledge was ripped from the secular arena and survived only in the one coherent institution left—the Church.

In the mid-300s, St. Basil the Great (c. 330–379) founded Christian monasticism. The founding of monasteries became an important source of preserving what learning there was in the Dark Ages, and monasteries became the West's libraries and foundations for the universities of the Middle Ages.

St. Basil was in favor of church vocal music: "Oh! The wise invention of the teacher who contrived that while we were singing we should at the same time learn something useful."[6] But he frowned greatly on instruments: "Of the arts necessary to life which furnish a concrete result there is carpentry, which produces the chair; architecture, the house; shipbuilding, the ship; tailoring, the garment; forging, the blade. Of useless arts there is harp playing, dancing, flute playing, of which, when the operation ceases, the result disappears with it. And indeed, according to the word of the apostle, the result of these is destruction."[7]

St. Augustine (354–430) was more deeply divided about church music and its seductive beauty. St. Augustine was born in Numidia in Africa (now part of Algeria and Tunisia). His father was pagan, his mother a Christian. He was a wild youth, especially in the big city of Carthage. At first he considered Christianity just another superstition among many. Then he met the future St. Ambrose (see Chapter 2). Augustine was converted to Christianity and personally baptized by Ambrose. Augustine wrote about this in his *Confessions,* which shows how deeply music affected him and his decision: "The tears flowed from me when I heard your hymns and canticles, for the sweet singing of your Church moved me deeply. The music surged in my ears, truth seeped into my heart, and my feelings of devotion over-flowed, so that the tears streamed down. But they were tears of gladness."[8]

St. Augustine wrote a dozen books regarding music. Still, he felt that at times he enjoyed music too much for his own good. He admitted that it was difficult for him to ignore the purely musical and concentrate only on the message in church music. He tried to keep his mind on track, but his senses took over in spite of his good intentions. He felt that for some people music in church was all right, but, like a recovering substance abuser, he realized that he was not one of them because his enjoyment was out of control. "I am inclined to approve of the custom of singing in church, in order that by indulging the ears weaker spirits may be inspired with feelings of devotion. Yet when I find the singing itself more moving than the truth which it conveys, I confess that this is a grievous sin, and at those times I would prefer not to hear the singer. . . . I beg you, O Lord my God, to look upon me and listen to me. Have pity on me and heal me, for you see that I have become a problem to myself, and this is the ailment from which I suffer."[9]

This ambivalence about the uses and abuses of church music would be a source of great debate throughout the Dark and Middle Ages, and St. Augustine was often brought up as a source—for both pro and con.

CHARLEMAGNE AND THE HOLY ROMAN EMPIRE

During the darkest period of the Dark Ages, two strong ethnic groups were left in western Europe—the Goths (both Visi- and Ostro-) and the Franks. In 732 the Frankish leader Charles Martel (i.e., Charles the Hammer) beat back Islamic armies that were invading Europe from Africa through Spain. Although he ruled like a king, Charles held only the office of "mayor of the palace" under the Frankish king. So did Charles's son, Pepin the Short, but Pepin wanted the real thing. His king, Childeric, was a "do-nothing" who took all the honors while Pepin did all the work. Pepin sent an emissary of friends to the Pope, who agreed that Pepin should be King instead. Childeric was deposed, and Pepin was crowned King of the Franks. In appreciation, Pepin not only defended Rome from its enemies—particularly a tribe called the Lombards ("Longbeards," after whom Lombardy is named)—but gave the Pope a large area of Italy for himself. This area became the Papal States, of which a tiny remnant—the Vatican—remains a separate state to this day. With the power of the Church as well as the power of the sword behind him, Pepin's tribe became the strongest in Europe. Pepin died in 768. He had two sons, Charles and Carloman. They ruled together until Carloman died. That left Charles, who would rule for the next 45 years and would become known as Charles the Great, or Charlemagne.

The realm Charles inherited was a huge, extremely disorganized area. But he was a brilliant soldier, and he absorbed the lesson of his father: that the combined power of the sword and the cross was practically unbeatable in the Europe of his time. He set up a win-win situation. If the Church would back his earthly policies, he would enforce the Church's policies. Armed on both fronts, Charles proposed a new empire based on the old Roman one. The Roman Empire, he reasoned, had not been all bad; at least it had had a central authority and a single set of laws throughout its vast territory. Charlemagne wanted that stability again, but under Christianity. Claiming that the office of Western Emperor had not been ended, but merely suspended, in 476 with the death of Romulus Augustulus, Charlemagne declared himself the next Emperor, within a Christian, or "Holy," Roman Empire. The Holy Roman Empire (Figure 1.1) remained a force in Europe until World War I.

Figure 1.1 This map of the Holy Roman Empire during the first half of the thirteenth century shows the fractional nature of Europe in the Middle Ages. Courtesy of Facts on File, Inc. Historical Maps I, Revised Edition © 2002.

THE FEUDAL SYSTEM

Taking his cue from Church hierarchy and his father, Charlemagne set out to standardize his empire. A stable society evolved, based on reciprocal responsibility between higher and lower ranks, known as the feudal system. The feudal system was a pyramid, with the Emperor at the top. Under him were kings who received their kingdoms from the Emperor and were directly responsible to him. Under the kings were lesser nobles: dukes, counts (or earls), barons. Then came their knights—their armored and mounted warriors. Each noble received land from his lord at the next higher level, to whom he owed military service. At the lowest level of nobility the lord of a single estate, or manor, ruled over the peasants on that land. The feudal system became the overwhelming form of government during the Middle Ages (even in countries such as England that were not part of the Holy Roman Empire). Everyone, from Emperor to slave, belonged to one of its categories and lived their lives according to its precepts.

Most people clearly see that the peasants were taking orders from everyone, civilians from the military, nobles from the kings, and the kings from the Emperor. What is not so often remembered—and what made the society so stable—is that the responsibility went both ways. The Emperor had to look out for the interests of the kings. The kings had to make sure that their nobles were prospering. The nobles had to supply the knights. The knights were supposed to protect the civilian population. And nobody was supposed to take the peasants for granted. Meanwhile, the charitable and hospitable works of the monasteries and churches provided a social safety net. As long as this system functioned fairly well, Europe was not going to backslide into its darkest hour again.

With a stable society regained, trade routes reopened. Agriculture re-established itself. Cities grew. The arts began to flourish. Although Charlemagne himself could hardly read or write, he promoted an education system. Monasteries looked over the education of outlying areas, while in the cities cathedral schools opened.

LIFE UNDER FEUDALISM

If one word could describe European life in the Middle Ages, that word would be stratification. There were definite layers to society, and virtually everyone belonged to one of those layers. Put into simplistic terms, everyone in feudal society was responsible *to* someone else and also responsible *for* someone else.

The Emperor and the kings were at the top of the stack. They held vast lands and had immense power. They could call up armies to fight other kings or other domestic or foreign enemies; they could lead campaigns to lands as far away as present-day Israel. They made the final decisions on the most important court cases. In theory they answered only to God. In real life, however, they had the most people to handle and, as cash rather than agricultural produce became more important in the Middle Ages, the most people to pay. Their campaigns cost a fortune, and if they were captured, their ransom cost another fortune. During a Crusade in 1250, King Louis of France had to pay a million gold bezants to buy his freedom from Egypt. Also, part of their prestige involved *largesse,* or conspicuous giveaways at certain times of the year, such as Christmas and Easter, and also for special occasions, such as a royal marriage. During those times royalty was expected to be ridiculously generous to the huge amount of people involved. Even peasants got clothing and a good meal. Also, in the real world there were weak kings and overly strong barons, absentee lords, and even peasant rebellions. In addition, if a King was really unpopular, he could be deposed, assassinated, or both (as was Edward II of England).

A great noble such as a duke received his land as a grant from a king or the Emperor. This land was known as a *fief* (through French, from Latin *feodum*, from which we get the word "feudal") and was held *for* the crown. The noble swore *homage* to the crown and promised to answer the call if the crown needed him. In the early Middle Ages great lords were pledged to serve a set amount of days for military service as knights. Later, as royalty needed cold cash more than people to feed, the military obligation changed to a yearly monetary fee. The lords raised that fee by encouraging settlement in "chartered" towns on their lands, with the inhabitants owing a variety of rents and taxes to the lords. In return, the lords were obligated to protect people lower on the social scale. The lord also acted as a court judge, deciding cases within his fief. Lords, like kings, had big expenses. They needed armor, weapons, equipment, and horses for battles and tournaments. They also had to pay their own knightly vassals and often "bought their robes, horses and arms." The lord paid all his servants, and furthermore he had to buy the "silks, furs, and precious vessels that displayed his dignity and grandeur to the world"[10] lest he lose honor in the sight of his fellow nobles. If a lord participated in some venture such as a Crusade, he had to pay his own expenses out of pocket.

Great lords received far more land than they could comfortably govern, and so they had vassals: lesser knightly lords, who held lands granted to them by the great lords. These might include younger sons of another lord, who had noble blood but little or no land of their own. The vassals swore homage and made the same basic promise to their overlords that the overlords had made to their monarchs.

There were a great variety of layers to the non-noble strata, and those layers were different for country folk and town folk. But one class was comfortable in both areas: the lord's servants. These people usually lived in the manor house or castle and were the domestic staff. In great houses, they were not necessarily uneducated or from a lowly background. In fact, it was a mark of honor to have polite, intelligent people as servants. They did not work the land and were paid for their services.

Villeins were people who lived in villages on lands owned by a lord. They were not slaves, but they were not free either. They were bound to the land and to the lord who owned it. In the early Middle Ages they pledged part of their services to their lord. Farmers would part with a percentage of their crops; shoemakers would make a certain amount of shoes for the lord and his family. If needed, villeins could also be called up for military duty as footsoldiers.

Freemen were not bound to land or to a lord. They were more like tenant farmers. They directly rented their land wherever they could, and they worked it themselves. If they were successful, they could hire help or even pay someone else to work the land.

Serfs were in a position similar to that of villeins, but a step lower. They were bound to the land and to the lord who owned it, and they were considered part of the lord's estate much as his cattle were. Unpaid, they were allowed to live on the land in return for services that could be almost anything. Usually they would work the lord's fields for a certain amount of time, but they could also be used for building projects, hauling cargo, or anything else that required relatively unskilled labor. Serfs had patches of land that they worked independently, but they were taxed by the lords for such things as permission for a serf's daughter to marry someone on another estate.

Cotters were free, but had no land at all. They actually worked *for* serfs. Living in the fields, literally, a cotter's ambition was to become a serf and belong somewhere.

Slaves were still known in the early Middle Ages, but there were fewer of them as time went on. These people were property. Usually they were captives from a non-Christian area. It was all right for an owner to have sex with a slave, but the slave did have some rights as well. A master's child born of a slave had the rights of a legitimate child of the master, and the woman also obtained some special privileges, which might include her freedom upon the master's death. By the later Middle Ages, most slaves managed to move up the social ladder to serfdom.

Each of these classes produced music suited to their particular lives and situations. The music of the lower classes has largely been lost because it was usually improvised on the spot and never written down. By far the largest share of surviving music from the Middle Ages is religious. The Church had a vested interest in keeping track of its music, and most of those who could read and write worked for it.

THE RISE OF TOWNS

One of the key factors of the Middle Ages is the rise of towns and cities, and the emergence of a middle class. There were many types of towns: spontaneous towns and leftovers from Roman outposts; castle towns and abbey towns that grew around a protective center; towns that were directly planted by a local lord and "grown" for his profit; river and bridge towns that provided avenues for goods; walled towns ringed with a protective manmade barrier; charter towns (also known as *bastides*), which had some self-governance but was still partially responsible to a local lord; and autonomous communes, which were so ignored by their "protector" that they were for all practical purposes self-governing. There were also "multifocal" towns, where a new town sprang up next to—or inside of—an older one.

The rise of towns was an effect of the changeover from paying a feudal overlord in goods and services, to monetary payments. Towns were a great way to raise cash. Towns ran on trade, and local lords did all they could to encourage it. There were weekly markets for villagers to sell their personal produce and animals, and also fairs at certain times of the year that drew people from a larger area. Peasants who sold their wares could pay their taxes and other obligations to their overlords, who could then pay *their* overlords, creating a "trickle-up" system that worked as a rule.

THE CHURCH AND FEUDAL SOCIETY

The Church, of course, had its own organization, which could also be called feudal. Just as each great lord received a fief from his king and in turn bestowed fiefs on his vassals, each bishop received authority over his domain (called a bishopric or diocese) from the Pope and conferred authority to priests over parishes within the diocese. The superiors of orders of monks and nuns likewise answered to the Pope and gave authority over individual monasteries to abbots and abbesses; monks and nuns were bound by strict vows of obedience. Of course there were clashes within this ecclesiastical society, and corruption at the top was a source of great concern during the Middle Ages. But the larger picture shows these two feudal systems working side-by-side, sometimes in cooperation (as in the Crusades) and sometimes in spectacular opposition (as in the case of Henry II and St. Thomas Becket).

Music of the Church was almost exclusively vocal during the Middle Ages, but it is the best-preserved music of the entire period. Through Church music, which was the earliest kind of medieval music to be written down in some form or other, scholars can trace the development of notation, harmony, and theory—and, from the twelfth century on, even identify individual composers.

MAJOR EVENTS OF THE MIDDLE AGES

During the Middle Ages (roughly 1000–1450), several events overwhelmed all of Western Europe. The Crusades began fairly early in the Middle Ages and periodically rose to the fore at various times. The other three events occurred relatively late in the Middle Ages—the fourteenth century—and had devastating results. Since all of these events occurred over all of the European arena, they are dealt with individually here and should be kept in mind as a background tapestry to later chapters.

THE CRUSADES

The Crusades resulted from several simultaneous factors: Western Europe's fear of being overrun by Moslem forces, a mixed sense of religious and feudal duty (God being the ultimate Lord of any feudal system!), and the rise of knighthood and chivalry.

The basic difference between a knight and other warriors was that knights were on horseback and therefore were more mobile and occupied higher "ground" than footsoldiers. Knights could kill an enemy who found it hard to reach them; their horses' hooves could finish off a fallen wounded foe; and, in a pinch, knights could retreat quickly and then wheel around for another attack.

Knighthood became, ultimately, the highest rung on the secular feudal ladder. Even kings were also knights. The value of loyalty to one's lord was written into the precepts of knighthood. A well-trod path prepared boys of noble birth for this occupation. At around seven years of age, a boy was sent from his own home to live in another as a *page* to learn service and obedience. At around fourteen, he would become a *squire*, serving a particular knight as what we would call a "go-fer." As a squire, he learned to care for the equipment and horses of a knight, and he also trained in weaponry. Squires sometimes went into battle with their knights and sometimes lost their lives. Those who survived became knights in a ceremony that started as a simple receiving of arms, but evolved into an elaborate, deeply religious ritual that lasted for several days.

Knighthood originally developed from the need to defend European territory from invasions of groups such as Vikings and Magyars, and because of internecine warfare such as the Norman invasion of England in 1066. But during relatively peaceful times, having roving bands of armed horsemen looking for someone to fight was counterproductive! One solution was to set up contests of skill, known as tournaments. Like the rodeos of the American West, tournaments took working skills and turned them into prize-winning enterprises. This effort was quite successful, and many a poor but skillful young knight made his fortune by defeating and ransoming his betters.

Another solution was to find someone outside of the European, Christian arena to fight. In 1096 the Islamic world provided that opportunity when the Seljuk Turks captured Jerusalem from the Arabs. The latter, who had seized the Middle Eastern part of the Byzantine Empire in 634, had certainly not been Christian, but they had been relatively tolerant of other faiths and their monuments. The Seljuk Turks, on the other hand, persecuted Christians and added insult to injury by destroying places considered holy to Christendom. Eastern Christians were alarmed, and the Patriarch of Constantinople called for help from the Pope in Rome. Pope Urban II saw an opportunity to defuse internal European strife, and simultaneously send thousands of armed men to use their aggression in the name of Christianity against someone other than one another.

The first Crusade, beginning in 1099, was possibly the most successful of all and resulted in the establishment of Christian states in the East including the Kingdom of Jerusalem. The second (1147–1149) was a disaster because of poor planning and internal arguments. The third (1189–1192) was a disaster because the leaders who called it died, and their heirs could not—or would not—work together. The fourth (1202–1204) was entirely a French effort that deviated from its original mission in Egypt and actually attacked Constantinople—a Christian city! The fifth (1217–1221) was fairly successful, but it ended up at the treaty table, where the Crusaders basically got a free retreat. The sixth (1228–1229) was nicknamed the "diplomatic crusade" because Jerusalem came into Christian hands entirely by negotiation—the marriage of a German king to the heiress of the Kingdom of Jerusalem. The seventh and last crusade (1248–1254) was another disaster. King Louis IX of France (St. Louis) was captured and ransomed with a huge price tag.

Other efforts were the People's Crusade and the Children's Crusade. The former was put together during the time of the First Crusade. At least four different groups of peasants set out, called together by leaders such as Peter the Hermit and Walter the

Penniless, to help recover the Holy Land from the Turks. They were totally unprepared and had very little idea of where they were headed, but they believed that because their hearts were pure and their cause good, God would take care of them. The ones who were not captured for slaves and did not starve were quickly killed. The Children's Crusade (1212) was even more pathetic. A French shepherd boy named Stephen decided that the adults were so corrupt that God had kept the Holy Land from them. It needed the purity of a child's faith to be successful. A German child with similar feelings led a second group to join Stephen's. They headed south, feeling that when they reached the Bosporus, God would part the waters just as He had for Moses. Instead, they were snapped up by slave dealers in the thousands.

One overall result of the Crusades was to shoot holes in the feudal system. The top of the power pyramid was hit particularly hard. Many knights were killed, mostly by Moslem archers who had no qualms about shooting the horses out from under knights, who disdained such tactics as dishonorable. King Richard the Lion-hearted of England was dispatched by an arrow that went through his eyepiece. Others simply never returned. But possibly the most ruinous effect came from the enormous ransoms demanded for a leader's return. Lords and their estates went bankrupt or deeply into debt over their ransoms. The European middle class, however, made out like bandits. They made the armor, sold the horses, and loaned the money. They also used the Crusades to obtain trade routes and start import-export businesses. Ultimately, the search for new trade routes would result in the discovery of the New World.

The other important result of the Crusades was the cross-pollination of European and Islamic cultures, which affected music. From Arabic roots, Europe picked up stringed instruments such as the lute and rebec, percussion instruments such as nakers (small, portable kettledrums), and reed instruments such as the shawm and bagpipe. Scholars also claim that Arabian-style poetry traveled through occupied Spain and into southern France, where troubadours began to write—and sing—a new cross-pollinated European style of song on the theme of "courtly love" (described in Chapter 3).

THE BABYLONIAN CAPTIVITY AND THE GREAT SCHISM

Although Italy would be recognized as the center of culture during the Renaissance, during the Middle Ages, that center was France. Although there was no unified French state, some of the greatest courts and most powerful monarchs lived there. Meanwhile, Rome was a backwater, but the Vatican was still where the Pope sat, and Popes made it quite clear that since the keys to the afterlife were in the Church's hands, they were more powerful than any earthly monarch. Some monarchs disagreed.

After Philip IV (the Fair) of France (1285–1314) had a series of standoffs with two Italian Popes, he engineered the election of a Frenchman as Pope. That done, Philip had the Pope's residence moved from Rome to Avignon in southeastern France. The outraged Italians called this move the "Babylonian Captivity" (named after the deportation of the Jews from Jerusalem by the king of Babylon in what is now Iraq in 587 B.C., described in the Bible), and they endured almost 70 years (1309–1377) of exclusively French Popes who lived in France. The Church had become in effect a partisan political entity, alienating Germans, English, and Italians. But the Popes in question preferred living in Avignon. After all, they were French, and France was the center of the European world. Why would they want to live in a slum like Rome?

The Great Schism was an outgrowth of the Babylonian Captivity. Even though the French Popes lived in France, they still had to be elected from the Vatican— in Italy. In 1378, when the cardinals gathered to elect a new Pope, Italians threatened to attack them all if they elected another Frenchman! The cardinals backed down in the face of physical harm. They elected an Italian whom they expected to be a puppet Pope. They were wrong. Pope Urban VI refused to leave the Vatican and live in Avignon, and he began making independent decisions— one of which was to cut the cardinals' salaries.

The cardinals met again, in Anagni, a province of Rome. Declaring that their last election was a fraud because they were being threatened, they elected another Pope, and this one moved to Avignon. Now there was a Pope in Avignon and a Pope in Rome. Neither would give up his seat, and each excommunicated the other and all his followers. Europe divided itself between the two (Figure 1.2).

In 1409, after thirty-one years of the Great Schism, 500 clerics and laypeople met to figure out how to solve this horrible situation. They found enough grounds to charge both current Popes with heresy, and elected Alexander V. But the other two would not budge, so now there were three Popes. Then Alexander died, and the cardinals elected the right man for their purposes this time. John XXIII (1410–1415) had been a pirate in his youth before discovering that the Church was a faster and safer road to riches. The first thing he did was take Rome by force. Then he raised an army and took over Avignon. So far, so good, but the plan did not last.

Apparently John's former occupation had not been forgotten. Although he petitioned to be declared the true Pope, the cardinals charged him with a few minor details such as heresy, sorcery, immoral behavior, the murder of Pope Alexander V, and selling John the Baptist's head for 50,000 ducats. He was deposed, arrested, and imprisoned.

The Great Schism ended only when one of the remaining Popes resigned, one was deposed, and a single Pope, Martin V, was elected by a special election of cardinals *plus* representatives of the five largest nations in Europe at the time. Ultimately a four-year Ecumenical Council from 1414–1418, called the Council of Constance, put the Great Schism to rest. John, the former pirate, was declared not to have been a true Pope, so the number XXIII went to the next Pope to take the name of John, over five hundred years later, in 1958.

The Great Schism's effect on music was to bolster the rise of secularism in the face of such abuses in the Church and to foster a generally cynical outlook in the poetry and music of the time. But there was also a flowering of music and art in Avignon during, and after the Popes' reigns.

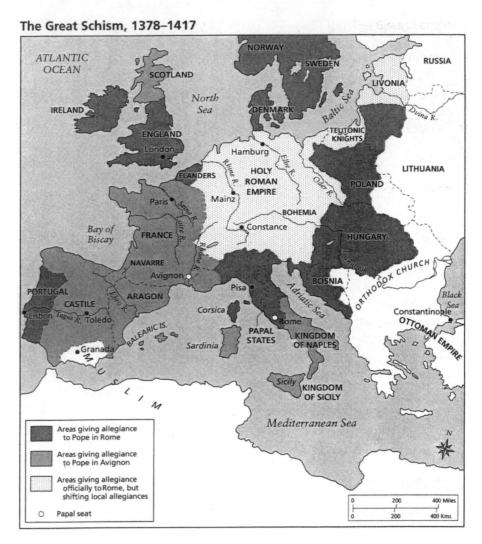

The Great Schism, 1378–1417

Figure 1.2 The Great Schism split Europe into factions, each of which recognized either the Pope in Rome or the one in Avignon. Courtesy of Facts on File, Inc. Historical Maps I, Revised Edition © 2002.

THE HUNDRED YEARS' WAR

Most modern wars have lasted about four years, and ten years is unusual and protracted. But what if a person today were still fighting a war in which their great-great-grandfather had fought? This was the situation from 1337 to 1453 in Europe (Figure 1.3).

Actually, the Hundred Years' War is a bit of a misnomer. It was not fought every day for 100 years; there were dozens of treaties, triumphs, and defeats. The main protagonists were England and France, but since other countries supported—morally,

Hundred Years' War 1337–1453

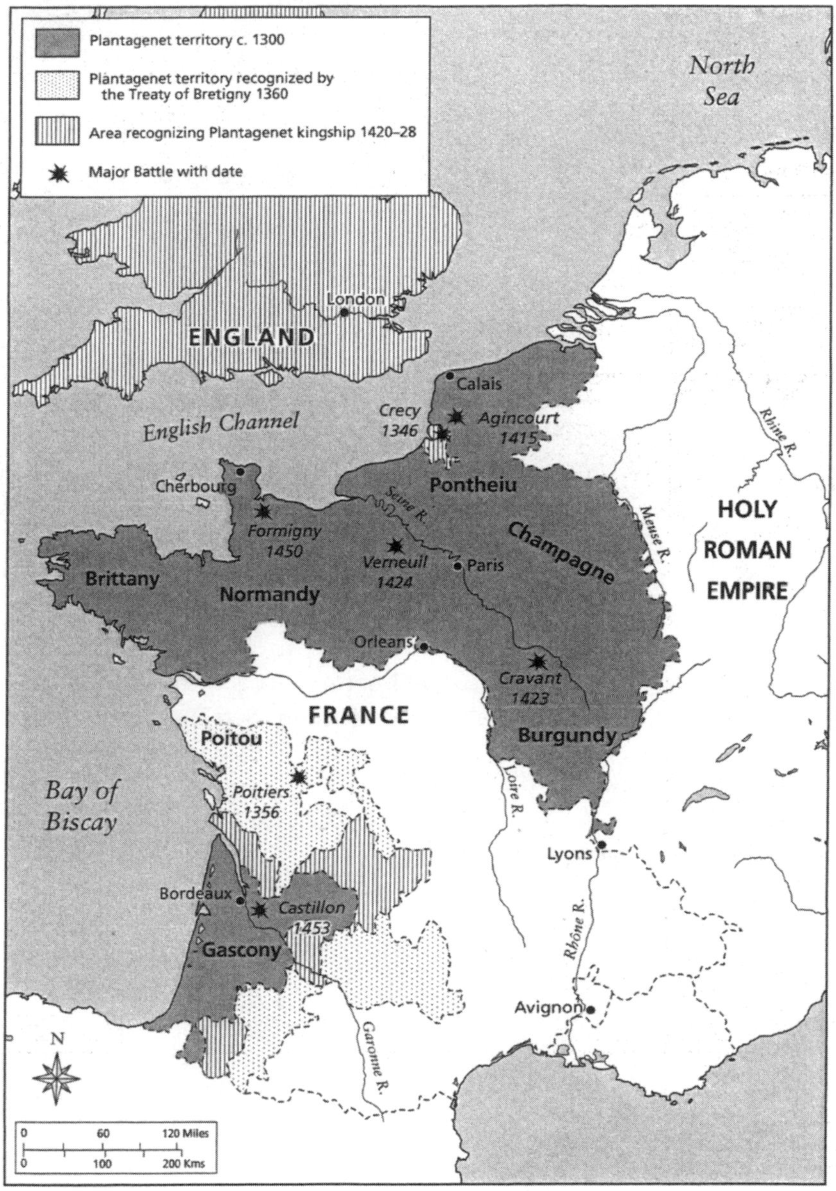

Figure 1.3 English (Plantagenet) territorial changes during the Hundred Years' War, which drew Europe into a seemingly endless series of battles. Courtesy of Facts on File, Inc. Historical Maps I, Revised Edition © 2002.

physically, or monetarily—one side or the other, it was the equivalent of a Western European World War.

It started with William the Conqueror, who established himself as King of England, but who was also of French royal background (though a bastard). English kings never forgot that they still had French blood, and through marriages and acquisitions, they eventually claimed that they had as much right to the throne of France as anyone else.

There were five main periods of war, listed here along with the outcomes:

1. 1337–1364: The English won most of the battles.
2. 1364–1380: The French recouped most of what they had lost.
3. 1380–1415: Both countries had internal conflicts that sidelined their efforts.
4. 1415–1429: The English won everything. Henry V of England became King of France. Then he died, leaving a 9-month old son.
5. 1429–1453: France got everything back except Calais and kicked England out.[11]

The effect of this enormous and protracted war was huge. It bankrupted both countries and was one of the nails in the coffin of the Middle Ages. It provided literature with many heroic figures, such as Shakespeare's Henry V. And it provided medieval history with its most famous heroine, Joan of Arc. It also provided England with one of its most famous non-Christmas carols: the Agincourt Carol, celebrating the English victory over the French in 1415.

Musically, the importance of the Hundred Years' War can hardly be understated. The musical traditions of England and France had followed quite different paths for hundreds of years. Tragically, it took a war to bring these two traditions together. But when it did, the cross-pollinating effect was an overwhelmingly better product that took a giant leap into the future, setting the groundwork for the great Burgundian School of music, which eventually supplied the Renaissance with most of its musicians.

PLAGUE (THE BLACK DEATH)

One of the most devastating epidemics on earth happened during the Middle Ages. It came relatively late in the era—the first (and worst) outbreak raged from 1347 to 1352 (Figure 1.4). But periodic outbreaks occurred from then on for over a hundred years. It was terrifying. Nobody knew where it would strike. It could kill a peasant or king with equal ferocity. Physicians and the Church were both helpless. It seemed to drop from the sky. Entire villages died. No one was left to bury the bodies. And lest one forget, this was happening during the Hundred Years' War and while two Popes—one in France and one in Rome—battled for supremacy. No wonder many people felt that the Black Death was a judgment from God!

Since the concept of germs was unknown in the Middle Ages, nobody could have guessed that fleas picked up the plague bacillus from infected rats and then spread it to humans. There were three types of plague, each a different course of the same infection: pneumonic, which was airborne and the most communicable; septicemic, which attacked the blood; and the most common, bubonic, which was characterized by blackened, swollen lymph nodes called buboes, which told the victim that he or she had a week or less to live.

The Black Death in Europe, 1347–52

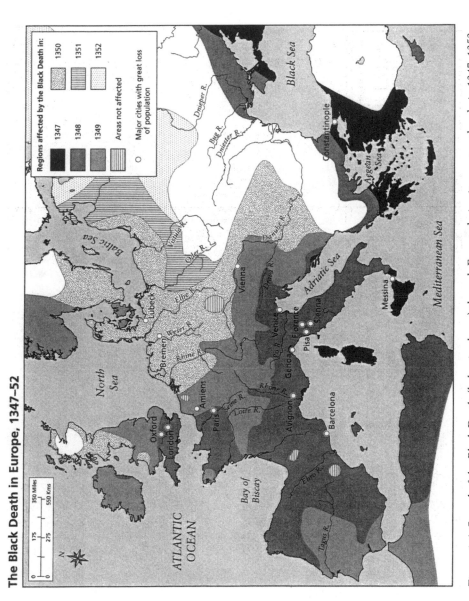

Figure 1.4 Spread of the Black Death (bubonic plague) through Europe during its worst outbreak, in 1347–1352; periodic outbreaks continued for many years thereafter. Courtesy of Facts on File, Inc. Historical Maps I, Revised Edition © 2002.

When plague hit an area, the first thing that people did was leave—which, of course, spread the disease. Over a three-year period, about one-third of the population of Europe died. The results were catastrophic. This plague cut through the feudal system like a scythe. It did not care whether you worked on a manor or owned one. Estates were left without owners or heirs. So few peasants were left to work the fields that those left were able to demand—and get—better working conditions. So many clergy died that new ones were quickly put into the system without proper training. Faith in the Church hit a new low as prayers remained unanswered; clerics refused to hear the confessions of the sick and dying for fear of catching the infection themselves; and their unsuitable replacements proved mostly corrupt. Education was affected. Two-thirds of the student body at Oxford died. As with the Church, educators also died and were replaced with poorly trained new people whose Latin was poor or non-existent. This contributed to the rise of classroom instruction in native languages instead of Latin.

Music and the poetry set to it were also affected. Satire leapt to the fore as the world seemed to have become the hell people were told to fear after death. Church music began to use secular works as part of the Mass music, and the "perfect" rhythmic timings based on groups of threes began to yield to "human" rhythms based on twos. One of the great names in medieval music—Guillaume de Machaut (discussed in Chapter 3)—lived through the plague years, described some of the scenes around himself, and also dedicated a work to the daughter of his patron who died of the plague in 1349.

NOTES

1. Albert Seay, *Music in the Medieval World*, 2nd edition (Englewood Cliffs, NJ: Prentice-Hall, Inc., 1975), p. 19.

2. Oliver Strunk, *Source Readings in Music History* (New York: W.W. Norton & Company, Inc., 1950), p. 88.

3. Gustav Reese, *Music in the Middle Ages with an Introduction on the Music of Ancient Times* (New York: W.W. Norton & Company, 1940), p. 62.

4. Ibid., p. 62.

5. Ibid., p. 65.

6. Piero Weiss and Richard Taruskin, *Music in the Western World* (New York: Simon & Schuster Macmillan, 1984) (selected and annotated), p. 265.

7. Ibid., p. 27.

8. Ibid., p. 29.

9. Ibid., p. 32.

10. Keith D. Lilley, *Urban Life in the Middle Ages 1000–1450* (Houndsmills, Basingstoke, Hampshire, and New York: Palgrave), p. 108.

11. John L. LaMonte, *The World of the Middle Ages* (New York: Appleton-Century-Crofts, Inc., 1949), p. 662.

CHAPTER 2

THE EARLY MIDDLE AGES AND CHURCH MUSIC

As the Dark Ages waned, the Church wanted stability, and so did Emperor Charlemagne. In quest of a stable and unified form for Christian worship, he looked back in time to find the type of Mass form and Church music that he felt was correct. The Pope who filled his expectations was Gregory I.

GREGORY I AND THE CHANT NAMED AFTER HIM

St. Gregory I, called The Great (c. 540–604) was from an old Roman family. He was Prefect of Rome before entering church life. After the death of his father, Gregory became a cloistered monk (a man who moves into a monastery to remove himself from the world, and devote himself to a rigorously religious life). In 579 he was sent to Constantinople as a representative of the Pope in Rome. When the Roman Pope died during an epidemic, Gregory was elected Pope by popular acclaim.

The Rome that Pope Gregory faced had suffered through decades of famine, plague, and wars. He had to bring some order into that chaos. Using the Church as the only functioning agency, he put it to work caring for the sick, making sure that city services functioned, taking care of the myriad beauracratic details that came up every day, and even mounting an armed defense of the city when it was necessary. As soon as order in Rome was restored, Pope Gregory branched out, trying to bring some organization to the rest of Western Europe. And as an extension of that effort, he also launched the Catholic Church's first missionary group, sent to preach the gospel in England.

Gregory was indeed a great Pope. But did he write—or even sponsor—the church chants named after him?

There was undoubtedly singing in the Roman church of Gregory's time. In fact, there is evidence of a *schola cantorum* (school of singers) in what would become the Vatican. But there is no connecting evidence that Gregory himself founded any of this. Although pictures of Gregory invariably show him taking music dictation from the Holy Spirit in the form of a dove (the origin of the phrase "a little bird told me"), the mention of Gregory and music came from sources 300 years later, such as John the Deacon. Even the dictation is under suspicion, since there was in Gregory's day no system of notation! The original term for the Church vocal music that we now call chant was *cantus planus* (level singing), *cantilena,* or *cantus ecclesiasticus* (ecclesiastical song). The term "Gregorian chant" came much later.

What is known about Pope Gregory is that he set up an order of the Mass that was to become standard, limited the length of the litany, and simplified some of the rites of the church. Rome started to revive *after* Gregory I's time, during the early 700s. It is possible—although historians disagree—that Gregory I has been mistaken for Gregory II, the Pope who refused to pay Byzantium any more taxes. Gregory II and several following Popes during the first half of the 700s actually did have an interest in Church music. What is the truth? No one knows. But although "Gregorian" chant is most likely a misnomer, it is one that will continue to be used.

And so, when the word "chant" or "plainchant" is used today, one automatically assumes Gregorian-style chant. Before Charlemagne, however, there were many other styles of chant throughout Europe. These were the styles suppressed by Charlemagne and the Church in a combined effort to standardize Europe's worship and music. Charlemagne took the simplified liturgies organized earlier by Gregory I and declared this Mass order to be the only one allowed. He also abolished any Church chants except those that are today called "Gregorian." Between armed enforcement and the threat of excommunication, Charlemagne and the Church generally got what they wanted. The effect on church music was electric. As part of a General Admonition put out in 789 A.D., Charlemagne insisted that clergy "should sing Roman chant in its entirety" and legislated that only the Roman form of Mass would be used.[1]

Charlemagne's rule took place before written notation had been pinned down to definite pitches. And during the suppression, oral tradition was completely disrupted. As a result, many pre-Gregorian forms of chant have been lost. Some were incorporated into the Gregorian literature and provide tantalizing glimpses of what might have gone before. The following paragraphs describe some of the major pre-Gregorian chant forms and what scholars have gleaned about them.

PRE-GREGORIAN CHANTS

Ambrosian Chant

This style of chant was partially written by and certainly encouraged by St. Ambrose (c. 340–397). Thus it is known as Ambrosian chant, although it is also known as Milanese chant.

St. Ambrose was not born into the church. In fact, his father had been a Praetorian Prefect of Gaul. Ambrose leaned toward the law and was under imperial service as a governor of Milan (in northern Italy) when Milan's bishopric became vacant in 370. By popular demand, Ambrose was drafted somewhat unwillingly into service. Already a Christian, he was quickly ordained and given the post. Ambrose used his lawyer's brain to set up a working administration for his diocese. His methods for ferreting out the truly needy from the only greedy, and for helping the poor without creating a welfare state, were eventually put into the Church's canon law and "formed the foundation of the medieval law of poor relief."[2] He was also an influential cleric and was, as mentioned in Chapter 1, the person who converted and baptized St. Augustine.

St. Ambrose was well acquainted with the then-more-sophisticated sacred chants of Constantinople, and he was greatly interested in Church music. When his bishopric was threatened by the Empress in Constantinople, who wanted a different style of worship, Ambrose kept his followers' spirits up through music. Inspired in part by Eastern techniques, he introduced a pattern of chanting that became common throughout the Western church. He also composed words and music for divine services. By the end of the fourth century, Milan had become one of the seats of the imperial government in the West, which made Ambrose one of the brightest lights in the Dark Ages.

Since Milan was a very early bishopric, it developed its own liturgical services and its own music. At one point, Ambrosian chant spread throughout the northern end of the Italian peninsula and even parts of the southern regions. Scholars disagree on the roots from which it sprang, and both Roman (Latin) and Greek influences have been pointed out. Ambrosian chant is one of the best preserved Western pre-Gregorian chants available, because although it was an oral tradition for hundreds of years, some of its melodies were notated during the twelfth century. A small amount found its way into Gregorian-style monastic chant music and music for Mass, but it is only a fraction of the overall literature. Milan was, for many years, a small holdout surrounded by overwhelming use of Gregorian chant before it eventually succumbed.

Scholars have found two distinct types of Ambrosian chant. One type is short and simple, with each syllable of text having only one or two notes apiece. Others, such as Mass *Alleluias*, are quite elaborate and may have been intended for special services. Those works are highly ornamental and have an enormous amount of notes on some syllables. Compared to Gregorian chants, Ambrosian are more elaborate. An elegant touch in some Ambrosian chants is known as "musical rhyme." This means that when a text phrase ends, it ends on the same series of note pitches every time.[3]

Old Roman Chant

This style of chant has been found notated as far back as the eleventh century, but it existed in oral form before that. As might be expected, Old Roman Chant is the pre-Gregorian form most closely related to Gregorian style. Scholars note small but telling differences. Through the ages, it has had many names other than Old Roman, such as Urban Roman, Special, Divergent, and Frankish. Some scholars claim that Old Roman is less of a chant variant than simply an early incarnation of Gregorian chant. They point out that the underlying melodies are virtually the same. Others, however, point to stylistic differences. "The gentle rise and fall of the typical Old Roman melody contrasts strongly with the more angular and assertive Gregorian melodic profile."[4]

Ravenna Chant

As pointed out in Chapter 1, Ravenna was once the seat of power for the Western Roman Empire, but by the end of the fifth century it was successively conquered by the Goths, the Byzantine Empire, the Lombards, and finally the Franks. Possibly because of all this destruction, Ravenna chant has largely been lost. The very few examples teased from various sources "reveal an elegance . . . not matched elsewhere in the West except among the more sophisticated chants of the Gregorian tradition."[5]

Beneventan Chant

This chant, named after the city of Benevento, was used in the southern part of Italy until it was finally suppressed in the eleventh century; it was at its most popular in the seventh and eighth centuries. For some time both Gregorian and Beneventan chants were used side-by-side in Beneventan regions, but finally the Gregorian pressure overwhelmed the older style. Since some Beneventan chants were written down, scholars have been able to study them. These chants are interesting because they do not seem to adhere to the same scale system (see "church modes") as other chants.

Gallican Chant

Gallican chant was one of the more severely repressed chants targeted by Charlemagne (and by his father as well). Since its repression occurred before written notation, scholars have been hard put to find any remnants. But there is evidence—by way of complaint—that instead of dropping Gallican chant, congregations and their priests tried to incorporate it along with the Gregorian literature. As the complaints were answered and reform continued, Gallican chant disappeared from the greater European arena. It appears that some remnant was still sung during the time of Charles the Bald (Charles II of France, and Holy Roman Emperor from 823 to 877), but the singers had to be brought in from Spain.

Mozarabic Chant

Mozarabes were Christians under Moorish (Islamic) occupied Spain. This chant style centered in Seville, Toledo, and Saragossa. Moslems generally did not concern themselves with such details of other religions as what chants they used. But when the Islamic forces were expelled from Toledo, Mozarabic chant, too, was suppressed by Rome in favor of Gregorian chants.

Since it was still being sung during the development of written notation, there are some complete manuscripts still available, as well as fragments. Unfortunately, the notation did not include staff lines and there are several styles of script, which added to scholarly confusion. But Mozarabic chant refused to die.

Some Toledan parishes had kept their practices even after the suppression, and there is some speculation that it may have continued in lands occupied by Arabic forces until their final expulsion from Spain in 1492. At any rate, during the late fifteenth century a Spanish cardinal revived the rite. The old manuscripts were recopied into notation that included pitches and rhythmic indications. In the late eighteenth and early nineteenth centuries, this revival continued. The Mozarabic chapel in Toledo Cathedral, Spain, still celebrates Masses using the Mozarabic rite and music to this day.

Sarum Chant

The name "Sarum chant" is a corruption of where it was sung—in Salisbury, England (its Latin name was *Sarisburia*). The Sarum rite was already in use before William the Conqueror made his way onto the British Isles. By being separated from the mainland plus never having been under the sway of Charlemagne, the Sarum rite and its chants were not affected by Gregorian suppression as other parts of Europe had been. The Sarum rite continued as an influential English liturgy through the Middle Ages and into the Renaissance. It even survived the first wave of religious Reformation in England until the Elizabethan era, when its basic liturgy was finally replaced by the Church of England's Book of Common Prayer. Even afterward, Sarum chant was the basis for many sacred compositions in England and contributed to their sense of "otherness" from Continental styles.

RESISTANCE TO GREGORIAN CHANT

As might be expected, the switch from variant to Gregorian chants was neither easy nor smooth. In fact, there was some sabotage right under Charlemagne's nose. This story was told in the *Life of Charlemagne* written in the tenth century by musician and monk Notker Balbulus:

Deploring the widespread variety in chanted liturgy, Charlemagne got some experienced chanters from the Pope. Like twelve apostles they were sent from Rome to all provinces north of the Alps. . . . [but] these clerics planned to vary their teaching so that neither the unity nor the consonance of the chant would spread in a kingdom and province other than their own. Received with honor, they were sent to the most important cities where each of them taught as badly as he could. . . . [6]

Fortunately for Gregorian chant, Charlemagne unmasked the plot. As the ruler of a great empire, he celebrated major feast days at a different court somewhere in his kingdom every year. Through his travels he heard what the clerics taught—or rather, what they had not taught! In a sting operation, he and Pope Leo III (795–816) smuggled two loyal chanters into the papal choir to ferret out the dissenters. The Pope exiled some of the culprits and imprisoned others.

THE GREGORIAN CHANT

The kind of chants commonly known as "Gregorian" were made for purposes of worship and carry with them a spirituality clearly felt to the present time. But this music was quite different from today's. For one thing it had only a melody. There was no harmony. For another, it was totally vocal. If an instrument was allowed, it played the same melody that the voices sang and was used only to keep pitches steady.

Except in convents of nuns, there were no women singers in medieval church choirs. All the singers in church choirs were men or boys. Also, in the early Middle Ages no one would be looking at written music, because notation had not been developed. In fact, people commonly believed that it was impossible to put something as insubstantial as music into black and white. Anyone who sang had to memorize the melody and text that he had been carefully taught, sometimes from childhood. The first notation, as will be discussed later in this chapter, consisted only of marks over the words to remind singers *whether* pitches should go up or down, but they still had to learn by ear *how far* up or down as well as the rhythms. Even in the later Middle Ages, after written notation had evolved, there was no printing press and therefore no sheet music for individual choir members. Instead, they would huddle around a single enormous book, on a sturdy stand, in which chants had been carefully copied by hand, often with beautiful decorations.

THE STANDARDIZED MASS

During the Middle Ages there was only one Church (in the West). You were either Catholic or a heretic. And thanks to Charlemagne, Europe gained a standardized Mass form (or lost variety, depending on one's point of view). Although changes have occurred through the ages, the Charlemagne-Gregorian standardized Mass has remained remarkably stable for over 1,000 years. While laying a foundation for worship based on regularity, it also had the flexibility of optional inclusions and special services for certain times of the year such as Christmas and Easter. And central to the Mass was its music—the Gregorian chant.

The Mass (*Missa*, in Latin) gets its name from the final words of the priest to the congregation: *Ite, missa est*, literally "Go, [the Church] is sent [out into the world]," but reinterpreted as "the Mass is [ended]." The early Christian Mass had two separate parts. The first was instructional, for both baptized Christians and those who were preparing to become Christians, who would leave after it was over. The second part was the Eucharist or Communion service, for baptized Christians only. By the Middle Ages, everybody in church was baptized, but the Mass still retained its two-part form, as it does today: a Fore-Mass or Synaxis (today called the Liturgy of the Word), and the Liturgy of the Eucharist. Each contained its own service. The basic order of the Charlemagne-Gregorian Mass was as follows:

The *Fore-Mass or Synaxis* included the Introit (entrance antiphon and psalm), **Kyrie**, **Gloria**, Oratio or Collect (opening prayer), Epistle, Gradual (psalm), Alleluia (replaced by Tract during the penitential season of Lent), Sequence (on special feasts), Gospel (Evangelism), **Credo**. Some sources also list the Offertory and Secret as part of the Synaxis.

The *Eucharist or Communion Service* included the Offertory, Secret (prayer over the gifts), Preface, **Sanctus**, **Canon**, **Pater Noster** (Lord's Prayer), **Agnus Dei**, Communion (antiphon), Postcommunion (antiphon), and **Benedicamus Domino** (Benediction).

Some of these parts, indicated by bold print in the preceding paragraphs, were known as the Ordinary of the Mass because their text never varied and these parts were included in everyday Masses on all occasions. The other elements were the Proper of the Mass, which were different for each day. All of the Ordinary sections except the Canon were originally meant for the congregation to sing, although trained singers eventually took over when the music became more complicated.

Gregorian chants could be sung in different ways. Sometimes they were sung in unison by all the singers at once. Other times they were sung antiphonally, in which the choir was divided into two halves that would alternate verses, or responsorially, in which a soloist would sing the verses and some sort of refrain (response) would be sung by the congregation.

Besides being "arranged" differently, chants differed in complexity. For instance some, such as the Gospel, were written mostly on a single note, with each syllable of text sung on one note at a time, so that the text could be heard clearly. Others, such as the Introit, Offertory, and Communion, were more complex. This is because they were sung while people performed other actions such as walking in, taking up offerings to the church, or receiving Communion.

The most complex chants were generally the Graduals and Alleluias. They tended to have more notes per syllable of text, and to be more dramatically presented—for instance, they might be sung responsorially between a choir soloist and the rest of the choir. One against eight or ten really stood out in a way that two halves of a choir did not.

Chants for Mass were generally composed anonymously. Since they were in essence offerings to God, advertising oneself as composer would have been arrogant if not sacrilegious. It was not the custom to write an entire Mass's worth of music. A composer might write one or more Glorias, or several Kyries, and never write a Credo. When choosing music for a service, officials could use any setting they wished for the Gloria, Sanctus, and other elements. It was not necessary to put together a unified "set." The idea of a unified Mass setting was born rather late in the Middle Ages.

Although almost all Masses and words to Mass music were in Latin by the Middle Ages, one part continued to be sung in Greek, a holdover from the Byzantine and early Christian services. That is the Kyrie. Its form is that of three times three—three being a sacred number, representing the Father, Son, and Holy Spirit of the Christian Trinity. First, *Kyrie, eleison* (Lord, have mercy) is sung three times, followed by *Christe, eleison* (Christ, have mercy) sung three times, and finally *Kyrie, eleison* (Lord, have mercy) sung three more times.

Even after they were written down, chant collections were generally kept privately. Monasteries and court chapels could lend books to be copied in other places or they could present a copy as a gift. Thus, chants spread from place to place, albeit slowly. Eventually two major sources emerged and remain to this day—the *Graduale*, and the *Liber Usualis* (the book containing the "use," or required actions as well as the chants, for both the Mass and the monastic Hours, discussed later).

THE REQUIEM MASS

One type of mass—*Requiem*, or Mass for the Dead—was different in its liturgy and music. Because of the solemn nature of this Mass, some of the normal Ordinary sections, such as the Gloria, were left out. Other sections, such as a possible Alleluia, were replaced by a more somber Tract. And there were special texts set to music for this special Mass. For instance its Introit text, from which it gets its name, was *Requiem aeternam dona eis* (Grant them eternal rest). Other additions included *Lux Aeterna* (Eternal light) and *Libera me* (Free me). The Requiem Mass also contains a chant recognizable by almost everyone—the sequence *Dies irae* (Day of wrath). Its chant melody has been used as a main or underlying theme in hundreds of later works, where it always carries a feeling of deepest doom.

MONASTICISM AND THE DIVINE OFFICE

The Mass was intended for both clergy and laypeople—that is, people living out in the world rather than dedicated to the Church. There were also, however, communities of men known as monks (or their female counterparts, nuns) whose lives were completely devoted to a rigorous religious life. They made sacred promises (took vows) of poverty, chastity, and obedience. That is, they renounced personal possessions and sexual relations, and they surrendered their lives completely to the authority of the superior of the community.

The practice of renouncing the world for the sake of serving God began in Egypt and Palestine somewhere around the second century A.D. with hermits, who lived alone in the desert. Contemporary writings report that these ascetics were far from being music-haters. In fact, they sang psalms as a central part of their worship. Eventually these solitary souls were joined by like-minded people. Thus communities of worshippers formed.

In Western Europe, people who wanted to retreat into a completely religious life had an alarming lack of deserts. Instead, they built walled habitats, known as monasteries, and their withdrawal from the world was known as being cloistered. The habit of chanting and praying solidified into worship forms known as Offices (meaning "duties"), which were held at certain times throughout the day, known as the Hours. Around 530 St. Benedict, who was the abbot (head of a community of monks) at Monte Cassino in Italy, wrote a manual for living the monastic life. Known as the Rule of St. Benedict, it includes (among many other things) information regarding where, when, and how music was to be sung.

The Hours occurred throughout a 24-hour period at roughly three-hour intervals. All involved the singing of Psalms. They were:

1. Matins: about 2 or 3 A.M.   (between 2 and 3 hours)
2. Lauds: at daybreak   (about 45 minutes)
3. Prime: 6 A.M.   (about 15–20 minutes)
4. Terce: 9 A.M.   (about 15–20 minutes)
   Mass was said between Terce and Sext and lasted about one and a half hours.
5. Sext: noon   (about 15–20 minutes)
6. None: 3 P.M.   (about 15–20 minutes)
7. Vespers: sunset   (about 45 minutes)
8. Compline: bedtime   (about one-half hour)

Monasticism was not an easy life. Monasteries were self-sustaining, which meant that they took care of all their earthly needs and even had cottage industries to raise funds. When not singing these prayers (their primary labor, which they called *opus Dei*, "the work of God"), working in the fields, making shoes, doing their laundry, taking care of livestock, or copying manuscripts, the monks were running some of Europe's earliest institutions of learning.

Monasteries in the Middle Ages became havens of civilization. Most medical knowledge was housed there. And in a time when perhaps one in ten men could read (Charlemagne could not) and almost no women could, monasteries housed precious volumes in their libraries and monks labored to make copies of holy works, works commissioned by patrons of their monasteries, and, later, music manuscripts. Monks and nuns also taught in monastery schools. In fact not all, but some of their charges lived their entire lives within monastery walls.

The Rule of St. Benedict was adapted for women, and convents of nuns became one place where females had some power. Not only could a female rise to become an abbess (head of the convent) but the self-sustaining convents meant that nuns balanced their own books, and administered the abbey's holdings. Those holdings could be considerable, even including rents from towns and villages that sat on their lands. However, women still needed a male priest to hold Mass and administer sacraments, and if a disagreement arose between an abbess and an abbot, the abbot generally won.

Though it seems incredible now, monasteries and convents were also seen as places to house unwanted or handicapped children. In a time when giving birth to 12 or 15 children was common, some families gave a "tithe" of their tenth child to the church. It didn't matter whether that child (called an "oblate," meaning someone offered) was fit for a religious life, and some scholars see the warehousing of those children as a hotbed for corruption.

These child oblates learned grammar and arithmetic, and they learned singing by memorizing what the monks beside them sang. Boys as young as 5 or 6, too, were at Matins every morning for a 2–3 hour service. Here is a passage from the *Costumal of St. Beningne,* written around 1050 in Dijon, France, which shows the pride this monastery took in the discipline of their charges:

> At Nocturns [the sections of Matins], and indeed at all the Hours, if the boys commit any fault in the psalmody or other singing, either by sleeping or such like transgression, let there be no sort of delay, but let them be stripped forthwith of frock and cowl, and beaten in their shirt only, with pliant and smooth osier rods provided for that special purpose. If any of them, weighed down with sleep, sing ill at Nocturns, then the master giveth into his hand a reasonably great book, to hold until he be well awake. At Matins the principal master standeth before them with a rod until all are in their seats and their faces well covered. At their uprising likewise, if they rise too slowly, the rod is straightway over them. In short, meseemeth that any King's son could scarce be more carefully brought up in his palace than any boy in a well-ordered monastery.[7]

Though monks were supposed to live rigorously, some monasteries bent the rules. For instance, monks might be restricted to one cup of wine a day, but their cups held about half a gallon each! Also, they had different ideas about some foods. For instance, on Fridays they were prohibited from eating meat, but fish and eggs were permissible. So they reasoned that anything coming out of the water was a "fish," and anything not born yet was an "egg." So a frog was a "fish" and an unborn pig, sheep, rabbit, or calf was an "egg" and could be eaten.

HILDEGARD OF BINGEN

One extremely musical—and powerful—monastic was the nun and abbess Hildegard of Bingen, who lived from 1098 to 1179. She was extremely learned, and moreover she had visions that, she claimed, were sent straight from God. These visions included music, and we are fortunate that Hildegard lived in a time when music notation enabled her to write these melodies down. Most plainchants have about an octave range and melodies that mostly move stepwise. Hildegard's melodies are quite different. The range is, for its time, huge (and challenging even for singers today), and pitches may make wide leaps, one after another.

Hildegard has another claim to fame. She wrote a play entitled *Ordo Virtutum* (Order of Virtues), the earliest known morality play that includes music and has survived. In a time when women's roles were narrow when they were noticed at all, Hildegard broke many of the Middle Ages' molds.

DEVELOPMENT OF NOTATION IN THE MIDDLE AGES

One of the most important developments in Western music was to come up with a way to write pitches reliably enough so that anyone could look at the written music and sing the piece. For many years, the monastery of St. Gall in what is now Switzerland was known for its excellent notation, and many other monasteries sent for monks from St. Gall to teach the monks in their own *scriptoria* (rooms where monks copied manuscripts) how to write music.

But music notation had its growing pains. The first notation, beginning around the ninth century, consisted of dots, strokes, and squiggly marks, eventually called *neumes*, over the syllables in the text to indicate changes in pitch (Figure 2.1), but it was not possible to know *how* high or low the pitches were meant to go without hearing the melody actually sung. Some scholars believe that these marks actually represent the motions, not of the voice, but of the director's hand, signaling the singers to make the pitch changes they had learned by ear. Around the turn of the millennium the neumes became more regular in shape. There was more care to place neumes so that the same pitch would be the same height. But pitch was still a matter of learning by ear. Then came one of Western music's brightest ideas: the staff line.

At first, the staff line was just that: a single line (like a walking stick, or staff) going across the page with neumes on, above, or below it. The line represented a particular pitch, and singers had more idea of how far away from that pitch they were supposed to sing. Later there were two lines: one yellow and one red. The yellow (or sometimes green) line represented the pitch of C, and the red one represented the pitch of F. (The origin of these ideas will be discussed in Chapter 4.) The next step was to write a letter C on the C line or an F on the F line—the origin of our clef signs. The F they used can still be recognized as the forerunner of our bass clef. The part of the bass clef that looks like a large comma used to be the back of the F, and the two dots used to be the two lines of the F. It still places the bass pitch of F between the dots. (The C clef is also used today for viola music, but it now looks much less like a C.)

Once these key innovations opened the floodgates, staff lines began appearing all over the place. In manuscripts across Europe, there could be anywhere from one to thirteen staff lines written. Obviously neither of these extremes was very satisfactory. Most written music from the Middle Ages ended up with four (not the five of today) staff lines.

	ST. GALL		METZ		CHARTRES		LIMOGES		NONANTOLA		MODERN NOTATION
PUNCTUM	◊ –	– –	•	⌒	ε	– ᵉ	◢	–	ε	–	♪ ♪̄ ♩
VIRGA	/	⌐	ʃ	ᵗ ʃ	/	//	√₂	–	/	1	♪ ♪̄ ♩
PES or PODATUS	⌄	√ᵉ√	ʃ	ᵃ ⌄√	⌄:	⌐	? ♪	⌐▶	ǀ	ᵗ ǀ	♫ ♫ ♫
CLIVIS	⋀	⌐⋏	⌐	⌐ ⌐	⌐	⌐ᶠ	: ♪	: :	⌃	⌐ᵖ	♫♫ ♫♫♫
TORCULUS	⋀	ʃ⋀	⋀	ᵃ	⋀ᴴ	⌐⌐	⌐	⌐ ⌐	⋀	ᵢ,	♫ ♫̄
PORRECTUS	Ν	Ν	⋁	ʃ	γ γ	⌐Μ	:ʃ	⌐ʃ	Ν	⌐	♫ ♫̄
SCANDICUS	/		ʃ	ʃ	/	ǀǀ√	ʃ	: :	ǀ	ǀ	♫ ♫̄
CLIMACUS	ǀ•.	⌐	::	⌐	: ⋀ :	: :::	⌐	ǀ;	♫ ♫̄
ORISCUS	ʃ ⌐		⌐		⌐ ⌐	ᴴ ⌐ ⌐	⌐ 3	♫♪
TRIGON	∴	⊓	•⌐	⌐ᵃ	••	– /⋀	••	⌐⌐	♪♪ ♫̄
QUILISMA	– ᴟ	ᴓ	2	ʃ ⋁	ǀ	♫
EPIPHONUS	⌣	⌄	⌄	⌄⌄ᵓ	ǀ	♫
CEPHALICUS	ρ	ᵗρ	⌐ ⌐	⌐ρ	ρ	/	•ᵓ	ρ	♪

Figure 2.1 During the Middle Ages there were many notation systems in use. This chart shows the neume shapes used in various regions and the pitch movements and rhythms they represented. *Source: Historical Atlas of Music,* Cleveland and New York: The World Publishing Company, 1968.

Written on the staff, the neumes ceased to look like squiggles and came to look like squares or diamonds as a result of being drawn with a flat nib held vertically or diagonally. And they may or may not have thin vertical stems on one side or the other, which indicate up and down voice movements. The shapes of the heads and the presence or absence of stems do not mean different rhythmic values as in modern notation; it is a whole different system. Notation in the Middle Ages was complicated, and the following description is a *big* simplification. In general, though, reading chant music of the Middle Ages is something like reading Shakespeare. Once you get the basic language down, it is not impossible to do, and can be quite enjoyable.

READING GREGORIAN CHANT NOTATION

First, a modern person must forget about a few things. Forget bar lines, time signatures, or counting beats. Forget key signatures; there are none. There will be a clef sign, but it will move about, and it may not mean the same pitch. There might be an accidental, but only one—and always on the same note.

First, look at the far left of any chant, such as that shown in Figure 2.2. The first item on the staff will be something that looks like a letter C with thick horizontals and a thin vertical. And it might have a mark to the left that looks like a number 7, again with a thick horizontal and thin vertical. Either way, that is a clef sign: a C clef without the piece on the left, an F clef with that piece, as described in the previous section. The middle of that clef sign will almost always be on a line. Wherever that is, whether on the top line, the bottom line, or anywhere in between, will be—for present purposes—middle C. This is hard for modern readers to grasp, because we are carefully taught only two kinds of clefs, which are always in the same place, so that lines and spaces have definite and immovable pitches. But this is music of the Middle Ages, and there are many more possibilities. So if the C clef surrounds the top line, then that line will be middle C, the space below it will be B, and the line below that will be A.

Now look at the neumes. Some will be plain rectangles, and they indicate a single pitch, whether lower or higher. Since we know where C is, we now know what the other pitches are. Just as in modern notation, notes higher on the staff are higher in pitch and notes lower on the staff are lower.

Sometimes two rectangles are stacked on top of one another, as if they are supposed to be sung together, and there is a thin vertical line joining them on the right. This pattern means singing the lower note first and then the higher one, both on the same syllable.

Another pattern has the rectangles stacked diagonally, the upper rectangle to the left and the lower rectangle to the right, again with a thin vertical line between the two. In that case, sing the higher note first and then the lower one. If there are three or more descending notes, usually a rectangle with a thin tail on the right is written for the first (highest) note, followed by a diagonal pattern of diamond-shaped notes.

Sometimes there are three rectangles connected with thin vertical lines, with the highest rectangle in the middle. Sing these just the way they look: lower note, higher note, lower note.

The opposite of the preceding pattern looks very different: a long, heavy diagonal black line sloping down from left to right and then connected to another higher note

Figure 2.2 An illustrated manuscript from the Middle Ages, using fully developed neumatic notation. Original manuscript from Sourthern Illinois University in Carbondale. Photograph by Skyla Sensahrae.

by a thin vertical line. This does not mean the voice is supposed to slide from one pitch to the next. Instead, start by singing the note marked by the top of the diagonal, then sing the note marked by the bottom, and then sing the higher third note.

At the end of each line of notes and text, you may see a small neume not connected to the rest of the line. It may be a different color, or a different size. If it is there, it indicates the first note of the next line.

You may also see some vertical lines that look like bar lines. They can be smaller or larger and mean different things. The very smallest, called a quarter bar, crosses only the top line of the staff and means that the singer(s) can take a breath there. A half-line, usually between the two middle staff lines, gives singers permission for a full breath. A single line that looks like today's bar line, indicates a pause of about a single syllable. Two lines that look like a double bar can mean the end of the piece (like a double bar today, but in chant notation both bars are thin), but if they do not stand at the end, the two lines indicate a point in an antiphonal or responsorial chant where the singing switches between one half of the choir and the other half or between the choir and the soloist.

How does one know whether notes should be shorter or longer? The simple answer is that, in general, we do not. But since Latin is a known language, one hopes that rhythms would follow language patterns. There are some hints. A dot to the right of the note, as in modern notation, means the note is lengthened, but to about twice its usual length. A horizontal line over a neume means the notes are lengthened somewhat less.

THE CHURCH MODES

The scale system of the Middle Ages was quite different from the major and minor keys musicians use today, but there are parallels. To get an idea of the thinking behind the scales used for chant, consider the white keys on a piano keyboard. If you start on middle C and go straight up to the next C, it will sound like a modern major scale. But if you start and end on G, or F, or A, or D, sticking to the white keys, the scale will sound quite different. These scales are the basis for the *modes*, in which musicians of the Middle Ages composed their chant melodies.

During the Middle Ages, there were eight scale systems, now known as Church modes, from which chant melodies were invented. They acquired names from ancient Greek scale systems. Four were called "authentic": Dorian (D–D), Phrygian (E–E), Lydian (F–F), and Mixolydian (G–G). Chants from these modes started and ended on the same note. Each of these had a corresponding "plagal" system that started a fourth below, and its Greek name started with "Hypo": Hypodorian (A–A), Hypophrygian (B–B), Hypolydian (C–C), and Hypomixolydian (D–D). A chant in a plagal mode starts on one note, but ends on a different one.

Modal scales, especially in Gregorian chants, are not a democracy—all their notes are not created equal (and this is also true of our modern major scale).

There are two notes more important than the rest: the *final*, which is the last note sung, and the *tenor* (or *reciting*) tone, which is the note to which most of the syllables in a psalm, for example, were sung.

No matter what note each mode starts on, the ending note, or final, of every plagal scale will be the same as the first note of its corresponding authentic scale. In other words, Dorian starts on D and Hypodorian starts on A, but their finals are both on D. Likewise, the final note for both Phrygian and Hypophrygian chants is E, for Lydian and Hypolydian scales it is F, and for Mixolydian and Hypomixolydian it is G.

The reciting tones of the pairs, however, are different. For authentic modes, the reciting tone is five tones above the final, but for plagal modes it is three notes above. For instance, to find the reciting tone in Dorian, one would count D, E, F, G, A; its reciting tone is A. But for Hypodorian, one would count D, E, F; its reciting tone is F.

Does this make a lot of difference when a person is listening to a lovely Gregorian chant? Not really. But if we want to understand the music and the minds of the composers of that time, understanding their scale systems is as important as understanding key signatures when studying music of the Baroque, Classical, and Romantic periods and the early twentieth century.

THE PROBLEM OF B

There was one sticky problem with the Church mode system, and it had to do with a particular interval (the difference in pitch between two notes). Recall that musicians of the Middle Ages took many ideas from Boethius and Cassiodorus (see Chapter 1), who got their ideas from ancient Greek writings. To all of them, the "perfect" intervals could be mathematically derived. They were the fourth, fifth, and octave. Octaves were no problem. But halfway between the perfect intervals of the fourth and fifth there is a middle interval known as an augmented fourth or a diminished fifth. In the Middle Ages, that interval was considered so disagreeable that it was known as the "Devil's interval."

To understand the problem, return to the white keys of the piano keyboard. Each of the white keys is a perfect fifth or fourth away from some other note: F to C, C to G, G to D, D to A, A to E, E to B. The terrible interval occurs on the way from B back to F to close the cycle. The perfect fifths and fourths have simple 3:2 and 4:3 ratios, but multiplying them together to get the ratio for the B–F interval produces a mind-boggling 729:512. It made composers of the Middle Ages crazy! They could not permit an important note to lead to this particular combination. They met this problem in several ways.

One was to change the rules. The Phrygian mode has a final of E, and it is authentic, so its reciting tone should be the fifth note above: E, F, G, A, . . . B, which was not allowed! So the reciting tone for this mode was moved to C. The Hypomixolydian mode had the same problem. Its final is on a G, and it is plagal, so its reciting tone should be up three steps: G, A, . . . B again! So theorists moved that reciting tone up a step, again to C.

Another way to avoid this particular interval was to attack the B itself. If B is lowered, or flattened, by a half-step, the fourth between it and F is no longer augmented but perfect. But how could one tell when to sing the B flat and when to leave it at its unaltered, natural pitch? The answer was to write the letter next to the note, using a round-looking "soft" B for the B-flat, and a square-looking "hard" B for the B-natural. This is where we get the modern flat sign, which looks like a small B, and the modern natural sign, which looks square. This is Western music's first "accidental." Also, even in the present day, some languages use the term *dur* (from Latin *durum*, "hard") to indicate a major key and *mol* (from *molle*, "soft") to indicate a minor key (for example, G major uses a B natural, while G minor uses a B flat).

CHANGES TO CHURCH CHANTS

Chant words were sacred and could not be altered. But chant notes were more fluid. Even in the earliest chants, there could be more than one note per syllable, and in some cases this took on heroic proportions. An example of this was called a *jubilus*, an extremely long sequence of neumes sung on a single syllable. Most often the jubilus is found at the end of the word *Alleluia*. This expression of joy—*jubilus* means song of joy—has been sung as far back as St. Augustine's time, as we know because he wrote about it: "It is a certain sound of joy without words . . . it is the expression of a mind poured forth in joy."[8] In a Gregorian chant using the text *Alleluia*, chances are that the last syllable will have anywhere from ten to forty "extra" notes.

SEQUENCES AND TROPES

As stated before, chant words were sacred and could not be altered. But they *could* be added onto. The man who gets the most credit for this lived a couple of generations after Charlemagne and before written notation had been nailed down. He was a monk from St. Gall named Notker, with the nickname Balbulus ("the Stammerer"). As a young man, Notker dutifully memorized his chants. But when it came to very long *melismas* (several notes sung on a single syllable of text), he became hopelessly lost. "When I was still young, and very long *melodiae*—repeatedly entrusted to memory—escaped from my poor little head, I began to reason with myself how I could bind them fast."[9]

The answer came with a visitor who was fleeing his own parish because of a Norman invasion. This visitor had a book with verses in it fitted to some of the long melodies. But the verses were terrible. Notker, excited about the idea, decided to try some verses of his own. If the long melismas had words of their own, he reasoned, then they would be easier to memorize! His idea was a hit. Notker was asked to write more, fitting proper syllables to the musical phrases. He turned out to be adept at this, and soon monks throughout Europe were using this device, now known as a *sequence*. A place was made in the Mass for sequences: just before the Gospel reading.

A later sequence composer was Adam of St. Victor (c. 1080–1150). A monk, but not cloistered, Adam was in a hotbed of musical knowledge in the Middle Ages—Paris. His sequential poetry is known for its elegance and power.

Tropes are very similar to sequences, and in fact some scholars call them interchangeable. But tropes were more radical in that either extra words or extra music containing extra words could be added to an existing chant. The important part of this development is the addition of extra music in a chant, which would open the door for more radical changes later in the Middle Ages.

Sometimes tropes were added at the beginning of a chant, like a kind of prelude. But other times they were added between parts of the chant. The music was original, and the words explained or commented on the chant text. So although the trope was new music and new text, it still was attached to an older, original Gregorian chant.

LITURGICAL DRAMA

Liturgical drama would have been impossible without the existence of troping, since it was text and music added to a Mass. This early form of Western theater was extremely simple at first, consisting of only a few lines sung independently either before the Introit, or during the Mass. This very special form was used on special occasions—the most obvious being Easter and Christmas. One of the very earliest dramas was a representation of the three Marys and an angel at Christ's tomb on Easter morning. The singers would have all been men, and the language Latin, so it is difficult to say how much of it the congregation understood. But the departure from normal spoken text before the Introit would have been startling, and so would the placement of the singers—three separated and singing antiphonally with a solo singer or choir.

The "angel" sang, "Whom are ye seeking, O servants of Christ?"

The "Marys" sang back, "Jesus of Nazareth, who was crucified, O servant of heaven."

Then the "angel" sang, "He is not here. He is risen as He said. Go and proclaim that He has risen."[10]

Once additions had been started, more things were added. For instance, a later drama added the Marys turning to the audience and singing "Alleluia, the Lord is risen. Today the strong lion, Christ the Son of God has risen. Give thanks to God, say *Eia*!" Another, even more dramatic, turn of events was to start the Easter service with a singer representing Christ himself, singing "I have risen" before the Introit.[11]

Christmas dramas had several built-in possibilities. Composers could draw upon the scene of the Holy Family in the manger of Bethlehem, the arrival of shepherds sent by angels, the visit of the Magi (the Wise Men) to the manger and presenting gifts to the new baby, and the extremely dramatic Slaughter of the Innocents, when King Herod decided to kill all the babies in Bethlehem under the age of two in order to rid himself of a potential future rival—the Messiah. Another popular

Christmas drama was *Ordo prophetarum,* or "Procession of the Prophets," in which both Old Testament prophets and pagan seers (such as the Roman Sybils) each predict the coming of the Christ Child.

Throughout the Middle Ages, liturgical dramas grew until they separated from the Mass itself and became Easter and Christmas plays complete with music, costumes, action, and scenery. One of the most famous, and one that is still performed today, is *The Play of Daniel.* Religious in nature, it is a tale from the Old Testament but not part of any Mass and not containing Mass music. The words are Latin, and boys whose voices are still high sing the parts of women. (In present-day performances these parts may be taken by a "countertenor"—a male trained to sing in a high voice known as "falsetto.") There is plenty of action—the Babylonian King Belshazzar's feast, which is interrupted by miraculous letters appearing on a wall foretelling the end of his kingdom (the original "handwriting on the wall"), the capture of Daniel, the arrival of Darius the Persian king and the slaying of Belshazzar, the betrayal of Daniel by Darius's jealous satraps, Daniel in a pit facing fierce lions, and the appearance of an angel both to protect Daniel and, later, to foretell the coming of Christ at the end of the play. There are colorful and exotic costumes for Persians, angels, and lions. There is scenery—the courts of Belshazzar and Darius, the feasting room, and the pit filled with lions. And there is music throughout, both sung and played by instruments. By the time of this play (the thirteenth century), music had acquired harmony and a definite rhythmic beat.

NOTES

1. Giulio Cattin, *Music of the Middle Ages I*, translated by Steven Botterill (Cambridge, UK: Cambridge University Press, 1984), p. 54.

2. Ibid., pp. 32, 33.

3. Gustav Reese, *Music in the Middle Ages with an Introduction on the Music of Ancient Times* (New York: W.W. Norton & Company, 1940), pp. 107–108.

4. Helmut Hucke and Joseph Dyer, "Old Roman Chant," *Grove Music Online,* edited by L. Macy (http://www.grovemusic.com/shared/views/article.html?section=music.11725, accessed September 7, 2006).

5. Kenneth R. Ley1, "Ravenna Chant," *Grove Music Online* (http://www.grovemusic.com/shared/views/article.html?section=music.22963, accessed September 7, 2006).

6. Piero Weiss and Richard Taruskin, *Music in the Western World. Selected and Annotated* (New York: Simon & Schuster Macmillan, 1984), pp. 44–45.

7. Piero Weiss and Richard Taruskin, *Music in the Western World. Selected and Annotated* (New York: Simon & Schuster Macmillan, 1984), p. 45.

8. Gustav Reese, *Music in the Middle Ages with an Introduction on the Music of Ancient Times* (New York: W.W. Norton & Company, 1940), p. 64.

9. Piero Weiss and Richard Taruskin, *Music in the Western World. Selected and Annotated* (New York: Simon & Schuster Macmillan, 1984), p. 46.

10. Richard H. Hoppin, *Medieval Music* (New York: W.W. Norton & Company, Inc., 1978), p. 176.

11. Ibid.

CHAPTER 3

THE MUSIC OF FRANCE IN THE MIDDLE AGES

During the Middle Ages, much of the history of Western music was centered in France. Whether one speaks of the southern or northern regions (particularly Paris), French territory became the front-runner in musical innovations. Because of so many French Popes and highly placed clerics (see Chapter 2), this dominance affected sacred music as well as secular.

FRENCH TERRITORY

The France of the Middle Ages was not the France that one generally thinks of today. Medieval France was a feudal kingdom with the feudal system's ties of loyalty outlined in Chapter 1. At its head was a king who was, until 1328, descended from the Capet family of the old Frankish tribe. Nobles throughout the Frankish kingdom did answer to the king according to the laws of chivalry, but over time and through marriages and conquests, leaders of some French territories gained as much power and wealth as the king himself, and, at times, more.

The fact that Paris was the center of a kingdom and held the king's court and main chapels is not news to a modern reader. The power and influence of areas such as Aquitaine, Normandy, Toulouse, Provence, and Burgundy, however, might come as a surprise. Also, it must be remembered that the Duchy of Normandy and the Kingdom of England were tied by William the Conqueror's Norman invasion of 1066. England's nobility and most of its royalty during the Middle Ages counted themselves as French, spoke French, and spent much of their lives in France (Richard the Lionhearted, for instance, spent very little of his time in England).

So, although England and its music will receive separate treatment, England and France had deep cultural and linguistic ties.

FRENCH LANGUAGE

Most sizeable countries have regional accents or variant dialects in their language. Even in a basically English-speaking country such as the United States, regional speech has had such wide varieties as a Texas twang, a Southern drawl, and leftover Shakespearean English in isolated Appalachian regions (at least before the smoothing of language in the face of nationwide television). But France in the Middle Ages went beyond dialect. There were two French languages: *langue d'oc* and *langue d'oïl* (both named after their words for "yes").

Langue d'oc, also called Occitan or Provençal, was the language of the south of France. For most of the Middle Ages it was considered the more poetic, sophisticated, and beautiful French language. *Langue d'oïl* was the French of the northern regions—Parisian French—which eventually became the modern French language.

The differences between northern and southern France went far beyond language, however. The north was much more tied to its feudal traditions. When the king put out a call, the north answered. Noble families in the south could not care less what the king did. In fact, they considered France a foreign country. Besides putting his name at the bottom of documents as a way of dating them, they paid very little attention to their nominal lord. Because the south could not be persuaded to join in the international troubles of the north, they had a relatively settled time in which to build trade routes, develop a middle class of some wealth, and take time for such niceties as music, art, and table manners.

Some poetic lyrics sung in both regions took potshots at one other. Northern verses sometimes describe Occitans as "poverty-stricken, avaricious brigands and courtly fools" with effeminate taste whereas they, the northern French, had better food, clothes, and armor and were better soldiers. Occitan poets paint themselves instead as generous, sociable, and polite to their guests whereas the (northern) French are "surly" militaristic animals, so inhospitable that a guest could "easily starve."[1]

AQUITAINE

The Duchy of Aquitaine in southern France was the birthplace of one of the Middle Ages' most popular music forms: troubadour music. Like Gregorian chants, troubadour music had a single melody with no known harmony. And like chants, some of these tunes were not written down for years. But unlike chants, we know who many of these singer-poets were. And this is some of the first secular (nonreligious) vocal music in the vernacular (native language) known in Western music.

William IX (1071–1126), Duke of Aquitaine, is renowned as Western music's first troubadour. At least he is the first whose name is known. As this fact implies, troubadour music was considered good enough for the upper classes not only to listen to, but to write words for—and even music. This meant that, unlike other secular music, the poetry and some music of the troubadours was recorded, copied, and kept. To date, over 2,500 poems and over 250 melodies have survived from an estimated 500 troubadours.

William IX's influence and patronage may have given troubadour music its start, but its spread depended largely upon his granddaughter, Eleanor of Aquitaine, one of the most remarkable figures of the Middle Ages.

Eleanor's father, William X, allowed his court to blossom with the sounds of poetry and music, and he brought up his daughter to appreciate all the arts. But when her parents died, Eleanor's life took a drastic turn. She inherited vast territory, but had already been betrothed to King Louis VII in a political move and was married the same year. This meant that she had to move to Paris to a husband who did not even speak her language. And the court in Paris seemed barren of the sophistication that Eleanor was used to. As a consequence, she regularly brought musicians north, particularly troubadours, so that she could hear her native language and admire the complexity of poetic form and musical excellence that she was used to.

Troubadour music had a direct influence on Parisian France, which soon wanted to hear the same types of performances in *their* language. Thus, by the middle of the 1100s, music using poetry in the *langue d'oïl* began to be composed. Of course, when the royal court favors something, other aristocrats want it too. And so the northern courts acquired their own singer/songwriters.

But Eleanor was hardly a stay-at-home queen. She quickly realized that she was the stronger half of her marriage. By 1152 Eleanor had had enough. She persuaded the Pope to annul her marriage, despite the fact that she and Louis had children (Marie de France and a son named Aelis). Not one to marry down, Eleanor next became the wife of Henry II, King of England.

In England, Eleanor met her match. She had more children—four boys: Henry, Geoffrey, Richard, and John. And even in chilly England with another husband who spoke Norman French, Eleanor brought as much sophistication as possible to the English court. Ultimately, she and Henry parted ways as well. In 1169 she returned to her homeland of Aquitaine (and its capital, Poitiers), where she supported the arts until her death.

Eleanor's artistic passions were inherited by several of her children. Her French daughter, Marie de France, was a strong patron of music and other arts. Because of Marie, many Arthurian legends were written down for later generations to enjoy. Eleanor's English son, Richard the Lionhearted, wrote and sang music himself and is counted as a troubadour, despite his mixed background. England, too, received the boost it needed for secular vernacular music of its own, when it finally blended its disparate peoples into one "English" language.

TROUBADOURS, TROUVÈRES, TROBAIRICES, JONGLEURS

Troubadours are the most famous of the secular musicians in the Middle Ages. When people today think of troubadours, most envision a singer. But in the Middle Ages, troubadours were really considered poets. Their verses were more important than the music they were set to. In fact, although some troubadours wrote and performed their own music to their own verses, others wrote only the verses and left the music to *jongleurs* (or *joglars*) who were hired to perform it. And the music wrapped itself around the form of the poetry, not the other way around (words written to fit the music)! This practice, known as *formes fixes*, was the overwhelming compositional technique throughout the Middle Ages and even into the Renaissance. The reason that some music forms have names such as "ballad" and "rondo" is because they came from the name for poems known as *ballades* and *rondeaux*.

It is a sad fact that while these forms were specifically written for the appreciation of their words, those words are almost completely lost on an English-speaking population. Even translations give only the poet's barest bones—a shadow of its skill, missing the puns, political swipes, and euphemisms present in the originals. Plus, translations lose the rhythmic grace and feel of the words, as well as shades of meaning implied by using one word rather than another. A person from the Middle Ages would be puzzled to find this subject in a book about music, as opposed to a book about poetry!

Although troubadour verses were written in the southern *langue d'oc*, this was not quite the language that normal people used on a daily basis. The poetic language of the troubadours was something like poetic language of today. How many times has a twenty-first-century person heard or used words such as "ere" for "before" or "whilst" for "while" in daily conversation? These conventions are used only in writing. And the language with which the troubadours worked was a specifically high-class, aristocratic, courtly language—a language used only in the highest society, and not for every day.

Talent was the key for success. Troubadours were one of the few Middle Ages personalities outside church life, who could "move up" in society. Although not the norm, there were cases of troubadours born into the middle or even lower classes. Two of the greatest were Bernart of Ventadorn and Marcabru. Bernart's father was a merchant, and Marcabru was a "foundling left at the gate of a rich man."[2]

Of course, owing to education, the cards were stacked. At least two-thirds of the troubadour population came from the noble class. By far the majority were aristocratic younger sons with no particular patrimony but with a good background and education. And there was a "top end" as well. Twenty or more names counted as troubadours were reigning princes. It is difficult to imagine during a time of feudal government, but princely troubadours were in direct competition with the offspring of merchants for their verses' appreciation!

As mentioned before, the troubadours' *langue d'oc* verses eventually traveled north. Northern France's center was Paris, headed by a king whose court spoke *langue d'oïl*. The northern courts had been too embroiled in wars, both among themselves and in foreign campaigns, to indulge in the kind of peaceful pursuits the South had developed. But they appreciated what the troubadours were doing. For awhile, they were content to import. But soon they came up with their own poets, using the *langue d'oïl*. Northern France's version of the troubadours are known as trouvères.

The jongleur, or joglar, was more of a performer than a composer. Usually considered as entertainers, and a step lower than troubadours or trouvères, the jongleurs got their name from the fact that some traveled to medieval market fairs and not only sang but did acrobatics and juggling. The variety of jongleur types is a little mind-boggling and includes everything from clowns and singers of obscene ditties, to instrumentalists, and from sycophants who slavishly followed any court that would have them, to entertainers who sang well and were hired by the best troubadours to sing their lyrics at the best courts.

Women could also join in this courtly pursuit. Remember that the south of France had bred women of power and stature, such as Eleanor of Aquitaine. From roughly 1150 to 1250, educated noblewomen wrote poetry of their own to be sung just as troubadour lyrics were. Such a woman was known as a *trobairitz*. Few of their works have survived—about 46 to date—but through letters and praise by other artists, some of their names have survived, such as Castelloza, the Comtessa de Dia, Clara d'Anduza, and Maria de Ventadorn. The trobairitz had "her own views on men, love, marriage, and power, and sometimes she wrote them down in verse, adopting and adapting the language of the troubadours to accommodate a female voice."[3] Some lyrics were rather tame, in the manner of troubadour/trouvère writing. One partial sample (in translation) is:

I cannot help myself, handsome friend, from
Asking you in song what I can expect from you,
Because you have been fair and loving towards me,
Sincere, and humble, and free of all deceit.
Is it lost, the strong desire
Which you had for me when we both parted,
Or have you given me up for another?[4]

Other samples, however, are frank to a degree that is still shocking. One translated sample (in part) follows, but readers are cautioned that this is still not the ultimate in poetic sexual frankness—in fact some other poems might qualify as pornographic!

I heard that a lady complained
About her husband, and I can tell you about her grievance:
He never put it in more than half way, when she gave herself to him,
And she insisted on her right to the rest of it[5]

TYPES OF SONGS

For simplicity's sake, the term *troubadour* will serve for all the versifiers already mentioned. Their poetry ranged from serious topics and historical subjects to entertaining lyrics telling stories more like today's sitcoms or soap operas. Songs were sung to fit the occasion and their differences were something like changing television channels today. The *forms* of poetry had their names according to how many beats came with each line and how the lines rhymed. But the *types* of poetry had their own names, according to their subject matter. The following paragraphs describe only a few of many song types.

The *sirventes* was a poem about a political personality, a literary figure, or the lord of the place in which the troubadour was staying. It could be complimentary, moral in nature, or satiric. Sirventes were so called because they were "served" up by the poet, and the poems were also "served" to the audience on melodies borrowed from older songs. The practice of setting new words to an old tune was known as *contrafactum*. (In fact, someone who sings words like "Batman Smells" to the tune of "Jingle Bells" is performing a contrafactum!)

The *Tenso* (or *Partimen* or *Joc-partit*) was a debating song, using the names of the "opponents." It could be a joint composition between two real-life troubadours, a pretend debate between the Troubadour and Love, or even a rhetorical debate between Government and Nature.

The *Planh* (Plaint) was a kind of obituary, mourning the loss of a military, religious, political, or other person of note. The best of these are intense, heartfelt poems that span the centuries to move people who read (or hear) them hundreds of years later.

The *chanson de toile* was a poem in the female voice, although not necessarily written by a trobairitz. In these, a woman describes where she is just at that moment, and then continues with a story of how she got there, or her feelings at that time.

The *Alba* was about two lovers who have sneaked off to make love in the night. Sometimes the poem described their parting at daybreak, but sometimes it was the voice of their frantic "lookout" trying to wake them up before they would be discovered.

The *Pastorela* had two main characters—a knight and a shepherdess. The knight was either out on an adventure or coming back from one and has come upon a lovely shepherdess. She is all alone. What happens next was the entertainment. Sometimes the clever shepherdess gets away with a trick or some well-phrased words. Sometimes the knight brags about having his way with her. Sometimes the knight is more persuasive and the shepherdess is not all that anxious to get away. The varieties of the situation were seemingly endless, and the Pastorela was very popular.

The *Lai* was a long poem that apparently was sometimes sung and sometimes recited. A subtype, the *Chanson de geste,* was a song of deeds, outlining a battle or campaign—particularly something including Charlemagne or King Arthur, but one or more Crusades could also serve as subject matter.

Balada (*dansa*) poetry was based on a dance form of the day. These poems were distinctly upbeat and usually refer to the coming of spring, a May Day celebration, or young love in bloom.

The *Canso* (*chanso, chanson*) was a song about a distinctly Middle-Ages phenomenon—courtly love. This was a formal, stylized verse meant to praise the wife of the troubadour's patron.

COURTLY LOVE

The phenomenon of courtly love flowered in the hyper-courtly manners in the south of France and spread out from there. It is a conceit in which the troubadour swears he has never seen a more beautiful, gentle woman in his life than the wife of his patron. Moreover, he is so infatuated with her that if she does not favor him in some way, he will die. He lovingly describes each and every one of her attributes and claims that he simply must have her. For many years it was assumed that the troubadours must have been "parlor snakes," making mad, passionate, illicit love to married women. But cooler heads have realized that this was yet another (very popular!) form of poetic flattery, with as much reality to it as the knight and shepherdess in the Pastorela.

The underlying idea of this type of love was that it made men into better people. By having a love object whose approval was important, a man would become a better person—even if the woman was unattainable, and even if his feelings made him miserable. In other words, by learning to think beyond one's basic needs and by learning to accept one's fate (for good or ill) with a certain grace, man ceases to be a higher form of beast and becomes a cultured human being.

Since the object of adoration was female, the status of women went up a notch. At times the adoring phrases sound almost religious. Females were only too happy to exchange powerlessness for a pedestal—even a fictitious one. Courtly love also became a basis for literature. This was the time, for instance, when the character of Lancelot, who loved King Arthur's wife Guinevere, entered Arthurian literature. And although courtly love was reserved for a certain class of women, the attitudes trickled down into a basic kindness. Knights changed from being merely the best killers around, into protectors of the weak—females, the elderly, and children.

Over time, the overblown phrases of courtly love began to sound trite and repetitive. Present-day people read the translations and roll their eyes. But anyone listening to the millions of variations on the theme of love in pop culture or country-western music will know how comforting and entertaining the same basic phrases can be. While the repetitive quality can be irritating to some, to others it is as relaxing as a comfortable pair of old slippers.

THE MUSIC

Troubadour/trouvère/trobairitz music is much rarer than its poetry. Copies of troubadour melodies seem to use the same modal system as church chants, but with more accidentals than the altered "B"s mentioned in Chapter 2. While some music contains E-flats, F-sharps, C-sharps, and even G-sharps, they may show up in strange places within a single work or in different places in different copies. Whether these are errors made by a non-musical copyist or regional variations is not clear.

The vocal range varies widely. One known instance uses a melody encompassing only a fourth, but other melodies can use as many as two octaves' worth of notes—a tour de force for the singer! Most melodies, however, lie around the octave range (give or take a note or two).

There are problems in modern scholars' understanding of this music. One problem is rhythm. There was no rhythmic notation for troubadour songs, and modern transcriptions are largely educated guesses. The other problem involves instruments. Paintings and tapestries of the time occasionally show a singer with an instrument. But if troubadour songs used only a melody, such as Gregorian chants, what was played on the instrument? No one knows for sure. Speculation is that the singer was accompanied by the same melody as the one sung, but with extra ornamentation added. It was, in other words, the same dress pattern, but with more buttons and bows. This is known as *heterophony*.

TROUBADOUR LIFE AND LIVELIHOOD

Many troubadours and trouvères were attached to a particular court and stayed there as part of the court's staff. For those who were not, their lives must seem haphazard and unstable from today's point of view. But their wandering was done mostly in the warm months. During the winter, they stayed home, teaching and writing more poetry for the next season. During those seasons they were as welcome to various courts as today's rock stars are welcomed to various cities. Gifts and payments were duly noted in court accounts. From that, one can read that troubadours not only received room and board but also clothes, horses fitted out with all the necessaries, and gifts of money. If a host was a cheapskate, they might find themselves on the receiving end of the troubadour's next sarcastic *sirventes* and ridiculed through song in a wide variety of courts!

THE END (THE ALBIGENSIAN HERESY AND CRUSADE)

What happened to troubadour life? In the southern areas of France it seems to stop almost at once. Some of the last troubadours are even found in other areas, such as Spain.

The cause was a different slant on Christianity known as the Albigensian or Cathar heresy. Some Eastern religious ideas arrived in the Occitan region somewhere before 1150. Ultimately they evolved into a sect of Christianity. The sect's precepts were largely secret and almost no writings have survived. In fact, most of what is known about their beliefs is from records of people who condemned them, not necessarily the most reliable source!

However sketchy, these beliefs seem to include dualism between good and evil— neither being more powerful than the other—plus ideas of reincarnation, many strict prohibitions on foods and sexual practices, and differences in the meaning, importance, and administration of sacraments such as baptism and the Eucharist.

Cathars divided themselves into *Perfects* and *Credentes*. Perfects were incredibly austere, with almost unbelievably strict rules by which they lived. Credentes were normal people who were not expected to live up to such rigorous demands but were bound to help Perfects with whatever they might need (such as vegetarian foods or shelter).

It seems that, besides differences regarding religious sacraments, the main problem was that of *consolamentum*—a rite (but not a confessional) that washed Cathar believers of all sins committed up to the time that the rite was given. Rumors quickly rose that Cathars thus committed all sorts of sins, had a consolamentum, and killed themselves before they could sin again. It was also said that Perfects starved themselves to death rather than risk any impurity by eating. But behind the rumours and accusations were the long-standing animosity between the North and South of France, and fears of all the souls (and revenue) lost to the Roman Church as the south of France gathered Cathar converts.

The Church declared Catharism a heretical religion and, after having little success with persuasion, ultimately decided to crush it out by force. The crusade against the "Albigensians" (named for the city of Albi, where a debate had once taken place between Catholics and Cathars) started by Pope Innocent III became an excuse for the heavily militaristic northern French to wage an almost unchecked war on those of the south from 1209 to 1229. The flower of art, music, and literacy was brutally ground out. The south of France never fully recovered, and by the mid-thirteenth century, the age of the troubadours was over. The observation has been made that a person leaving the Occitan in 1154 and returning in 1204 would find things pretty much the same, but a person leaving in 1204 and returning in 1254 would find things so fundamentally different that the person would feel as though he or she had landed on Mars.

The art of the troubadour remained in the hands of the trouvères, and lived on in other areas, such as with the German minnesingers (see Chapter 5).

WHERE THE TROUBADOURS' SONGS ARE AND HOW MANY SURVIVE

Because the troubadours' art was admired, and because it was presented at courts where at least some people were literate, much of their poetry has been preserved. Unfortunately, the same cannot be said of the music. Over 2,500 troubadour lyrics (words only) have been kept in about thirty-five collections from the thirteenth to the sixteenth century, but only about 270 of the tunes were written down.

The trouvères of Northern France fared better. In about twenty-four sources, scholars have found about 4,000 verses, and about 2,100 of those have kept their music. These works were kept in collections called *chansonnières*. Though sometimes the same work was copied several times, and sometimes a troubadour work is found inside a trouvère collection, the chansonnières are a treasure trove of Middle Ages culture. Some chansonnières were in the private libraries of noble families, some have been found in religious libraries, and some are now in state libraries. The Spanish courts of Alfonso IX and X enjoyed collecting troubadour poetry and music, so a large number of works have also been preserved in Spain.

SOME FAMOUS TROUBADOURS/TROUVÈRES

A few names stand out in the ranks of troubadours and trouveres, by the excellence of their poetry, the frequency with which their works were copied and preserved, and sometimes by their rank in society or other special circumstance.

William of Aquitaine

King William IX is credited as being the first troubadour (at least he is the first known). Certainly he supported the art with his own works, as well as funding other artists. He could afford it; in 1086, when William was fifteen, he inherited almost all of southwestern France, more territorial square footage than held by France's northern king. But most of his rule shows that his character remained that of a willful fifteen-year-old. Starting and then abandoning project after project, William seemed interested in two W's: war and women.

Scholars surmise that William's poetic urges were inherited from Arabian Spain, since part of his family had married into the Aragon royalty. William was well-known for his wit and comic spirit, as well as his devil-may-care brand of bravery. And his music making was often commented on. After a close escape as a Crusades prisoner, he was asked many times to sing—that is, to personally perform—before "kings and magnates and Christian assemblies" the account of "the miseries of his captivity in rhythmic verses with funny measures."[6]

His verses tend to be off-hand and often scatological. Almost always they were about the vicissitudes of love, and they sometimes related a scene or story still amusing today. One must have sympathy for translators, who must reveal not only the sense of William's words but their sense of play. Here, in part, is William's basic philosophy about love, life, and poetry:

> Friends, I'll write a poem that will do:
> But it'll be full of fun
> And not much sense.
> A grab-bag all about love
> And joy and youth.
> A man's a fool if he doesn't "get it"
> Or deep down inside won't try
> To learn.
> It's very hard to escape from love
> Once you find you like it[7]

Another poem, too long to quote, describes an amorous adventurer who runs into a couple of women ready for a bit of love play. He pretends to be a mute and, as he surmised, the two women quickly realize that they have a "boy toy" who can never tell what happened. They take him home, feed him, and begin a petting session. But first they decide they must test him out to make sure he is not faking his muteness. So they find the biggest cat they can, pull its tail to get it angry, and rake it over the adventurer's back to see whether he will scream. He grits his teeth but manages to stay quiet. Satisfied, they strip him down for a bath. He stays in the lap of luxury and delight for eight days, bragging that during that time he satisfied them 188 times and never walked quite the same again![8]

Bernart de Ventadorn

In Medieval times (and well into the Renaissance), what look to us like last names indicated where a person was born; Bernart was from the castle Ventadorn. His background is legendary for its lowliness, as his father was reportedly the man who kept the castle bread oven hot. But the Viscount of Ventadorn took a liking to this handsome, bright young man and had him educated. Some of Bernart's first works were in praise of the Viscount's wife, but apparently his admiration went too far, and as a consequence Bernart was asked to leave. Thus he began his life as a wandering troubadour. But his talents made him welcome in many courts, even in England (where, if one will remember, the court spoke and considered itself French). Bernart's artistic philosophy is quite different from William IX's and, translated in part, is:

> It is no wonder if I sing better than any other singer; for my heart draws me more than others towards love, and I am better made for its commandments.[9]

For one of Bernart's most poignant and beloved songs we are fortunate to have both words and music preserved. The sentiments of its second verse echoes hundreds of today's pop lyrics:

> Methought that I knew every thing
> Of love. Alas my lore was none!
> For helpless now my praise I bring
> To one who still that praise doth shun,
> One who hath robbed me utterly
> Of soul, of self, of life entire,
> So that my heart can only cry
> For that which it ever shall require.[10]

Richard I of England and Blondel de Nesle

Richard was not slated to be the King of England. True, he was the son of Henry II and Eleanor of Aquitaine, but he had two grown elder brothers, Henry and Geoffrey, in front of him.

When Richard's father got into extremely hot water with the Catholic Church over the murder of Canterbury's Archbishop, St. Thomas Becket, Richard's eldest brother Henry was crowned king. But Henry never actually ruled, dying of dysentery in France during a military campaign. (This is why he is referred to as Henry the Young King instead of Henry III.) Next up was Geoffrey, but this elder brother was trampled by a horse and died. That left Richard.

Richard ruled 10 years (1189–1199), but spent almost all of his time in France and never spoke English. He was, technically, a trouvère and not a troubadour, since the English court used *langue d'oïl*, even though his mother spoke *langue d'oc* and Richard spent a good deal of time in Aquitaine. Only two of Richard's poems survive, and only one with music. That poem was, in country-western parlance, a prison song from an incarceration where his ransom was unanswered:

No one will tell me the cause of my sorrow
Why they have made me a prisoner here
Wherefore with dolour I now make my moan;
Friends had I many but help have I none.
Shameful it is that they leave me to ransom,
To languish here two winters long.[11]

Richard's troubadour fame is tied to a favorite fellow-trouvère of Richard's whose name was Blondel de Nesle. According to legend, Richard and Blondel had composed a song together that had never been sung publicly. Only Richard and Blondel knew it. When King Richard was held for ransom in Austria in 1194, legend says that Blondel traveled from castle to castle in Europe, singing one part of that particular song. While in Austria, he heard a voice singing the rest of it and knew that this was where Richard was being held. Legend says that Richard escaped. History says that he was finally ransomed—a king being an expensive commodity—for almost one-fifth of the total wealth of England.[12]

FRANCE AND POLYPHONY

No one knows why, or even when, the sound of a single melody became the sound of two melodies sung simultaneously. Anyone listening to a typical church congregation knows that there are some people who follow hymn notes up and down, but not at the same up and down as their fellows! Perhaps this happened in the medieval world of chant. Perhaps it was strangely appealing—a happy accident later taken up purposefully. Or perhaps, as human nature would have it, musically inclined people wanted to add something to the existing literature.

For whatever reasons, a second voice began to be added to plainchant melodies. In modern terms, the name for having two or more melodies *of equal importance* performed at the same time is *polyphony*. It is important to emphasize that polyphonic melodies are equal in importance. If monophony with its single voice is an absolute ruler, then polyphony is a musical democracy. This point is crucial to the understanding of music in the Middle Ages. Even when there are two, three, or four voices, the people of that time heard vertically and not horizontally. In other words, modern ears may hear a "chord" from time to time, but the participants and listeners in the Middle Ages did not! They heard two, three, or four separate lines interweaving around and among one another.

The practice of polyphony has been traced back to somewhere in the ninth century, where texts speak of more than one tone being sung at the same time, and its spread occurred over the next 250–300 years. The development of polyphony in church and secular music is long and complicated. What follows is a simplification that, one hopes, can give the reader a foundation upon which to build a deeper knowledge, if wished, by further reading.

ORGANUM

Although polyphony is the modern term, musicians of the Middle Ages first called their new invention *organum*. It had nothing to do with the instrument known as an organ. It had to do with the root word for "organization." This music was—had to be—carefully organized.

New voices needed new names. The original chant was now the *vox principalis*, *cantus firmus*, or *tenor* line. The word *tenor* comes from the Latin *tenere*, "to hold," from which the word tenacious is formed. The tenor in organum had nothing to do with the tenor voice range of today. It was simply the voice that "held" the original melody. The added line was known as *vox organalis*, or organum voice.

Although the addition of a single new voice to an older, existing tune sounds incredibly simple, it actually opened a world of possibilities for medieval musicians. For one thing, it was now possible to have voices moving in parallel motion (both voices moving in the same direction), oblique motion (one voice staying the same while another moved), or contrary motion (two voices moving in opposite directions). Parallel motion is still used today to give a "medieval" feel to music. For instance, by striking the notes C and F simultaneously on a piano and then, using only the white keys, moving up and down the keyboard, anyone can get a "monkish"-sounding music. (Later polyphony developed rules forbidding parallel motion in fifths.) But one must not suppose that entire works used only one kind of motion, which would be boring! Musicians used a few notes of one motion and then switched to another, creating a graceful "weave" of interplaying notes.

Another possibility had to do with text. While the original text was retained in the cantus firmus (at least for a number of years), it was now possible to have either the same words or different words in the other voice (or voices). In fact it was even possible to use more than one language.

And third, there were rhythmic possibilities. Both lines could follow along note by note (or more properly in the earliest instances, neume by neume) at the same time, which was a practice known as organum *discant*. Or one line could have more notes, seeming to move faster or be more florid than its partner. This was known as organum *purum*, or florid organum. But this second set of possibilities presented a problem. Although by this time music had staff lines, neumes, and even accidental markings that pinned down melodies nicely, there was still no rhythmic notation.

THE SCHOOL OF NOTRE DAME

During the Middle Ages, the Parisian cathedral of Notre Dame was a hotbed of musical innovation. Two of the brightest musical lights of the late twelfth and early thirteenth centuries worked there: Masters Leonin and Perotin. Leonin's fame came from his collection of two-voiced organa to be used for both church Masses and Offices. This tome is known as *Magnus Liber Organi*, or The Great Book of Organum, and was completed by about 1180. Perotin's fame came a generation later, from developing organum with three voices, and even four voices.

But Leonin and particularly Perotin needed to pin down rhythms in order to make music from potential chaos. The School of Notre Dame's fame comes from meeting this problem head-on. Taking a cue from the Church's melodic modes (see Chapter 2), musicians at the School of Notre Dame came up with *rhythmic* modes.

There were six rhythmic modes, all based on groups of three beats. Three was seen as a "perfect" basis for rhythm, since three was the number for the Father, Son, and Holy Spirit of the Christian Trinity. Using "short" for one beat, "long" for two beats, and "very long" for three beats, the modes were as follows:

- Mode 1 (Trochaic): long, short = three beats altogether
- Mode 2 (Iambic): short, long = three beats altogether
- Mode 3 (Dactylic): very long, short, long = six beats altogether
- Mode 4 (Anapaestic): short, long, very long = six beats altogether
- Mode 5 (Spondaic): very long, very long = six beats altogether
- Mode 6 (Tribrachic): short, short, short = three beats altogether[13]

Just as musicians mixed voice motions within a single work, they also mixed rhythmic values. Musicians realized that an entire work in only one mode would be hypnotically boring. But with no bar lines and only neumes to work with, how could a person know when one group of modal threes was turning into another? The full answer is much too complicated for inclusion here, but it involved *ligatures* which are "sticks" tacked onto the rectangular notes, making them look somewhat like notes of today. Depending on where the ligatures were placed, and how many unmarked notes followed, musicians knew which rhythmic mode to use.

For modern ears, this music acquires a rather skipping or "sing-song" quality because of the short and long beats that always add up to groups of three. But for listeners in the Middle Ages, this music must have been as exciting (and possibly as disturbing) as atonal works were at the start of the twentieth century.

Three-part organum with rhythmic modes became the rage of thirteenth-century Church music. With the addition of a third voice, the names of the parts changed once again. Everything was still based on an original Gregorian chant, and that voice, placed on the bottom, was still known as the *cantus firmus*. But now the *vox organalis* became the *duplum* (second voice) and was directly above the original chant. The *triplum* (third voice) sat on top of the others. Again, all the voices were of equal value.

It is important to remember that every line, no matter how many, related *only* to the cantus firmus. It didn't matter whether the top two lines clashed, as long as neither line clashed with the cantus firmus. (Remember, listeners heard the lines horizontally and not vertically.) These voices fitted together, largely because all the notes fell into groups of three beats, and yet they each had their own independent rhythms. The cantus firmus began to slow down and acquired the longest beats. Soon it became impossible to use the entire chant at this snail's pace. So a portion of chant was used, known as a *clausula* (just as a clause is only part of a complete sentence). Eventually this line's note values became so long that historians believe it might have been played on an instrument. This idea is bolstered when the cantus firmus line has no text printed on its part. But that is only one theory.

The top two voices acquired more independence. They could mirror one another's rhythms, or one (usually the top voice) could become still faster. But with three voices, a rhythmic style called *copula* evolved. In this style, one voice would relate to the cantus firmus in the neume-to-neume *descant* style, while the other voice would simultaneously relate to the cantus firmus in the *florid* or *purum* style. Thus, two styles were being sung simultaneously. A modern mnemonic device to remember this style is that the musicians were using a "couple of" (copula) styles at the same time.

While most Church music clung to some form of Gregorian chant as the cantus firmus—its "home base"—one type of Church music became unusually independent. The *conductus,* music performed during church services but not part of the Mass, was sung while priests went from one place to another during the service. These melodies were freely composed and had nothing to do with any precomposed music. There was no cantus firmus. This was entirely newly composed material. By the thirteenth century, the conductus was being treated polyphonically—that is, two or three voices of freely composed music made into a musical work. Although the conductus certainly did not undermine or destroy the idea of having a cantus firmus, it offered an outlet for creative freedom that was unusual in its time.

THE MOTET

But church music was not simply about the music—its text was paramount. And having two-, three-, or four-voiced works made a variety of texts possible as well. Remember Notker Balbulus's idea of the sequence, or trope (see Chapter 2)? The idea of adding new words was spread to organum voices, and words were added to the duplum, triplum, and (if there were one) quadruplum voices. The cantus firmus still had its original Latin, but the other voices might be in Latin or French. Further, one line might have a sacred text and another a secular text.

These multi-texted offerings became known as *motets*, from the French word for "word," *mot*. One would think that this might sound like "cats in January," and yet, because listeners were hearing separate lines, the motet rapidly gained popularity among musicians and listeners alike.

Motets could be sacred or secular—or, in a time when there was no separation of church and state, a mix of both. Sacred motets were not part of Mass ordinary movements, but they used Biblical texts or dealt with sacred topics. Two-voiced sacred motets usually used Latin lyrics, but three-voiced could include a line of French. Secular motets used a wide range of texts and subjects, from love topics to scathing political rants. They usually used part of a Latin chant in the bottom voice, but the upper voices were usually in French, and there is a theory that the bottom line might have been played on an instrument rather than sung in Latin.

Motet titles appear confusing to the modern reader. What is one to make of a title such as *Quant voi/Au douz tans/Hodie*? This type of title is known as an *incipit*, from the Latin word for beginning, and it is the first few words from each line of text included in the motet. In other words, while the triplum voice is singing "Quant voi," the duplum is singing "Au douz tans" and the cantus firmus is "*Hodie*," part of a Gregorian chant.

In this case the texts are rather mild. The "Hodie" text is from a biblical phrase, "Today it has purified." The duplum voice, translated, begins, "In sweet, pleasant weather, when birds are happy." The triplum translates as, "When I see winter return and also the cold."[14]

But as time went on, musicians began to slip texts and even melodies of a much more secular type into their motets. It was a sly, rather tongue-in-cheek maneuver to put the most questionable text—sometimes with its original melody, though embellished—into the middle voice, where it was less likely to be identified by persons not carefully listening. One example of this is *Mout me fu grief/Robins m'aime/Portare*. The cantus firmus, *Portare* (to carry) is in Latin, part of an old chant. The top voice is a trouvère song of a fairly innocuous type, the words translating "It grieved me greatly, the parting of my loved one . . ." But the middle voice retains both the words and original melody of a song that has Maid Marian singing of Robin Hood, "Robin loves me, Robin has my love, Robin has asked for me, he may have me."[15]

Multiple voices also left room for some musical tricks. One popular technique was the *hocket*, coming from the French word for "hiccup." Voices would be singing along until suddenly, all except one would stop and the "leftover" voice would seem to pop out. Or, two upper voices would seem to sing every other note for a few beats, creating a sort of early stereo effect that must have been startling in its time.

Another effect was *stimmtausch*. This was a form of voice exchange where one voice would "steal" notes from another's melody for a few notes. In fact, both voices might switch into one another's territory for a few notes before returning to their own. It had the effect of a musical raid.

FRANCO OF COLOGNE

The system of neumes, which had held sway for so long, needed updating to be used reliably for the more complicated rhythms that were developing. Franco did just this in his treatise written around 1260, *Ars Cantus Mensurabilis* (The Art of Measurable Music). His method of notation set forth a written rhythmic notation that was less complicated than that of the School of Notre Dame. Although still too complicated to be explained in full here, the idea was to introduce a method for writing duple rhythms as well as triple ones. In other words, one could now count in either threes or twos. The rhythms in threes were "perfect," and those in twos were "imperfect." Also he included a method for *rests*—areas of silence in music. Using different shapes and the presence, or lack of, a "tail" (ligature), Franco could write everything from what we would call a dotted whole note (six beats) right down to a diamond-shaped note that lasted half—or a third—of a beat. This was the "semibreve" (half of a short note). Over the succeeding centuries, finer and finer note divisions were added, beginning with the "minim" (smallest; written with an upstroke on a semibreve), and the older notes came to take more and more time. Today the semibreve and minim are our whole and half notes.

ARS NOVA

The wheel of history turned rather quickly from the thirteenth to the fourteenth century. As seen in Chapter 1, several major events turned the fourteenth century into a more cynical era. Life itself, cheapened by the slaughter and political upheaval of the Hundred Years' War, was even more uncertain thanks to the terrifying pandemic of the Black Death. And in the daily face of death and destruction, even belief in life everlasting was badly shaken by the Babylonian Captivity and Great Schism. Both earthly and heavenly kingdoms seemed to have failed.

Art, as a reflection of life, was enormously influenced. The humanism so hailed as a Renaissance institution began as a seedling of lost faith during the fourteenth century. As hallowed institutions faltered and failed, artists and musicians began to ignore the old rules or create new ones. This time artists were looking earthward as well as heavenward.

Two treatises, put out at almost the same time, put some of the musical changes that had already been occurring into words. One was Philippe de Vitry's *Ars Nova* (The New Art) from about 1322. The other was *Ars novae musicae* (The Art of the New Music) by Jean de Muris from about 1321. Because of the similarity of their titles and contents, French music of the 1300s became known as *Ars Nova*.

Jean de Muris played it safe in his treatise by outlining why rhythms in threes should be called "perfect." Then he outlined a way to make those perfect rhythms imperfect, or duple. Philippe de Vitry came up with the first real time signatures, which included both duple and triple rhythms as equals. His method was known as *mensuration*.

MENSURATION

Vitry used two key words for his rhythmic scheme: *time* and *prolation*. Time could be perfect or imperfect—that is, in threes or in twos. Prolation could be major or minor—major for threes and minor for twos. The combination of time and prolation became the foundation of our modern time signatures.

Time as Vitry presented it, was how the notes were grouped. Perfect time was represented by a circle. Imperfect time was represented by a half (i.e., broken) circle.

Prolation was how many beats were contained in each group. Major prolation was represented by a dot. Minor prolation was represented by the absence of a dot.

After that, it was all mathematics (see Table 3.1). A circle with a dot was three groups of notes, each group having three beats. It added up to our 9/8 time. A circle without a dot was three groups of notes, each group having two beats. This added up to our 3/4 beat. A half circle with a dot was two groups of notes, each group having three beats. This added up to our 6/8 beat. And a half circle without a dot meant two groups of notes with two groups each—our 2/4 beat.

One of these signs is still present today. The half circle with no dot has morphed into our present-day sign for 4/4 time, later explained as "C" for "common" time.[16]

Vitry further contributed to the decline of the reign of triple rhythms by introducing *coloration* of notes. A series of notes that were to be sung in duple rhythms were literally a different color: red.

All voices in a two-, three-, or four-part work did not need to be in the same mensuration. In fact, the Flemish composer Ockeghem wrote a Mass during the last part of the Middle Ages that included a section in which each of four voices sang in a different mensuration! It only lasted for a portion of time, until all the voices came out "even" at the end, but it is still studied as a remarkable example of this inventive rhythmic scheme.

Table 3.1 Rhythms in Ars Nova

Time	Prolation	Modern Time Signature		Notation		
Tempus perfectum	Prolatio maior	9/8	⊕	■ = ♦ ♦ ♦ =		
Tempus perfectum	Prolatio minor	3/4	○	■ = ♦ ♦ ♦ =		
Tempus imperfectum	Prolatio maior	6/8	⊕	■ = ♦ ♦ =		
Tempus imperfectum	Prolatio minor	2/4	C	■ = ♦ ♦ =		

ISORHYTHM

The upheaval of Vitry's time may perhaps be understood better by looking at a more familiar period: Germany between the World Wars I and II. At that time, Germany's population was uprooted, dispirited, and angry. Government institutions, customs, and even the monetary systems were in chaos. Religion seemed to be no help. Long-held artistic "rules" were breaking down, and new forms such as cubism in visual arts and atonality and serialism in music both freed the arts from old bonds and forged new ones.

France during the fourteenth century suffered a similar uprooting of its culture. And the radical new musical concepts of France's Ars Nova period—Franconian notation and Vitry's rhythmic mensuration and isorhythm—mirror its own discontented times.

Isorhythm consists of two components: a *color* (with the accent on the second syllable), and a *talea*. The original chant line (cantus firmus) in the tenor, which was by now only a portion of chant anyway, was further cut down to a few notes of its melody. These notes were repeated over and over throughout the work. This was the color. There was also a separate rhythmic pattern, known as the talea, which would also repeat in the tenor line, over and over throughout the work. Sometimes the talea and the color were set up evenly (for example, two taleas for every color), or sometimes they overlapped in ways that created new possibilities in the tenor, and thus new possibilities for the voices over them, with every repetition.

For readers familiar with twentieth-century serialism, it may not be entirely accidental to find a similarity between the concepts of isorhythm and those of serialist music. The concept of an overlapping color and talea, and a modern work with a set of tones and a set of rhythms overlapping seem to be twins, born 600 years apart.

It is important to remember that isorhythm showed up only in one voice—almost always the tenor. It is also important to know that it was all right for the talea to change in a relative way. That is, it could become twice as fast or twice as slow, but keeping the rhythms in the same relative balance as before (e.g., using modern terms, a half note followed by a whole note would become a quarter note followed by a half note). These changes were neatly taken care of by using the new mensural time signatures and notation innovations.

PHILIPPE DE VITRY

Although little is known about his personal life, Vitry (1291–1361) is still famous for his musical innovations and treatises. A cleric, Vitry was closely tied to Avignon (not Rome) and also served as an administrator and diplomat for the French royal court. As a keen observer of both church and secular abuses, Vitry's observations found their way into his motets. Vitry's verse writing was widely admired, not only in France but also in Italy, and he was praised as "the only true poet among the French" by no less a poet than Petrarch.[17]

One of Vitry's most interesting works may be found in a scathing political denunciation entitled *Roman de Fauvel*. The word *roman* in this sense only means "story," and this work was a play for which several composers wrote musical works. Thus, the musical styles found in this play vary from one-line monophony to Middle Ages avant-garde. Vitry's most famous contribution was a motet entitled *In nova fert/Garrit Gallus/Neuma*. It has three vocal lines, three texts, and uses isorhythm in the bottom (tenor) voice.

The *Roman de Fauvel* is the story of a world gone mad. In this tale, good, honest people fall to the bottom of society's ladder while Fauvel, who was literally an ass, rises to a ruling position. Fauvel's name stands for what was most valued in this world: F = *Flaterie*, A = *Avarice*, U = *Vilanie* (guile), V = *Variété* (instability), E = *Envie*, and L = *Lacheté* (cowardice). Everyone tries to make Fauvel happy to get what they want. The best way to get Fauvel in a good mood is to brush and comb his mane, from which comes the expression "to curry favor" (originally "curry Favel," English for Fauvel). Allegorical figures are mixed with actual (though unnamed) contemporaries in this wicked send-up of corruption and helplessness in the face of evil. Not only is the music a study in medieval styles, but the texts show the depth of cynicism and despair present in this pointed satire.

GUILLAUME DE MACHAUT

Machaut (c. 1300–1377) was equally known in his own time both as an important poet, having written many works not set to music, and as an excellent musician. By his time, polyphonic music was well established, and Machaut took the techniques developed by his predecessors to develop further genres that would be used in the late Middle Ages and into the Renaissance.

Machaut was a churchman, but was connected to a long list of noble houses and, particularly in his early career, traveled widely with those houses. Some of his long poems (called *dits*, "things said," or stories) are of great interest to historians, as they describe events contemporary to Machaut. One of the more chilling is a description of a plague epidemic, through which he lived, in 1348–1349.

Machaut wrote both secular and sacred works. Most of his motets use the traditional three voices, but the absence of text for the tenor voice indicates that this line was taken up by an instrument. A small portion of his motets were written for four voices: two sung lines, and two instrumental lines.

The use of four lines, so familiar to the present day, was innovative to the French Middle Ages. It involved the addition of a line under the tenor, known as the *bassus* or *contratenor*. At that point, the tenor voice took the spot that it occupies to this day.

Machaut also showed that although the basic *formes fixes* idea for vocal forms such as the ballade, rondeau, and virelai was still firmly in place, the possibilities of embellishment made these forms more interesting and vital. One of his rondeaus, *Ma fin est mon commencement* ("My End Is My Beginning"), is a masterpiece that can be sung from start to end, or backward from end to start and sounds the same either way!

But Machaut's biggest call to fame was his *Messe de Nostre Dame* (Mass of Our Lady). Before Machaut, Mass movements were written separately (see Chapter 2). In this work, Machaut wrote the first unified Mass (that scholars know about)— that is, all the Mass movements belong to this particular Mass and not to just any Mass. Nowadays, when a composer writes music for a Mass, it is taken for granted that the composer will write music for all the movements. Machaut's Mass also uses four voices, and the voices are more delineated than was usual. The upper voices, in particular, point to the use of boys or countertenors (no women sang in a church choir during the Middle Ages). This delineation would, in time, become our typical set of SATB (soprano, alto, tenor, bass) voice ranges, and the four-part writing would become standard.

AVIGNON STYLE AND ARS SUBTILIOR

During the Babylonian Captivity and Great Schism, the area of Avignon became a center for musical experimentation. French and Italian composers both brought their styles here and pushed musical intricacy to the end of its possibilities. In this style, used mostly in secular music, rhythms became incredibly complex and might even include sounds such as shouts, cries, and even bird calls. Some of the works were physically shaped, such as a three-part love song written in the shape of a heart, or a *caccia* (literally, "chase," a form of round) in the shape of a circle. Only the most highly trained singers could handle this music, probably intended for performance before the small amount of people who could appreciate its intricacies.

Known as *Ars Subtilior* (the more subtle art), this music is sometimes counted as a subtype of Ars Nova and sometimes as an altogether separate style. To modern ears it sounds discordant and strange. When Avignon lost its power, Ars Subtilior lost its sway. It remains a sample of how far the notation and theory of the Middle Ages could go before French music gave way to the Italian Renaissance.

NOTES

1. Linda M. Paterson, *The World of the Troubadours: Medieval Occitan Society*, c. 1100–1300 (Cambridge, UK: Cambridge University Press, 1993), p. 6.

2. Francis Hueffer, *The Troubadours* (London: Chatto & Windus, 1878), p. 54.

3. Carol Jane Nappholz, *Unsung Women* (New York: Peter Lang Publishing, Inc.), p. 2.

4. Ibid., p. 107.

5. Ibid., p. 93.

6. James J. Wilhelm, *Seven Troubadours: The Creators of Modern Verse* (University Park and London: The Pennsylvania State University Press, 1970), p. 33.

7. Ibid., p. 43.

8. Ibid., 39–41.

9. Rev. H. J. Chaytor, *The Troubadours* (Cambridge: The University Press, 1912), p. 48.

10. Harriet W. Preston, *Troubadours and Trouveres, New and Old* (Boston: Roberts Brothers, 1876), pp. 186–187.

11. "Richard I Coeur de Lion" (Britannia.com, 2005, http://www.britannia.com/history/monarchs/mon27.html, accessed November 28, 2006).

12. Ibid., p. 222.

13. Jeremy Yudkin, *Music in Medieval Europe*, Prentice Hall History of Music Series, edited by H. Wiley Hitchcock (Englewood Cliffs, NJ: Prentice Hall), 1989, p. 367.

14. Ibid., pp. 396–397.

15. Ibid, pp. 406–407.

16. "Mensural Notation" (http://www.answers.com/topic/mensural-notation).

17. Margaret Bent, Andrew Wathey, "Vitry : Life, Position, Reputation; Literary Works," *Grove Music Online* (http://www.grovemusic.com/shared/views/article.html?section=music. 29535.1, accessed November 29, 2006).

CHAPTER 4

THE MUSIC OF THE ITALIAN STATES IN THE MIDDLE AGES

The first thing to remember about Italy during the Middle Ages is that there *was* no "Italy." The area now known as Italy was divided among republics, oligarchies, dukedoms, and principalities, all with their own territories, their own loyalties, and their own leaders with their own armies. Add this to the fact that most of these territories were at war with one another, that outbreaks of plague haunted the Italian Middle Ages, that many men from all classes were lost to Crusades, and that in their midst were the Papal States—the center of Western Christianity, with its own set of problems—and one can begin to see why Italy was not the forerunner of cultural innovation during the Middle Ages that it would become during the Renaissance.

THE PAPAL STATES

The last vestige of Roman power in Italy was ruled by the Church. Central Italy was an independent area given to the Pope and the Church government by Pepin the Short in 754 (see Chapter 1). The Papal States' musical contributions to the Middle Ages were distinctly minor in comparison to France's. Most musicians during the Middle Ages were connected in some way with the Church, as priests or as clerics working for a cathedral or church, or singing in a chapel. But sacred music, including motets, was surprisingly static in the Middle Ages. Still, top musicians knew one another from having sung in the Vatican choir, a coveted position that served as a launching pad for future composers.

GUIDO D'AREZZO

One of Italy's most influential musicians lived during the earlier Middle Ages, from about 995 to 1050. Not much is known about his early life—even whether he was born in Italian or French territory—but, because of where he worked, he is identified with Italy.

Although Guido's birthplace is unknown, it is known that he was educated in a Benedictine monastery—in the order in which the Rule of St. Benedict first outlined music's place in monastery life (see Chapter 2). Eventually, Guido was sent to a Benedictine abbey near Ferrara, Italy, and given the task of training singers. This work was usually a formidable and rather boring task of repeating the most-used melodies again and again so that the learner could memorize everything by rote, but it soon became clear that Guido's choristers were learning much more music at an astounding rate. What was his secret? This was what Pope John XIX wanted to know. And so Guido wrote out what he had been doing, and changed Western music forever.

In Guido's time, music was written with staffless neumes (see Chapter 2). Recall that, using staffless neumes, singers could tell whether they were to sing higher or lower, but the question was how high or how low. Guido wrote that he had noticed how even small boys, as soon as they learn to read, have the entire Bible—indeed, all of written literature—at their fingertips, and yet they must spend years learning to sing even a fraction of the Church's melodies. So he devised a reliable way of writing pitch into melodies in the same way that literate people write letters, words, and sentences into thoughts. He made rows. Each row, and the spaces between each row, corresponded to a certain musical pitch. "The sounds, then, are so arranged that each sound, however often it may be repeated in a melody, is found always in its own row."[1] What Guido meant by rows are staff lines, still used today.

Guido further pinned down pitches by giving them letter names. Because of Pythagoras's and Boethius's writings (see Chapter 1), the concept of the octave was well-known. Guido's letter names are the same as today's: A, B, C, D, E, F, and G, then starting over again at the octave. He also colored two of the lines. "Wherever, then, you see the color yellow, there is the third letter, C, and wherever you see the color red, there is the sixth letter, F, whether these colors be on the lines or between them."[2]

Further still, Guido developed the concept now called *solfege* or *solfeggio* for teaching purposes. These are the syllables *do, re, mi,* . . . that schoolchildren still use today when learning to read music. Guido's original scheme did not include *ti*, and what we now call *do* had a different name: *ut*. (People who work crossword puzzles will know "ut" as the answer to the clue "Guido's note"!) As a monk and a

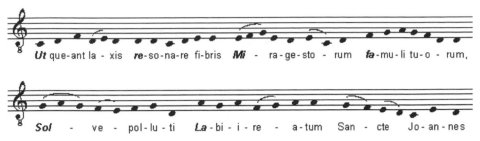

Ut que-ant la - xis re-so-na-re fi-bris Mi - ra-ge-sto - rum fa-mu-li tu-o - rum,

Sol - ve - pol-lu - ti La-bi-i-re - a-tum San - cte Jo-an-nes

Figure 4.1 The hymn *Ut queant laxis*.

musician, Guido got these syllables from a chant hymn, *Ut queant laxis*, sung on the feast of the birth of John the Baptist. In this hymn each phrase begins one note higher than the phrase before it (Figure 4.1). *Ut* is on C, *re* is on D, *mi* is on E, *fa* is on F, *sol* is on G, and *la* is on A. The only syllable missing is the one for B, the Middle Ages' problem note (see Chapter 2).

Guido wrote down an antiphoner (a collection of Church music) using his new system. It was an enormous improvement. "To sing an unknown melody competently as soon as you see it written down or, hearing an unwritten melody, to see quickly how to write it down well, this rule will be of the greatest use to you."[3]

Musically speaking, this is one of history's biggest understatements. Although music theory has changed many times, Guido's staff lines, letter names, and solfeggio syllables remain bedrock in learning to read music. Beginning piano students start by finding middle C on the keyboard, and in solfeggio, *ut* (now *do*), *re*, *mi*, *fa*, *sol*, and *la* are still on the same notes where Guido put them.

Because he was using both men's and boys' voices, Guido tended to use the scale starting on G (now the bottom line on the bass staff) for training. This scale (and eventually all scale systems) became known as a *gamut* from a combination of the Greek letter gamma and the note *ut*.

As if all this were not enough, Guido also devised a system to help his choir remember what to sing, by using parts of his hand to correspond to one or more notes of music. All he had to do was point to some specific place on his hand, and the choir knew where the music was supposed to go. (Remember that this was before polyphony, so there was only one melody. When there was more than one melody sung at the same time, Guido's method had to be used to teach each part separately.) For instructional purposes and to learn melodies quickly and well, Guido's hand was a phenomenally innovative tool. Guido's hand did allow for both "hard" and "soft" B (see Chapter 2) but no other "accidentals." Therefore, for the next several hundred years, if a note was altered by a half step up or down (say, an E flat or an F sharp), those notes were said to be "outside the hand."

Figure 4.2 shows Guido's hand with both the letter in the gamut (G, A, B, etc.) and also the solfeggio letter(s) that one was to sing at each position. Note that some joints have two or three syllables written on them. These alternatives

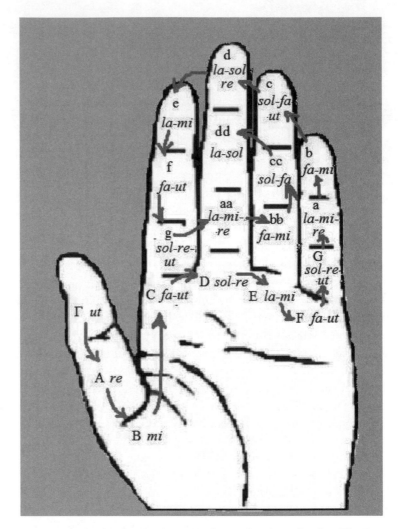

Figure 4.2 Guido's hand. From "Guidonian hand," *Wikipedia: The Free Encyclopedia*, retrieved from http://en.wikipedia.org/wiki/Guidonian_hand. Image by Lukas Pietsch.

enabled *ut* to be sung on F and G as well as C—the beginning of our system of multiple keys and key signatures. For example, the B (written "b" because it was on the second octave) at the tip of the little finger has both *fa* and *mi*. When *ut* was sung on G, the B was *mi*, so it was hard (natural). When *ut* was sung on F, the B was *fa*, so it was soft (flat).

Eventually Guido was sent to Arezzo, from which he got his place-name, and near which he lived for most of his life.

Musical developments in Italy for the next two centuries remained largely unremarkable. They did develop polyphony, but the few examples left are not of the highest quality, and the lion's share of innovations were happening in France. Most early Italian polyphony was unwritten improvisation and thus lost to history except when mentioned in treatises or in contemporary letters. Possibly because of its improvisatory nature, music did not hold as important a place in the educational curricula as it did in France. Italy's oldest universities tended toward medicine and law. Serious study of music was not high on their list. So there was no chance for something to develop in Italy such as the School of Notre Dame did in France.

Instead, Italian history was most innovative socially, in the religious movement of St. Francis of Assisi (1182–1226), who founded the Franciscan order. Rather than remaining cloistered away from the world as Benedictine monks were, Franciscan friars were missionaries. The growth and spread of the Franciscans was a phenomenon of the thirteenth century.

The rapid spread of the Franciscan order, promoting a life of simplicity, seemed to have struck a chord with many Italians. Musically too, Italians preferred a certain clarity in their music and were less interested in the complex rhythms and intricately interwoven musical lines of French innovations. In Italian music, the main melody was generally put into the top line, not the bottom (tenor, cantus firmus) line. Thus the tenor line did not have the same importance as in French music. In Italian works using three voices, the two lower lines supported the top line, instead of the French custom of having all the voices line up with the tenor.

Musically speaking, outside influences arrived rather late in Italy. During and after the Albigensian Crusade (see Chapter 3), refugee musicians from the south of France, particularly troubadours, brought their music into Italy. The styles that came in at that time influenced Italians, who began to incorporate some French aspects into their own music. Thus, music in Italy seems to spring from nowhere, coming into its own somewhere in the fourteenth century. The proper name in Italian for the number 1300 is *mille trecento*—one thousand, three hundred. Eventually the name was shortened, and Italian music of the 1300s (the same century as French Ars Nova) has become known as *trecento* music.

THE ITALIAN TRECENTO

During the Middle Ages, the various Italian city-states became Europe's middleman for trade with the East. It was during this time that Marco Polo returned from his travels all the way from China to tell fabulous tales of the possibilities open to traders. Trade routes went both by land and by sea, and Italy, being a nation of coastlines, also became a center for shipbuilding. Eventually the revenue that began coming into the Italian states began to trickle down from its wealthiest ruling families to the arts.

Though the Renaissance was yet to come, the Italian 1300s produced some important artists. Painting flourished in the works of Giotto (1267–1337), and Italy was also building some of its most impressive architectural achievements during this century. But more important to musicians were Trecento writers: Dante

Alighieri (1265–1321), Petrarch (1304–1374), and Boccaccio (c. 1313–1375). The works that they produced convinced Italians that their own language was worthy of being used as musical text. These writers' skillful use of the Italian language became known as the *dolce stil nuovo* (sweet new style).

All was not rosy, however. This was also the century of French dominance over the Western Christian Church, which eventually lead to the upheaval of the Great Schism. This was also a time when almost every city-state was warring with its neighbors—that is, when they were not being cut down by the Black Death. The plague hit all of Europe, but Italy particularly hard, in 1348 (see Chapter 2).

Italian reactions to their chaotic and uncertain daily lives was split into two camps: (1) a deep depressive mood centered on death (the end of the world was a popular theme), and (2) the idea that life was so unpredictable that one should rush to savor all its possibilities now, on earth, instead of taking a chance on heavenly bliss.

NOTATION OF THE ITALIAN TRECENTO

Italian notation was different from France's. The Italians did not use Franco's new notation system or Vitry's mensural signs. Although the details of the notation they used are much too complicated to cover in this brief chapter, for many decades Italian musicians used a "dot of division" as a way of delineating certain rhythms. Eventually they developed a system that stemmed from a single long note and broke into a first, second, and third division of notes. Each division had a *binaria* (a system of duple rhythms, that is, rhythms divisible by two) and a *ternaria* (a system of triple rhythms), and each division broke down into smaller and smaller note values.

When French styles and ideas of French notation came into Italy, an Italian theorist named Marchettus wrote a treatise called the *Lucidarium* (1317–1318). In it he proposed using both Italian and French notation systems within the same work. When the French system was to be used, they would put a small letter "g" into the part, standing for *gallica* (from Gaul, the old Roman name for what we call France).

TRECENTO MUSIC FORMS

During the fourteenth century, music in the Italian states began to come into its own. The moods mentioned in the preceding section, plus influences from other arts, added to patronage from wealthy families, all affected Italian music in various ways. The marriage of troubadour influences and native traditions gave rise to several forms of vernacular music, that is, music using the native Italian language. This was secular vocal music, although its texts varied widely from the religious to the profane. Several styles in particular spread throughout the Italian city-states and found their way into other parts of Europe—the caccia, the lauda, the ballata, and the madrigal. The first two were popular mainly in the Middle Ages; the third style lasted well into the Renaissance; and the last, which took its first baby steps in the Middle Ages, became the dominant secular vocal style of the Italian Renaissance.

THE CACCIA

Technically, the caccia is a canon at the unison. Known as a "round" by anyone who can sing "Row, row, row your boat," the caccia differentiates itself by having three voices, only two of which are alike. Caccia means chase, and the top two voices chased one another while the bottom voice moved freely. The top two voices also had text while the bottom voice had none, which leads scholars to believe that this line was played on an instrument.

What could be more natural to a chase song than one of the Middle Ages' most vital occupations—hunting? Of the twenty-five or so surviving trecento caccias, many describe some sort of hunt. Not realistic, these scenes were entertaining and sometimes quite humorous. They could also include such extra-musical effects as "shouts, bird calls, [and] hunting cries."[4] Other caccia texts described sailing, a fire, or even street scenes.

Caccias typically contained an element called a *ritornello*—a piece of text and music that returned, that is, was sung more than once. The idea of a ritornello would grow over the next several centuries until it became a key element in certain musical forms of the Baroque and Classical eras, such as concerto and symphony movements in "ritornello form" and the rondo.

A partial translation of one Middle Ages caccia gives an idea of its sense of urgency and action:

> "Now here, companions, here with great enjoyment, call the dogs here immediately!"
> "Black-mouth, fetch, fetch!" "White-skin, stay here, stay!" "I think I see a chamois!"
> "Where is it coming from?" "From here, from here!" "Which way is it going?"[5]

THE LAUDA

The Lauda was a vernacular vocal work with a biblical text. This form came about from religious organizations made up of laymen, known as *laudesi*, who specialized in the singing of laudas. Some of these organizations were affiliated with a particular church order, such as the Franciscans or Dominicans, but the members were not monks themselves. Church and civic life in the Middle Ages blended one into the other, and though their text was religious, laudas were not meant to be sung in church. Lauda organizations put on religious events with the blessing of the Church, ranging from simple processions to fairly elaborate dramatic representations. The dramas used music known as *laude dramatiche*, performed by members known as *disciplinati*. All the vocalists were men; the high parts were sung by boys.

Laudesi poets wrote their texts without thought to the music. If music was needed, the organization commissioned a professional musician to write it, or they might simply use a familiar tune that happened to fit. Texts of this type have a note at the end of the poetry, saying that the work was to be sung to the tune of this or that contemporary vocal work that someone in the Middle Ages would have known.

Surviving examples of laudas are in collections known as *laudarii*. Unfortunately for musicians, although there are about 200 of these collections with texts, only two include music notation. Laudas could be either monophonic or polyphonic. Though they were sung in many Italian city-states, Florence was a major producer. By the last years of the Middle Ages, polyphonic laudas were being written and set to music independently of any organization; the lauda was just another form of vocal piece. And eventually the form faded into history.

THE MADRIGAL

The madrigal is such an integral part of the Italian Renaissance that many people are surprised even to find them during the Middle Ages. There are very early examples of single-voiced (monophonic) madrigals, however, from as far back as the thirteenth century. Scholars believe that they began as texted tunes sung by shepherds or peasants and were later picked up by higher social circles and began to be officially composed by the thirteenth century. Two- and three-voiced madrigals were composed for the courts of various Italian city-states. Surviving examples have a wide range of complexity from the very simple to ornate examples containing what would today be known as sixteenth-note values.

Madrigals had texts for all voices, indicating that all the lines were sung. There are some passages of imitation—areas where one voice copies what another voice has already sung—that are like short echoes of the caccia form. However, madrigal music (like troubadour music) was absolutely subservient to its text. In fact, madrigal music has been described as "draped across its text."[6] Poetic lines generally coincide with some sort of musical cadence (ending point), and if there is a repeated stanza, it is not only treated with a musical ritornello, but separated by using a different meter—that is, if the verses are in a duple meter, the ritornello will be in a triple meter.

Madrigal writers tended to be from territories in the northern half of Italy, such as Padua, Verona, Milan, Florence, and Bologna. Three big names in medieval madrigal writing were Giovanni de Firenze from Florence, Jacopo of Bologna, and Magister Piero, both of whom worked in Milan and Verona.

One interesting device of the time has to do with a madrigal's text rather than its music—the *senhal*. The senhal was the name of a person, who might be a patron, a friend, or a political personage, hidden in the text. When the texts were sung, the names remained secret. But if one looked at the text closely, the name could be ferretted out. For instance, look at this sentence and reward yourself if you see the name "Andrew"!

BALLATA

During the trecento, the ballata was an extremely popular form of secular vocal music. It had many relatives, namely the French virelai, the English carol, and the Spanish cantiga. Scholars believe that all of these forms sprang from dances, and they all are somewhat similar in form, with verses and refrains of some type. Indeed, Bocaccio's most famous work, *The Decameron,* describes people dancing to a sung ballata: "Immediately Lauretta began to lead the others in the dance, while Emilia sang the following ballata in amorous tones."[7]

Ballata texts varied widely "from the erotic, the pastoral, the descriptive to the contemplative, the moral and the political."[8] There are monophonic ballatas as well as two- and three-voiced polyphonic ballatas. However, ballatas of both types may have an untexted part, indicating that instruments may have taken one of the lines. Also, while a caccia or a madrigal would change from duple to triple rhythms and might use some complicated rhythms among its voices, ballatas tend to be simpler. This is not to say that ballatas were composed with less skill, but they were more restrained than their companion forms.

FRANCESCO LANDINI

The greatest composer of the trecento ballata was the Florentine composer Francesco Landini (1325–1397). His life is described in a history of Florence begun by Giovanni Villani (1275–1348) and continued by Giovanni's son, Filippo Villani (1325–1407). Since they were contemporaries of Landini, much more is known about Landini's early life than about those of other Middle Ages composers.

Landini's father was a painter who had studied and worked with Giotto. So it must have been especially horrible when little Francesco caught smallpox and was left blind from the scarring. Since painting was out of the question, Francesco turned his artistic bent to music. He sang and learned to play the organ. His contemporaries admired his organ playing to the point of adoration. "In particular, he began to play the organ, with such great dexterity—always accurately, however— and with such expressiveness that he far surpassed any organist in living memory."[9] Eventually Landini added designing and building organs to his playing skills. Both a small portrait on an illuminated manuscript and a carved portrait on his tomb-stone show Landini playing a portative organ (see Chapter 10 for that instrument).

But although the organ was his main instrument, he also played others: fiddle, lute, and wind instruments, and a stringed instrument called a *serena serenorum,* which he invented and that was once described as a cross between a lute and a psaltery (see Chapter 10 for lute and psaltery). He both sang and directed other singers, and he composed both poetry and music. Because of his fame among contemporaries, much of his music has survived—eleven madrigals, two caccias, and 141 ballatas. It is fairly obvious that the ballata was a favorite form for Landini.

Landini's music was praised many times by eyewitnesses for its sweetness. And indeed, it is possible to listen to Landini's music without undue stress even in modern times, where it sometimes emerges in rather unlikely venues. (The author first heard Landini's music as a youngster on an album by the folk singer Judy Collins!)

Landini wrote both two- and three-voiced ballatas. Most of the two-voiced ballatas have text in both voices. The three-voiced ballatas have either text in all three voices or one line sung and two others played on instruments. Landini was connected with the church as a clergyman, but did not feel that his art must lean toward the sacred. In fact, all of Landini's songs are secular. The texts vary, but they sound rather like troubadour songs in that love and its joys and pains are a main topic. For instance one, in part, translates:

> Do you enjoy—since I loved you,
> And still love you so much that I have no other happiness———
> Holding my life in such torment?

Its repeated refrain is:

> Lady, if I deceived you,
> Or ever followed another love but you,
> I would willingly die at your own hands[10]

Landini's ballatas have also been studied as samples of how French elements began to introduce themselves into Italian trecento music by the end of that era, particularly in Florence. One of Landini's ballatas even uses the French language (which technically makes it a virelai!). Besides being famous for his ballatas, Landini is also famous for how he ended most of his works, with a convention that became known as the "Landini cadence."

THE LANDINI CADENCE

The endings of Landini's works are so typical that having heard one, most people can spot a Landini tune from then on, by hearing its last few notes. In addition to the rhythms, which sound syncopated to our ears, at the very end both (or in the case of a three-voiced work, two out of three) voices approach their final note from a half-step below, suddenly moving in parallel fourths, reminiscent of parallel organum. Those half steps are called leading tones because they lead so strongly to the ending note, one half-step above. Thus, the Landini cadence has a "double leading tone"—one from, say, a B natural to a C and the other from, say, an E to an F.

FLORENCE

Although other Italian city-states were musically active, Florence stands out among them even in the Middle Ages. Florence's artistic leanings had something to do with its combination of urban identity, wealth, and the intermingling of sacred and secular life. Florence's leading family, the Medici, were bankers and were famous already as patrons of the arts (although their full flowering would culminate later in the Renaissance with Lorenzo de Medici). Other wealthy Florentine families followed in their footsteps, and even on a purely personal level, an upper-class male was not considered well-bred if he did not indulge in some sort of amateur music-making. Clerics participated fully in Florence's urban life, and most of the music teaching was left to their care. Although still churchmen, clergy musicians were perfectly free to compose secular music or poetry and felt no guilt about writing a madrigal, caccia, or ballata. Florentine poets, too, felt that the madrigal was a perfectly fine vehicle for their work. The most popular poetic texts set to medieval madrigal music in all the Italian city-states were those of Sacchetti, a Florentine.

THE FIFTEENTH CENTURY

Winds of change were blowing into Italy from the outside during the last part of the trecento, and they picked up speed during the first half of the fifteenth century. French influences continued to come in, and another new musical area was beginning to have its influence felt: Burgundy. The Burgundian court was beginning to turn out excellent musicians, known as Franco-Flemish. The Burgundians were as interested in trade as the Italians (see Chapter 8), so there were plenty of opportunities for cross-cultural contact. Franco-Flemish musicians eventually were imported into Italy, where they blended their musical techniques with local music practices. They also fostered native-born talent and were excellent educators—all of which helped to boost Italy into becoming the dominant musical force of the Renaissance.

NOTES

1. Oliver Strunk, *Source Readings in Music History* (New York: W.W. Norton & Company, Inc., 1950), p. 118.

2. Ibid., p. 119.

3. Ibid., pp. 124–125.

4. Albert Seay, *Music in the Medieval World.* 2nd edition (Englewood Cliffs, NJ: Prentice-Hall, Inc., 1975), p. 156.

5. John Caldwell, *Medieval Music* (Bloomington and London: Indiana University Press, 1978), p. 186.

6. James McKinnon, ed., *Music and Society: Antiquity and the Middle Ages from Ancient Greece to the 15th Century* (Englewood Cliffs, NJ: Prentice Hall, 1991), p. 253.

7. Jeremy Yudkin, *Music in Medieval Europe. Prentice Hall History of Music Series*, edited by H. Wiley Hitchcock (Englewood Cliffs, NJ: Prentice Hall, 1989), p. 523.

8. Reinhard Strohm, *The Rise of European Music, 1380–1500* (Cambridge, UK: Cambridge University Press, 1993), p. 86.

9. Piero Weiss and Richard Taruskin, *Music in the Western World* (New York: Simon & Schuster Macmillan, 1984), pp. 74–75.

10. Jeremy Yudkin, *Music in Medieval Europe. Prentice Hall History of Music Series*, edited by H. Wiley Hitchcock (Englewood Cliffs, NJ: Prentice Hall, 1989), p. 542.

CHAPTER 5

MUSIC OF THE GERMANIC LANDS

In some ways, Germanic lands of the Middle Ages were similar to the Italian ones. As with Italy, there was no "Germany" in the sense that one knows it today. If anything, Germany was even more fragmented than the Italian city-states. But just as Italy had the Papal States as an area of some power to look toward, the Germanic lands were at least loosely glued together by the power of the Holy Roman Empire.

Since German-speaking areas were so widespread and included not only Germany but what is now Austria and parts of the Netherlands, Belgium, and even parts of France and Italy, this text will refer to "Germanic areas" and not to "Germany."

THE HOLY ROMAN EMPIRE

The Holy Roman Empire (see Chapter 1) was a solidifying force that helped Europe climb out of the Dark Ages. The Emperor's chair was supposedly an elected office, with Electors—heads of major areas—voting for the next Emperor each time the last one died. But in practice, during the Middle Ages many of these elections were rubber stamps for what was essentially a hereditary lineage. The following paragraphs provide a rough outline of the major houses and their rulers.

The Carolingian Empire set up by Charlemagne disintegrated after his death in 814. His son, Louis, was overwhelmed by powerful dukes who turned their feudal territories into hereditary duchies. Worse, Louis's own sons fought among themselves. The ensuing civil wars and territorial grabs split the Empire into two main parts, which became the seeds of Germany and France.

While France dealt with its own fractious territories, the Germanic areas came up with another strong leader—Otto I, who broke up the powerful duchies by transferring much of their hereditary territory to the Church. Since clerics had no heirs, these territories once again became fief-like and tied to Otto's royal court. The Ottonian Empire lasted from 936 to 1024, under Ottos I, II, and III. Its downfall came mainly through an obsession with controlling Italy, particularly the Vatican.

After the Ottonians came the Salian Emperors from 1024 to 1125. Under Ottonian rule, Popes had been nominated and backed by the Holy Roman Emperor. Then in 1059, the Vatican ruled that its own Cardinals would decide who would be Pope. Now the Holy Roman Emperor and the Vatican were at odds. Salian rule was marked by church/state conflict and civil wars.

Next came the Hohenstaufen Emperors. They ruled from 1137 to 1254. Their most famous member was Frederick I, known as Frederick Barbarossa (the "Barbarossa" nickname referred to his red beard). He considered himself equal to the Pope in religious matters, and it was Frederick who added the "Holy" to the title of Holy Roman Emperor. He too was obsessed by controlling Italy, but the Lombards spoiled his agenda. Frederick Barbarossa died in the Third Crusade and was succeeded by his son, Henry V, and then his grandson Frederick II—an outstanding leader known by the Latin title "Stupor Mundi" (Wonder of the World). Unfortunately, Frederick II inherited the family obsession with Italy. He actually invaded and occupied the Papal States for a time. But during his absence, the Germanic nobility gained strength.

After Frederick II's death, several contenders, some of them from as far away as Spain, claimed the title of Holy Roman Emperor, and the period from 1254 to 1273 is known as the Great Interregnum (the time between kings). By 1273, the fighting had settled into three basic families: the Luxemburgs, the Wittelsbachs, and the Habsburgs. This time the Electors held a real vote instead of their usual rubber stamp, and chose a minor Swabian prince, Rudolf of Habsburg, to become the Emperor.

The Electors were not being altruistic. Rudolf was elected because the Electors thought he was too weak to bother them; they were wrong. Rudolf acquired more and more territory by various means until the Habsburgs were as powerful as any other family. Moreover, he ruled from Austria. Historically, this solidified Austria's capital, Vienna, as the capital of the Holy Roman Empire.

By 1356, seven areas were designated as courts whose rulers would always be Electors. Some of these areas belonged to the Church, and others had secular rulers. This move set up a church/state balance of sorts, and it also set apart several Germanic areas as most powerful. The Electors would be the archbishops of Mainz, Trier, and Cologne, the Count Palatine of the Rhine, the Duke of Saxony, the Margrave of Brandenburg, and the King of Bohemia.

Although the individuals died and were replaced, these titles remained and are sprinkled throughout the history of music from the Middle Ages into the Classical era. For instance, during the Baroque era (1600–1750), George Frideric Handel worked for the Elector of Saxony (the same Elector of Saxony who subsequently became George I of England), and J. S. Bach wrote his Brandenburg Concertos for the Margrave of Brandenburg.

The Holy Roman Empire was dissolved only when confronted with Europe's most irresistible force—Napoleon—in 1806.

LIFE IN THE MEDIEVAL GERMANIC LANDS

Underneath all this strife, ordinary people had to live their lives, not an easy task. For one thing, the country was not united by language. A dialect known as High German was spoken in southern areas, while Low German was spoken mainly in the north; meanwhile, the Old forms of the languages were turning into the Middle forms. These two sets of categories—Old/Middle and High/Low—mixed and matched throughout history. For the time covered in this book, the form most used was Middle High German.

Because the Germanic areas were so loosely connected, defense was constantly on the minds of the leaders in each area, court, town, and even religious institution. To this end, Leagues formed for defense. Most famous was the Hanse, or Hanseatic League, of states on the Baltic Sea in Northern Germany, but throughout the country there were Town Leagues with their own militias. Instead of being protected by the knightly class, Town Leagues were *attacked* by the leagues of knights! By the fifteenth century, most Leagues were mainly fighting one another and, except for the Hanse (which lasted until 1688), they disintegrated. Some areas formed Republics and relied on outside forces hired for protection. There were plenty of soldiers for hire because of the constant fighting and shifting loyalties in Germanic areas. Not confined to their homelands, these soldiers were hired all over Europe. And of course, in more tightly controlled areas, feudalism was still working. Areas owned by the Church relied especially heavily on feudalism for their defense.

Music was a thread woven through the badly shredded cloth of Medieval Germany. Whether in Latin, German, or a mix of the two, music played an important part in both sacred and secular spheres.

GERMAN SACRED MUSIC

Sacred music in Germanic areas had been codified during Charlemagne's reforms and tended to be conservative. Most Germanic contributions were theoretical writings (in Latin) and not actual music. The monastery of St. Gall was a center of this art, and one of its monks was Notker Balbulus, "The Stammerer" (see Chapter 2), the early medieval musician, composer, and theorist. In addition to the usual Latin, some of Notker's writings were in Old High German. And, as has been mentioned, he was responsible for the development of texted sequences, a milestone in Middle Ages sacred music (see Chapter 2).

One notable area of sacred writing, curiously, is a series of detailed descriptions of organs, organ pipes, and development of various organ *tablatura* (special notation for playing organ music). This Germanic fascination with the organ continued through the Middle Ages, the Renaissance, and eventually it would lead to the most famous line of organists known throughout the world: the Bachs.

Since European innovation in church music centered mainly around Paris during the Middle Ages, far-seeing Church musicians tended to go there. Franco of Cologne was one such German-speaking musician who is counted as French (see Chapter 3). Although the development of time signatures was incredibly important to music history, it had little effect in his homeland, where even polyphony made few inroads until the end of the Middle Ages.

There was an exception, who again has already been mentioned. This exceptional figure wrote not only newly composed text and music not tied to Gregorian chants, but occasional organum. Moreover, the composer was female.

HILDEGARD OF BINGEN

One of the earliest Germanic medieval composers was female: Hildegard of Bingen, who lived from 1098 to 1179 (see Chapter 2). As an abbess, Hildegard headed a convent of nuns that she founded in Bingen, a Rhine Valley area.

Hildegard claimed that her music, just like her visions, came to her straight from God. Thus, it is unapologetically different from that of her contemporaries. Hildegard was a Renaissance woman who lived well before the Renaissance. Keenly intelligent, she wrote on a wide variety of topics in addition to music, including medical and scientific treatises as well as the lives of saints. Her religion, solidly Catholic, leaned toward—but was not exclusive to—female saints and celebrations involving the Virgin Mary. For these she composed hymns, sequences, and other musical forms.

But even without her other accomplishments, Hildegard's place in music history would have been cemented through her 1152 work, the morality play *Ordo Virtutum* (Play of the Virtues). Although she may not have invented the morality play genre, she is credited with having been the first to put one to music. Also, this drama did not come from a Bible tale, but concerns the soul of a woman and her choices between sixteen personified Virtues and the Devil's myriad temptations. The work takes about ninety minutes—an extraordinarily long effort for its day. All the Virtues were represented by women from the convent, and they sang their parts. The Devil was the only male character—probably played by the monk Volmar, Hildegard's secretary—and never sang but shouted. There was also a narrator, and this part was likely taken by Hildegard herself.[1] Still performed by early music groups today, this play is rich in symbolic gestures, both in its words and in its music.

GOLIARD MUSIC

A link between secular and sacred music is that of the Goliards, a loose group of minor clerics and wandering students who gave homage to a possibly fictitious patron, "Bishop Golias" (Goliath). They were most active in the twelfth and early thirteenth centuries. Much of their music has been lost, and their few surviving tunes are in staffless neumes, which makes reconstructing them difficult. However, many of their lyrics remain. The languages of Goliard texts range from High and Low German and good Latin to a corrupted Latin-German mix. Their subject matters were as varied as their languages and include everything from praising the Virgin Mary to songs about love, the coming of spring, and the joys of drinking.

For example, the words to a song entitled *The Confession of Golias* are, translated in part,

> In the public-house to die
> Is my resolution:
> Let wine to my lips be nigh
> At life's dissolution[2]

Goliards and their wandering ways earned them a sort of "Friar Tuck" reputation. They were seen as unreliable and borderline heretics, and their pranks and especially their satirical writings against the Church and its foibles finally led to having their "privileges of clergy" rescinded by the church. Also by the mid-thirteenth century, wandering students had settled into established universities. Under this double blow, the Goliards dwindled out. However, 800 years later, the Goliards had a revival of sorts. A collection of manuscripts of their poetry from the thirteenth century, kept in Benediktbeuern Abbey near Munich, had its texts published in an 1847 book entitled *Carmina Burana*. Several of these Goliard texts were re-set to new music by Carl Orff, creating the Carmina Burana familiar to concertgoers worldwide.

MINNESINGERS

The early thirteenth century was marked by two giant leaps forward in German-language literature: Wolfram von Eschenbach's *Parzival* and Gottfried von Strassburg's *Tristan*. Both stories are Arthurian legends, and thus British in origin. Scholars believe that these were recited as after-dinner entertainments, likely sung in a formulaic pattern in the same manner as French chansons de geste (see Chapter 3). Both tales were written for the enjoyment of secular courts, and both share a trait common in a country as divided as the Germanic lands—borrowing from other countries.

Minnesingers were secular musicians who sang for the entertainment of Germanic courts during the Middle Ages. Their works were called *minnesang* (love songs). It is no accident that this description sounds extremely similar to French troubadour and trouvère traditions. The Minnesinger's art was directly borrowed from France and included several possible sources. When Frederick Barbarossa married Beatrice of Burgundy in 1156, his new wife came with her servants, including her personal

Table 5.1 French and German Forms

Troubadour-trouvère form	Minnesinger form equivalent
Alba	Tagelied
Jeu (or joc)-parti	Wechsel or Geteilteyspil
Chanson de geste	Kreuzlied (Crusade song)
Lai	Leich
Sirventes	Spruch
Ballade	Barform

trouvère. Also, Germanic crusaders listened to French secular musicians on their travels to and from the Holy Land and even during battle campaigns. In addition, troubadours and trouvères were often invited to perform in Germanic areas. This must have encouraged German-speaking nobles to want the same type of music for their own courts, but in their own language.

However it came about, Minnesingers became the Germanic equivalent of the French troubadours and trouvères, even borrowing the forms of their songs. In fact, there is some evidence that on occasion a lord or lady would give a Minnesinger a French melody and ask him to put German words to it! Scholars point out that in the early years, Germanic Minnesinger music forms were direct equivalents to French ones, as shown in Table 5.1.

However it started, the Minnesinger tradition long outlasted its French ancestors. This is because polyphony came late to the Germanic areas. While France was experimenting with three-, four-, and five voiced-works in their church and secular music, Germany was not so eager to jump into this new and confusing world. Thus secular monophony became "old hat" in France but still was appreciated in Germany until the end of the Middle Ages.

WALTHER VON DER VOGELWEIDE

Walther von der Vogelweide (c. 1170–1230) is believed to have been born into the lower aristocracy, but during his lifetime he was honored as being the greatest poet-composer-singer of his era. In Gottfried von Strassburg's *Tristan*, the author takes time to name a dozen poets from whom he had personally taken inspiration. Although all are hailed as geniuses, Gottfried states that the "nightingale of Vogelweide" heads them all.

One of the aristocrats Walther served was no less than Frederick Barbarossa, who took Walther with him on a Crusade. From this we have a surviving Kreuzlied in which Walther describes his feelings upon seeing the Holy Land for the first time. Its words are, translated in part:

Now is my life fully blessed,
Since my sinful eyes have seen

The Holy Land and the earth
Which has been so honored.
What I have always wanted has happened:
I have come to the city
Where God appeared as man.[3]

One of Walther's best accomplishments was in breaking the dead-end of troubadour lyrics: courtly love. In courtly love (see Chapter 3), a man is in love with a woman he can never have. Walther made love a mutual affair, and thus brought to it a humanity lost in French lyrics, while still keeping its Germanic-language poetry on the highest level of skill.

TANNHÄUSER

The name Tannhäuser usually brings about thoughts of the Romantic era composer Richard Wagner, who wrote an opera of that name. But the real Tannhäuser was a late-era Minnesinger whose birth name is unknown. This artist wrote in both the older, French-inspired forms, and newer Germanic styles that developed during the thirteenth century. One of the texts of this minnesinger provides a wonderfully upbeat prayer, translated in part:

Today is a wonderful day.
Please care for me, You who watch over all,
That I might live a blessed life
And repent me of my great offenses
. . .
And when I have to leave my companions,
May I find friends in the other world,
Who are so happy with my songs
That I shall win fame amongst the knights in heaven.[4]

MEISTERSINGERS

Along with the Minnesinger tradition came another, parallel movement: that of the Meistersinger. Meistersingers were the middle- (and occasionally lower-) class equivalent of Minnesingers. They were not professionals in the sense of making a living at singing, but being a Meistersinger was a serious avocation. The Meistersinger tradition was tied to trade guilds, and this is why it sprang up in Germanic areas.

In many areas of Europe during the Middle Ages, merchants were looked down upon. This part of society, the merchant class, was a small one, strung between the nobility and the lower classes. But Germanic areas saw the merchant class more positively. Because of this, they developed a larger, more affluent middle class than other areas.

These citizens were organized, moneyed, and interested in cultural events. Most individual trades (such as goldsmiths or shoemakers) developed guilds. Guilds may be compared with unions of today. Each guild specified how people in their particular trade were to be trained, tested to see whether they were good enough, and policed to prevent price gouging, undercutting, or production of shoddy goods. Guild members paid dues, had officers, voted on referendums, and supported various causes with monetary help. Nowadays, a union might have a bowling league. In the Middle Ages, guilds had Meistersingers.

It is no accident that towns with stronger trading guilds were known as centers of Meistersinger activity. Nuremberg, Augsburg, and Frankfurt in particular were three thriving trade areas in the Middle Ages, and all were known for their Meistersingers. Just as they had in business, the guilds had severe restrictions concerning what should (or should not) happen in Meistersinger music and lyrics. Inspiration and creativity were not the cherished yardsticks here. The trick was to "color within the lines" and do it with style.

The Meistersinger tradition began after that of the Minnesingers, but it lasted longer. Their heyday started in the early fourteenth century, but lasted through the Renaissance and into the Baroque. In fact, there were still some Meistersingers in the nineteenth century, and the last genuine Meistersinger died in 1922![5]

The songs they composed and sang were called Meisterlieder. They were generally monophonic (one melody, with no harmony). But near the end of the Middle Ages (around 1450), one type of polyphonic song gained popularity. This type of song was known as a *Tenorlied*. It was so called because its melody was still in the tenor line, although composers elsewhere in Europe were putting the principal melody in the top voice by this time. True to Germanic conservativism, this hearkened back to the traditional cantus firmus, in which voices were added around the main melody, which was a Gregorian chant sung in one of the lower voices (see Chapter 3).

Meistersingers were nothing if not thorough, and guilds kept manuscripts of its members' best works. To date, about 16,000 manuscripts of their words and music have been preserved. Many were signed, but that does not necessarily mean that scholars know who wrote the work because something like "written in the meter invented by Hans" might mean that Hans wrote it, or that someone else did it in the style of Hans.

Although scholars know that the works were buried under a plethora of rules, these restrictions varied from area to area, contradicted one another, were "corrected" again and again, or were lost altogether. But they do know that poetry was the main concern: how many lines, how many syllables in each line, and what the rhyme scheme should be. Meistergesang poetry, usually written in Middle High German, could be amazingly intricate and complicated. According to one source, "Stanzas with intricate rhymes and thirty to fifty lines of varying lengths are frequent." Add to that the fact that certain meters were considered appropriate only for certain subjects, and one gets an idea of how complicated this form could get.[6]

This thicket of rules is one of the reasons that one does not hear Meistergesang in the same way that one might hear a troubadour song. For the Meistersinger, the poetic form was the challenge, and the music was not as important. Tunes were borrowed freely from earlier times, some were written in now-obscure tablatura, and others were simply written out in a sloppy manner. It is believed that no instruments were used.

The list of subject matter is impressive, and includes both sacred and secular matters. Some verses reflect a Germanic flirtation with mysticism. Others are allegorical. Some are eulogies, some are satirical, and some are "debats"—that is, descriptions of a contest between two poets. Others are riddle poems. A *Lügenlied* describes a topsy-turvy fantasy world. Aesop's fables were also a favorite verse subject. Still other songs dabble in the Middle Ages' hobby of making lists. Of course there are lists of grand-scale matters such as virtues, vices, saints, or heroes. But one of the most interesting is a listing of household utensils.[7]

The Meistersinger whose name lives on is that of a shoemaker from Nuremberg named Hans Sachs, who is remembered as the main character in Richard Wagner's opera *Die Meistersinger*. Unfortunately, he lived during the Renaissance (1494–1576) and thus cannot be included in this work. He does have surviving texts ascribed to him, however, and one is a set of list verses, listing items he knew very well: the tools in a shoemaker's shop.

GERMAN PLAGUE SONGS

When the Black Death came to Germanic areas in 1349, panicked citizenry joined penitent societies in the hope that a pleased God would take away this curse. Because they whipped themselves as penance for a wicked world, they were known as flagellants (in German, *geissler*). *Geisslerlieder* described their activities and ceremonies in verses set to music. They are considered folk songs. Some used tunes from older songs, related to the Italian "lauda" of the Middle Ages (see Chapter 4). One chilling set of lyrics, translated in part, is:

Oh Mary mother, Virgin mild,
Forget not Christendom thy child
. . . .
Our refuge here alone art thou;
From sudden death defend us now.
We have no help but him and thee,
Thy Son who reigns eternally:
Oh Mary, hear thy children's cry;
Have mercy on us, or we die[8]

STADTPFEIFEREI

Stadtpfeiferei were literally "town pipers," although they played instruments of all types, not only bagpipes. These musicians were hired directly by the town in which they played. Records show payments beginning somewhere around the mid-fourteenth century as a per-service arrangement. By the fifteenth, there were formal contracts spelling out the rights of both the town and the musicians. Stadtpfeiferei played for holidays and public celebrations, the dedication of buildings, important visitors (especially royalty), church and school functions, and for parades—generally any occasion called for. If they lived today, Stadtpfeiferei would play at mall openings. Moreover, they were responsible for training future Stadtpfeiferei.

For being "on-call" any time, musicians received a salary paid either by the year or by the half-year. They could also take up monetary collections at certain times of the year (such as New Year's Day), receive donations (fuel or grain, but not money), they might be exempt from taxes, and sometimes they got their instruments, music, and working clothes paid for. Of course, each city and town had different contracts, so all of these privileges were not granted in every place. In smaller, less wealthy areas, Stadtpfeiferei might have to wear more than one "hat," such as doubling as an organist, as an instrument maker, or even as a night watchman in the town tower.[9]

In short, music in Germanic areas lagged behind other, more innovative lands. Their heyday would come later, during the Baroque era.

NOTES

1. Craig Wright and Bryan Simms, *Music in Western Civilization* (Belmont, CA: Thomson Schirmer, 2006), p. 40.

2. Gustav Reese, *Music in the Middle Ages with an Introduction on the Music of Ancient Times* (New York: W.W. Norton & Company, 1940), p. 200.

3. Jeremy Yudkin, *Music in Medieval Europe. Prentice Hall History of Music Series*, edited by H. Wiley Hitchcock (Englewood Cliffs, NJ: Prentice Hall, 1989), p. 317.

4. Ibid., pp. 323–324.

5. K Marie Stolba, *The Development of Western Music*, 3rd edition (Boston: McGraw-Hill, 1998), p. 101.

6. Archer Taylor, *The Literary History of Meistergesang* (London: Oxford University Press, 1937), pp. 55 and 68.

7. Ibid., p. 103.

8. Gustav Reese, *Music in the Middle Ages with an Introduction on the Music of Ancient Times* (New York: W.W. Norton & Company, 1940), p. 239.

9. Heinrich W Schwab, "Stadtpfeifer, 1. Employment and Duties," in *Grove Music Online*, edited by L. Macy (http://www.grovemusic.com, accessed June 11, 2007).

CHAPTER 6

MUSIC OF THE BRITISH ISLES IN THE MIDDLE AGES

Almost everything we know about English music stems from the year 1066. It was at this time that Duke William from the French region of Normandy invaded England and took over the throne from its Saxon (Germanic-speaking) rulers. The success of William the Conquerer threw England into a strange dichotomy of French-speaking rulers and a Saxon-speaking population. Its land ownership, laws, military obligations, and religious institutions were deeply affected by the changes brought in by William's twenty-one-year reign.

The Conquest also put England into a love-hate relationship with the most musically advanced population of the Middle Ages—France. During that entire era, English nobility considered itself French and spent considerable time, effort, and money trying to hold onto its French lands or claim the French throne. Thus there were at various times intermarriages and wars, in which kings and princes on both sides were captured at one time or another, and it finally ended up drawing most of medieval Europe into a war that lasted a hundred years (see Chapter 1).

But England's isolation as an island also made it somewhat independent of the Continental mainland's musical dominance. The eventual cross-pollination of English and French music was the wellspring from which modern music sprang, just as the cross-pollination of the Saxon and French languages gave rise to modern English.

Though the Middle Ages were a time of divisiveness and wars for England, it was also the time when St. Thomas Becket was murdered and subsequently canonized, when Richard the Lionhearted became the stuff of legends, when the fictitious exploits of Robin Hood were born, when King John was forced to sign the Magna Carta, when the great tales of King Arthur and his knights were written, and when Geoffrey Chaucer wrote *Canterbury Tales*. During all of that time, music was an integral part of English life.

Much of England's music comes from the latter part of the Middle Ages. Outside of the Church, very little English music prior to 1200 has survived. Some types are known about only through literary sources. Even English Church music from the Middle Ages is scarce because of the destruction of Roman Catholic properties during the Reformation.

ENGLISH CHURCH MUSIC BEFORE THE NORMAN INVASION

When the Roman legions left Britain in 410 A.D., many of the people they left behind were Christian, as was the case elsewhere in the Empire. From such a family came St. Patrick, who had been captured and enslaved by Irish raiders in his youth but, some twenty years after the departure of the legions, returned to Ireland as a bishop to win the island for Christianity, in the process bringing the Latin alphabet and (according to legend) expelling Ireland's snakes. In the meantime, however, Britain's Celtic population was being overrun by pagan Germanic tribes: the Angles and Saxons. By 597, though, a St. Augustine (not the same one discussed in Chapter 1) came to what could now be called England as a missionary to the new-comers, founded a Benedictine monastery in Canterbury, and became its first arch-bishop. Benedictine monasteries spread throughout the British Isles, and as seen in Chapter 1, music had a central place in their worship. Benedictine cathedrals such as Canterbury, York, and Worcester were centers of musical activity. And as other abbeys such as Westminster and St. Albans were established, they, too, brought their influence to English Church music.

Of course, all of these churches were Roman Catholic, as were all Christian churches in the medieval Western world. But while Charlemagne's Church reforms on the European mainland stamped out alternate forms of worship by stan-dardizing the Mass and banning all chant forms except Gregorian, the British isles escaped more or less unscathed. Thus, they continued to use liturgy and chants from Salisbury—known as "Sarum" chants, mentioned in Chapter 2—instead of the continent's Gregorian chants.

As Anglo-Saxon settlements and government grew, there was a surge of cultural development during the seventh and eighth centuries. But waves of Viking (Danish) invasions put an end to that progress for almost 200 years. Then, shortly before 900, the Saxon ruler King Alfred tried to stem this devastating cultural brain drain by once again centering activities in and around Benedictine monasteries. These monasteries are where the first manuscripts of any kind of British music may be found.

During the tenth century there were two outstanding names in English music: Bishop Dunstan (c. 908–988), and Bishop (and Abbot) Ethelwold (c. 963–984). Both were cultural giants of their times and intensely interested in religious music.

Dunstan was concerned enough to invite a continental monk named Abbo from Fleury (France) to live in a Ramsey, England, abbey for two years to teach those monks proper Benedictine rule, including proper singing for Masses and the monastic Offices (see Chapter 2). Dunstan also wrote the rules down for English Benedictine monastic life, and this is where scholars have gotten information about when, where, and what types of church music were used in pre-Norman England. Ethelwold took a slightly different tack. Rather than importing a monk, he sent English monks to Fleury to learn proper execution of chant there and return with the knowledge.

By the late tenth century, English churches were using organum (see Chapter 2). In the *Winchester Troper*, which is a c. 1050 copy of an earlier lost collection, there are examples of tropes (see Chapter 2) added to liturgical chants that include two-part organum (see Chapter 2). This is some of the earliest surviving organum examples anywhere. The bad news is that the staffless neumes make it impossible to know exact pitches, so scholars are still not sure about what intervals or rhythms were used. Some scholars believe that these organum samples traveled from the continent. But others point to tropes (see Chapter 2) that honor saints identified with England, and in cases where comparison can be made with a French source, scholars point to differences where music may have been altered to suit English tastes.

Not much survives of early English church polyphony. Fragments have been found in various large Benedictine abbeys, and also some early works were copied into later collections such as the *Winchester Troper*. But there are no large surviving collections. In fact, the surviving fragments can thank their very survival to recycling. Many pages of older books were used as book bindings for other, later works. Since these were cut from larger papers, the notation and lyrics left on them are incomplete. Besides these scraps, scholars have combed through church writings to glean information there, mostly from angry clerics railing against singing in three parts, using voice ranges unnatural for men (falsetto), singing too many fast notes and fancy passages, and using special effects such as hockets. Only by reading what clerics wished to condemn do we know what existed!

It may seem strange that even scraps of music lean so heavily toward Church music, but it must be remembered that monastery scriptoria were the places where music was copied, and sacred music would be their first concern.

PRE-NORMAN SECULAR MUSIC: SCOPS AND GLEEMEN

There was, of course, music in the courts of England before the Norman Conquest. At Saxon courts musicians called *scops* played for nobles. The scop was not just an entertainer but a historian who sang of the great deeds of men, and scops were treated as persons of great respect. A scop would be attached to a certain court and work for one particular noble family.

Wandering musicians not attached to a specific court were known as "gleemen." They and instrumental harpers were a step down from the scops, but still respected for their talents. No music or lyrics have survived from any of these pre-Norman-Conquest musicians. Scholars only know about them because of literary writings. For instance, the anonymous "Gawain Poet," in his introduction to the Arthurian tale *Sir Gawain and the Green Knight*, states, in modern translation:

If you will listen to my lay but a little while
I will tell it all, and at once, as I heard it told in town,
Rightly, as it is written
A story swift and strong
With letters locked and linking,
As scops have always sung.[1]

At the end of the twelfth century a monk called Gerald of Wales (Giraldus Cambrensis) described an ear-witness account of close-harmony Welsh singing. He said they picked it up from the Danes, so it was apparently a long-standing tradition by the time Gerald heard it. Thus, even though no music survives, pre-Norman secular music may have been sung with harmony, which of course uses more than one part.

After the Conquest, both the scop and gleeman positions were incorporated into a "minstrel" tradition. But although not one piece of music from either scops or gleemen remains, the identification of gleemen lives on in glee clubs—singing organizations—worldwide.

Two less-known sources for pre-Conquest songs were textbooks: the *Older Cambridge Songbook* and the *Younger Cambridge Songbook*. The former was a schoolbook used at St. Augustine's monastery in Canterbury to teach Latin and was copied sometime in the middle of the eleventh century. It includes Latin song lyrics and even some notation. However, the notation is, again, staffless neumes. Some have instructions for the student to sing the lyrics to a particular tune that is named, but the tune has been lost to us. Most songs are religious, but apparently this songbook also includes some love songs, fables, and political verses as well. The latter songbook comes from post-Norman Conquest—the late twelfth or early thirteenth century—but it includes some earlier works. It contains thirty-five songs. Twenty-two songs are monophonic, but twelve use two voices and one uses three voices. This book uses Latin lyrics but shows a much wider range of topics than its predecessor. This book also uses lyrics "from devotional hymns and sequences to biting moral satire, intense love poetry, philosophical debates and humorous fabliaux."[2]

MUSIC NOTATION IN BRITAIN

Early notation in England, as elsewhere in Europe, was staffless neumes, and even those are quite scarce. There was an English mensural notation, and also some evidence of using the alphabet as a means of notating pitches. But the mensural notation of Franco of Cologne (see Chapter 3) overtook every other written notation, seeing that the copyists were working for the Norman French upper class and heavily influenced by French trends. However, instead of using square note heads, the English sometimes used a more round, "lozenge" shape for some note heads. Also, a fragment of music in England contains the earliest known keyboard *tablature* (a type of notation specific to its instrument). Scholars believe that its origin was French, and that it had something to do with the King of France being held prisoner in the English court from 1357 to 1360 during the Hundred Years' War.

THE POST-CONQUEST ENGLISH CHURCH AND SARUM CHANT

In Evesham Abbey, a Benedictine monk named Walter Odington (definitely not a French name!) wrote a music theory treatise around the year 1298. Written in Latin, the language of the church, it was in six parts and put together both theories of the past and then-current methods of religious composition. Given the scarcity of materials available for early English Catholic Church music, this treatise is a valuable tool for scholars.

As the French-based nobility took over and Church institutions became tied to the throne, English church music closely followed developments in France. But some areas were more affected than others, and the subjects of praise were sometimes Anglo-Saxon saints or even figures of reverence such as Dunstan and Ethelwold.

The English Church of the Middle Ages used the continental cantus firmus idea (see Chapter 2) of building independent musical lines around an older chant form. The difference was that their cantus firmus used Sarum, not Gregorian, chant and tended to be placed in a middle voice, not at the bottom. The English also had a preference for harmonies in thirds and sixths, which were "imperfect" consonances, instead of the "perfect" fourths and fifths of the Continent.

Also, while Continental musicians occasionally allowed separate voices to cross into one another's vocal "territory," the English did not like to do so. In instances where the (Sarum) cantus firmus line had to do so, musicians preferred to place that line temporarily in another voice rather than have the middle line singing within the upper or lower vocal areas. This development is known as a "migrant" cantus firmus and was a technique later used in continental music. One of the best surviving collections of English Church polyphony has been the *Old Hall Manuscript*. The copy itself is from around 1420–1460, but contains earlier music.

Besides music for actual Masses, English Church composers also wrote motets (see Chapter 3). Only one English motet of the Middle Ages has been found using the Middle English language, and only a very few use Norman-French. An English motet of the Middle Ages would ordinarily use the Latin language, and it almost always covered a sacred topic. Secular motets were invariably copies from France. Of course, English composers, writing for a nobility that considered itself French, knew about the Parisian-based styles and motet setups. But as a rule, they did not like the incredibly complicated rhythms of the French. They leaned heavily toward perfect time and major prolation (what we would now call 9/8; see Chapter 3).

English motets used three or four voice lines. If there was anything truly "English" about these motets, it might be found in their tenor lines. Although Latin lyrics are used rather than English ones, the tunes to such popular English songs as "Hey, lure lure" or "Dou way Robin" sometimes provided the "plainsong" line instead of a chant.[3]

Sometimes the English continued using musical forms that France had abandoned long before. Even though churches used newer techniques for big occasions, they continued using two-voiced organum long after the continent had left it behind. The English Church musicians also continued writing conductus music (see Chapter 2) right on into the fourteenth century.

The *Old Hall Manuscript* and other partial sources show several techniques used in English Church music of the Middle Ages. One technique rarely written out, but apparently used often, was "faburden."

FABURDEN

Faburden was a polyphonic music technique providing harmony for a chant line. The chant (at least until the fifteenth century) would be in the middle of three voices. Above and below that line would be voices following along in exact rhythm, but on different parallel pitches. To modern ears, these pitches sound like chords, moving in parallel motion.

This is how it worked. Let's say that the chant line note is a G. The top voice would sing four notes higher, a C (count G, A, B, C). The bottom voice would sing three notes lower, an E (count G, F, E). All three notes together are C-E-G—which we recognize as a C major chord. This was possible in England rather than on the continent, because the English liked the sound of notes in thirds. In France, this chord would be considered dissonant (an unpleasant sound), which they would have to "resolve" quickly to a perfect interval of a fourth or fifth. Another term for this practice was "English discant." Technically, the English discant (or descant) was the chant line in the middle, and the faburden was the term for the outer voices that shadowed the chant line.

Later, when English music came to the Continent during the Hundred Years' War, the French picked up the idea and created Fauxbourdon. However, by the early fifteenth century, the French were putting the melody line (chant line) in the top voice, so their fauxbourdon was all underneath. So if their chant line note was a G, it would be in the top line. The next voice underneath would sing four notes below, a D (count G, F, E, D), and the bottom voice would sing six notes below, a B (count G, F, E, D, C, B). Thus, the French fauxbourdon would create a G-B-D chord, G major, instead of the C major chord that the English faburden would have produced on the same cantus firmus note.

In either faburden or fauxbourdon, the opening and ending notes do not conform to the pattern. That is because in the Middle Ages' three-voiced harmony, it was normal to start and end with an open fifth and an octave. That is, if the last note were a G, the other voices would sing Cs—one a fourth above, and the other a fifth below. Although this may seem strange to modern ears, it was no less common to the Middle Ages than the inevitable "Amen" chord at the end of most modern Western Christian hymns.

During the fifteenth century a curious thing happened. After the English technique of faburden crossed over and became French fauxbourdon, the fauxbourdon crossed back over to England! By that time, English nobles (who, remember, considered themselves French) had brought back collections of French music using Ars Nova techniques, which were rapidly incorporated into English Church music techniques.

ENGLISH VERNACULAR SONG

The oldest known Middle Ages English song with an English text came from St. Godric, a Saxon hermit who lived during the last part of the 1100s. It is a piece of music in local language that was put into an already-existing Latin Church chant. This type of mix is known as an English "farse." Several nonliturgical songs in the English language survive from the thirteenth century. Their titles are: *Worldes blis ne last* (The world's happiness does not last), *Man mei lone him lives wene* (Long may man want his life to be), *Mirie it is while sumer ilast* (Merry it is while summer lasts), and a love song entitled *Byrd one brer* (Bird on a briar). *Bryd one brere* was a particularly miraculous survival. Both words and music were found on the back of an old legal document.

THE RONDELLUS

Scholars could call the rondellus a canon at the unison, which sounds very complicated. But a canon is only a tune starting at one time, and then the same tune starting a little later and following along, like a line of melodic ducklings. A canon "at the unison" only means that every voice comes in on the same starting pitch. We know it as a round.

A rondellus uses several phrases sung in canon. Think about the well-known round, "Row, Row, Row Your Boat." Now think of "Row, row, row your boat gently down the stream" as one phrase and "Merrily, merrily, merrily, merrily—life is but a dream" as a second phrase. It is easy to see how each voice shares both phrases, one after the other, after the other, after the other. The difference between a round and a rondellus is how they end. Rondellus voices all end at the same time, not one after the other.

ROTA

The English rota is a combination of two types of music. The first is a four-part rondellus in Middle English. This is sung over a two-part *pes* or "foot," which is a simple—but separate—two-part canon. Sung together, an English rota is a double-round. Both complicated and simple, the most famous example for this form is still enjoyed. Its title is *Sumer Is Icumen In* (Summer has come in).

The earliest known copy of this rota is from the late thirteenth century in a collection called Manuscript Harley 978, thought to have been used in Reading Abbey. It has two sets of lyrics. One is in Middle English, and one is in Latin. This is the first known work anywhere to contain six voices singing at the same time. Its organization was startlingly advanced for its time. The *pes* apparently uses a tune borrowed from an earlier Marian antiphon, but the words in the English text version are "sing cuccu" (Sing, cuckoo). The top four voices rollick along in a bouncy 6/8 to the following Middle English lyrics:

Sumer is icumen in,
Lhude sing cuccu!
Groweth sed and bloweth med
And springeth the wde nu.
Sing cuccu!
Awe bleteth after lomb
Lhouth after calve cu.
Bulluc sterteth, bucke verteth,
Murie sing cucu!
Wel singes thu cuccu.
Ne swik thu naver nu![4]

The modern English translation is, roughly:

Summer has come, loudly sing cuckoo. Now is the seed growing and the meadow flowering and the forest springing to life. Sing cuckoo. The ewe bleats after the lamb, the cow lows after the calf, the bullock leaps, the buck breaks wind ("farts"). Merrily sing cuckoo. Well dost thou sing cuckoo, never cease now.[5]

In an interesting note, the same manuscript where *Sumer Is Icumen In* was found also contains an index of what is supposed to be in this particular collection—which has been lost. It is heartbreaking, like finding a table of contents, without the book.

THE ENGLISH CAROL

Today, the word "carol" in the musical sense is almost always preceded by the word "Christmas." But this was not at all true in the England of the Middle Ages. A carol was a song usually—but not always—of a religious nature that incorporated both English and Latin languages. Verses in English alternated with a "burden" or "burthen" in Latin. The English verses had different words each time, but the burthen was the same, like a refrain.

According to scholars, the earliest English carols, from around 1150 or so, were dance songs. They point out literary references such as the Prologue to *Sir Gawain and the Green Knight*, written by the Middle Ages' anonymous "Gawain Poet." Describing the Christmas revels at King Arthur's court, this poet wrote (in modern translation):

Tournament trumpets rang there time and again,
And knights jarred knights, with jubilant hearts, in the joust,
And later they came into court to dance caroles;
For the feast was in full swing for fifteen days[6]

Dancing to carols, according to some scholars, might have, at least in England, been an ancestor of the later Dance of Death, Europe's most morbid dance form, connected with the belief that the Black Death could be averted by sweating out its "humors" through dancing.

Very few early carols have survived. These monophonic carols were lost because they were not written down. The only reason that scholars know they existed is through literary writings. But from 1300 to 1500, there are about five hundred surviving carols. Carols were popular both in and out of court settings, but they were composed for the upper classes. Burdens for these carols were sometimes in Latin, but could also sometimes be in English, or in a mixture of English and Latin known as a "macaroni."

One of the most famous English carols of the Middle Ages was written to celebrate a famous victory of the Hundred Years' War: the Battle of Agincourt in 1415. Definitely not a Christmas carol, these words practically stick their tongue out at the French. But since the English, under Henry V, had traveled overseas and won a battle over an army four times their size, perhaps they can be forgiven. It is also a textbook example of carol form.

Its words are:

(Burden) *Deo gratias, Anglia, redde pro victoria* (England, give thanks to God for the victory)

(Verse 1) Our king went forth to Normandy
With grace and might of chivalry
There God for him wrought marv-lously,
Wherefore England may call and cry
Deo Gratias
(Burden sung here)

(Verse 2) He set a siege, forsooth to say,
To Harflu town with royal array;
That town he won and made affray
That France shall rue till Domesday (Doomsday)

Deo Gratias
(Burden sung again)

(Verse 3)   Almighty God he keep our king,
His people and all his well-willing
And give them grace withouten ending:
Then may we call and safely sing
Deo Gratias
(End with Burden)[7]

Some of the "rhymes" at the end of the Agincourt Carol bring up a big fact of Middle Ages life. Their English was not the same as English today. For one thing, their alphabet had some different characters. For instance, they had a specific letter for the sound of "th." At the beginning of the Lord's Prayer "Father" would have been spelled with five letters, not six. Pronunciation was quite different as well. The words "marvelously" and "cry" would have actually rhymed six hundred years ago, because the word "cry" would have been pronounced "cree." Words such as "we" were pronounced with a short "e," not a long one. The word "we" would have sounded like "weh." Also, as a holdover from Saxon, words such as "might" and "knight" would have pronounced the "gh" as a "kh" sound, and the beginning "k" would not have been silent. Thus, "a mighty knight" would have sounded like "ah mikhtee kanikht." Some plurals were quite different as well, such as the plural for "shoe," which was "shoon," or "eyen" for "eyes." Thus, the words "moon" and "shoon" could have been used as rhymes.

In the Middle Ages, poetry was the proper literary form. Prose was used, but not often. One interesting poetic form used in England was alliterative poetry. Instead of having a specific rhyme scheme and rhythm, the poetry was set up according to words that started with the same letter. This gave a certain rhythm and force to the words, while diminishing the need to make everything rhyme at the end. For instance, here is a sample from the late fourteenth century *Alliterative Morte d'Arthure,* a partial description of a tournament between Arthur's knights and some knights from Rome:

Then the Romans and the royal knights of the Round Table
Drew up again in array, both the rear and the rest,
And with heavy weapons of war they hacked through helmets
And cut with their grim steel through glittering mail. . . . [8]

The Gawain Poet's sample preceding the Agincourt Carol was also written in alliterative style, translated into modern English.

The English carol of the Middle Ages never crossed the channel onto the Continent. Early carols are believed to have been monophonic (one melody without harmony), but later carols used one, two, or even three voices. We know this because English carols were written out in "score" form, not in parts. In other words, all the voices were written onto a single page which could be seen at once, and not divided into part books for separate voices. Carols of course thrived through the Middle Ages and the Renaissance and are with us today.

OTHER VERNACULAR SONGS

This is one place of some confusion, because of the Franco-Saxon dichotomy. The French-speaking upper class never made any attempt to learn or record what the lower classes were doing, and the lower classes never adopted French models.

The upper classes' songs are in the Norman French vernacular—the language of royalty. Henry II and Eleanor of Aquitaine patronized the arts, but neither ever bothered to learn to speak English. Neither did their children. Henry owned more land in France than the French King of his time, and he spent a total of only four-teen years out of his thirty-four-year reign in England. His son Richard the Lion-hearted spent even less time in England—about ten months total during his ten-year reign. The rest was spent either on Crusades, in captivity, or in France.

Their English musical contributions were more the patronage of household minstrels. Through royal and noble household accounts, we know something of who was playing what kind of music for what occasions at noble courts. This is also how scholars know about musicians traveling to and from the continent, particu-larly during the last hundred years of the Middle Ages. At that time there was a particularly active interchange of English and Burgundian musicians.

The Church turned out to be a sort of middle-man between the classes, and it is thanks to local churches and abbeys that any English language songs from the Middle Ages survive. While there were plenty of Latin verses to be set to music, one enterprising Franciscan friar named Bozon started inserting Middle English words into these songs—and, apparently, into his sermons as well—in order to encourage his congregation to pay attention.

The story of English language songs in the Middle Ages has both good news and bad news. The good news is that many of the lyrics have survived, about two thou-sand of them. The bad news is that the music has not. It simply was not written down. Apparently the tunes were so familiar that it would have been like writing down the tune for "Happy Birthday." Instead, a source might simply give the name of the tune.

One important Middle Ages English genre was the lullaby—particularly lulla-bies put in the mouth of the Virgin Mary singing to the Christ Child. The verses are about the sweetness of the sight of Mary and her newborn, and the Refrain holds the words of the lullaby that Mary is singing. For instance:

I saw a swete semly syght,
A blisful birde, a blossum bright,
That murnyng made and mirth of mange;
A maydin moder, mek and myld,
In credil kep a knave (boy) child
That softly slepe; scho sat and sange

Lullay, lullow, lully, lullay,
Bewy, bewy, lully, lully,
Bewy, lully, lullow, lully,
Lollay, baw, baw, my barne,
Slepe softly now.[9]

GEOFFREY CHAUCER

A seemingly unlikely source of information about music is the literary giant, Geoffrey Chaucer (c. 1340–1400). Credited with writing the first major work in Middle English—*Canterbury Tales*—Chaucer was also an Esquire of the King's Household. As such he was required to write texts set to music, and it is possible that he collaborated with the musician(s) on this task and it is even possible that he had to sing some of them. Besides that, *Canterbury Tales* is sprinkled with musical information.

In his real life, Chaucer was definitely moving in upper-class (French) circles. But in *Canterbury Tales*, not all of his characters are from that circle. The *Canterbury Tales* is a fictitious account of a group of English pilgrims on their way to the shrine of St. Thomas Becket in Canterbury, who decide to tell stories along the way to pass the time. Each pilgrim was to tell one tale on the way to the shrine, and one on the way back. Then they would vote on which was the best, and the winner would get would get a free meal at the end, paid for by the others. There were a total of twenty-nine pilgrims, giving modern readers a rare glance into the cross-section of English society, both religious and secular.

Even in his Prologue, Chaucer makes mention of the musical abilities of some of these pilgrims, by way of compliment. The knight, for instance, was described as singing, playing the flute, and composing songs, as well as dancing, painting, and writing well:

Singing he was, or floytinge, al the day;
He was as fresh as is the month of May.
Short was his goune, with sleves longe and wyde.
Wel coude he sitte on horse, and faire ryde.
He coude songes make and wel endyte,
Just and eek daunce, and well purtreye and wryte.

Chaucer poked a little fun at the Prioress (a nun) for her nasal singing: "Ful wel she song the service divyne, Entuned in hir nose ful semely." The Friar was ready for music-making at almost any time. He "certeinly . . . hadde a mery note; Wel coude he singe and pleyen on a rote" (*rota*, a medieval fiddle). In fact, even after the Friar had finished singing, he enjoyed instrumental playing:

And in his harping, when that he had songe,
His eyen twinkled in his heed aright
As doon the sterres in the frosty night.

The Pardoner sang secular tunes with a set of lungs that could drown out a trumpet:

> Ful loude he song, "Com hider, love, to me."
> This Somnour bar to him a stiff bourdoun:
> Was never trompe of half so greet a soun.

Even the Miller, a huge and uncouth man, lead the procession out of town blowing on a bagpipe: "a baggepype wel coude he blowe and sowne, And therewithal he broghte us out of towne." And within the Pardoner's tale, one even learns what the young folks in Flanders were playing on a night out on the town living a riotous life in beer halls and whorehouses ("stewes"):

> In Flaundres whylom was a companye
> Of yonge folk that haunteden folye,
> As ryot, hasard, stewes, and tavernes,
> Whereas, with harpes, lutes, and giternes,
> They daunce and pleye at dees (dice) bothe day and night.[10]

By the late Middle Ages, English bourgeois traders got into music-making, forming guilds and establishing a yearly festival. It is not unthinkable to suppose that this was inspired by the Germanic trade guilds and their music-making abilities. Scholars know from London Guildhall records that there was a Court of Love set up with a competition for the best song composed. Just as in the Germanic guilds, composers had to write according to a minefield of rules in order to win.

CHAPEL ROYAL

During the Middle Ages, the English Royal Chapel (Chapel Royal) grew from a few people into a national institution. That this dramatic growth was inspired by the French King Louis IX's chapel of Sainte Chapelle is a possiblity, since it began not long after Sainte Chapelle was founded in 1248. And since English royalty considered itself French, a kind of keeping up with the (French) Joneses is entirely believable.

During the 1270s, under Edward I (reigned 1272–1307), the Chapel Royal went from three to sixteen men. It included four "choristers"—enough to sing either three- or four-part polyphony with one voice on a part or, of course, to sing chant together monophonically. By the end of the Middle Ages, the size of this staff had grown to forty-six, and it was famous throughout Europe for the excellence of its singers and composers.

Besides the King's chapel, other royal personages also had household chapels. During Henry V's time (reigned 1413–1422), his mother and three brothers also had "royal" chapels. Also, several institutions had chapels supported by the crown, such as St. Stephen's at Westminster and St. George's at Windsor.

The Chapel Royal is important to English music of the Middle Ages because its account books have survived. From them, scholars know who was paid what, and when. They can pin down when music was performed, relative importance of musicians (from their salaries), names of performers—and sometimes whether those performers had been imported from another country.

According to scholars, before 1450, boy singers would have been used to sing chant but would not be used for polyphonic works. For that, men's voices would be used—the modern baritone, tenor, male alto, and/or countertenor (depending on whether there were three or four parts to be sung). Most polyphony would have been of the improvised faburden type except for special occasions, when written-out, composed polyphony would be performed.

ENGLISH COMPOSERS OF THE MIDDLE AGES

Unfortunately, early English composers all had the same name—Anonymous. After the creation of the Chapel Royal some of England's greatest composers acquired both the means to create outstanding music, and names! There are three English composers of the Middle Ages who will be considered here: the lesser-known John Aleyn, and two giants of their age: Lionel Power and John Dunstable.

JOHN ALEYN (ALENUS)

John Aleyn (d. 1373) shows up in the account books of the Chapel Royal between the years 1364 and 1373. He served Edward III (reigned 1327–1377), and may have also worked for a noble who served the Black Prince (Edward III's oldest son) in France. Scholars believe this, because Aleyn's most famous work—a three-voiced motet with the incipit *Sub Arturo/Fond cithariyancium/In omnem Terram* was found in a manuscript in France, not in England.

Admittedly, the work is not English in style, but it is an example of how an English composer could handle the most sophisticated French contemporary styles of his day. In addition, Aleyn's work is also a scholar's delight. It has six stanzas, two of which are particularly interesting. One describes the work's own setup: The Tenor is to be performed three times—each time with shorter mensuration signs (see Chapter 3). It moves from Perfect major to Imperfect major to Imperfect minor. That is, the same melody is sung first in 9/8, then in 6/8, and finally in 4/8 (or 2/4). Another stanza uses all three voices to praise musicians of the past and present. While the Tenor line sings the text "They are springs from which streams flow to irrigate every kingdom in the world," the middle (Duplum) text lists famous musicians of the past such as Tubal, Pythagoras, Boethius, Pope Gregory I, Guido, and Franco of Cologne, while the top (Triplum) line lists singers working in the Chapel Royal at that time—names that probably would have otherwise been lost.

LIONEL (LEONEL) POWER

Lionel Power (c. 1375–1445) is believed to have served as a Gentleman of the Chapel for Thomas, Duke of Clarence, one of Henry V's brothers. After the Duke's untimely death (at age 33), Power served other noble houses. Though he had close ties to Canterbury and its church, there is no indication that he was a cleric. About forty of his works have survived—twenty-three of them in the *Old Hall Manuscript*.

Power's calling card was in tying together Mass Ordinary movements into polyphonic "Mass cycles." Usually, composers of the Middle Ages simply wrote one or more Mass movements. For masses, any of the appropriate movements were used regardless of styles, composers, or when they were written. Powell differed in that he wrote his movements in ways that clearly indicated that two or more movements were meant to be used within the same Mass. He did this in several ways: (1) using the same style of composition to match the movements, (2) using the same chant for each movement, either as a cantus firmus or by putting it in the top voice, (3) opening each mass movement in the same way with a "head motive." He also made use of occasional isorhythmic techniques (see Chapter 3). Power's techniques were picked up by the Burgundian court and became a staple of their later Mass movements.

Scholars have pointed out that although Power obviously knew all the latest Parisian techniques, he fitted them to a sound preferred by English ears. His sonorities were more full (chordlike), and his use of thirds and sixths makes his works sound more "normal" to modern ears.

JOHN DUNSTABLE (DUNSTAPLE)

John Dunstable (1390–1453) was a singer in the chapel of John, Duke of Bedford, another of Henry V's brothers. While Henry conquered France during the Hundred Years' War, he put his brothers in charge of large swaths of the country. Thus, Dunstable's employer became Regent of France from 1422 to 1429 and Governor of Normandy from 1429 to 1435. (He was also the man responsible for paying for Joan of Arc to be turned over to the English, who eventually burned her at the stake). John brought his court with him, including musicians, and so scholars believe that Dunstable was in France for at least part of those years.

There are about sixty surviving works of Dunstable's. Most of his works were sacred and the texts are Latin, but there is one carol, two rondeaux, one ballade, and a modified ballade for which he is famous—*O Rosa Bella* (O beautiful rose). Another Dunstable favorite is a motet entitled *Quam Pulchra Es* (How fair you are). Both are works still performed today, and both sound as lovely now as they did over six hundred years ago.

Dunstable was a true musician in the ancient Greek sense—he was a mathematician and an astronomer as well as a musician. One of his works is a triumph of mathematics. It is a "pan-isorhythmic" work, in which all voices (not only the tenor) are written in isorhythm (see Chapter 3).

But despite his general excellence, Dunstable's lasting impact had more to do with the Hundred Years' War than his fame as a composer.

LA CONTENANCE ANGLOISE

Through his employer's military conquests, Dunstable did something unusual for an English musician. He ended up composing English-style music while living in France. (As has been mentioned before, most of the musical trafficking had gone the other way, French music being imported to England.)

Because of his proximity and the political situation described in Chapter 8, Dunstable's music came into contact with contemporary Burgundian composers Guillaume Dufay and Gilles Binchois. They were stunned by the beauty and power of Dunstable's style and called it *la contenance angloise* (the English Face, or the English Way). The differences between Continental and English music have already been discussed, but in short they were:

- Treating intervals of the third and sixth as consonances, not dissonances
- Adding a note within the interval of an open fifth, creating a triad
- Keeping all lines consonant with one another, not only with the tenor line
- Writing pan-rhythmic sections in which all voices move at the same time
- Using faburden, creating parallel chord-like passages
- Foreshadowing homophonic writing, by putting the main melody in the top line and treating it as more important than the other voices
- Adding a fourth (bass) voice underneath the tenor line and creating the SATB (soprano-alto-tenor-bass) arrangement still familiar today
- Mixing the textures of four- and five-voiced works for more variety
- Using more than one singer for each vocal line, choral style

When French composition styles met the English face, it changed music history. The fusion of the intricacies of French music added together with the denser, more chordal, four-voiced English music was perfected in the court of Burgundy, which during the late Middle Ages became a new center of musical excellence (see Chapter 8). Because of the beauty of their music, Burgundian composers were hired all over Europe and thus spread their new, cross-pollinated style everywhere they went.

The new style pushed music from the Middle Ages into the Renaissance in several ways. For one thing, it began the process of thinking in terms of chords rather than in terms of several lines of music traveling from left to right. Also, when the addition of a bass line weakened the strength of the cantus firmus by burying it among three outer voices, it began the death knell of what had been the Middle Ages' major composition style for religious music. As Burgundian composers moved into southern Europe and further fused their music with local Italian styles, their music became the music of the Renaissance. And in that way, one can say that Dunstable was responsible for kicking off Renaissance music.

NOTES

1. John Gardner, ed., *The Complete Works of the Gawain Poet, in a Modern English Version with a Critical Introduction* (Chicago: University of Chicago Press, 1965), p. 224.

2. James McKinnon, ed., *Music and Society: Antiquity and the Middle Ages from Ancient Greece to the 15th Century* (Englewood Cliffs, NJ: Prentice Hall, 1991), p. 181.

3. Reinhard Strohm, *The Rise of European Music, 1380–1500* (Cambridge, UK: Cambridge University Press, 1993), p. 81.

4. Edmonstoune Duncan (collector and editor), *Lyrics from the Old Song Books* (New York: Harcourt, Brace & Companz, Inc., 1927), p. 1.

5. John Caldwell, *Medieval Music* (Bloomington: Indiana University Press, 1978), p. 202.

6. John Gardner, ed,, *The Complete Works of the Gawain Poet, in a Modern English Version with a Critical Introduction.* (Chicago: University of Chicago Press, 1965), p. 225.

7. *Music of the Early Renaissance* (USA: Turnabout, a Vox Production [LP Record], TV34058S, n.d.).

8. John. Gardner, ed., *The Alliterative Morte Arthure and Five Other Middle English Poems* (Carbondale: Southern Illinois University Press, 1971), p. 57.

9. Richard Leighton Green (ed.), *The Early English Carols* (Oxford: Clarendon Press, 1935), p. 98.

10. All quotes in Chaucer section from *The Canterbury Tales by Geoffrey Chaucer*, selected, edited, and translated by A. Kent Hleatt and Constance Hleatt (New York: Bantam Books, 1964).

CHAPTER 7

MUSIC OF THE IBERIAN PENINSULA IN THE MIDDLE AGES

During the Middle Ages, the areas of present-day Spain and Portugal were in an even more fractured situation than the rest of Western Europe. Not only was this area cut off from the rest of Europe by the Pyrenees mountain range, but it encompassed several different languages and three major religious groups. Iberian languages included Basque, Catalan, Gallego-Portuguese, and Castilian in addition to the Arabic and Hebrew languages spoken in Moslem-held Spain. In fact, the entire peninsula was a patchwork of kingdoms that did not coalesce until the Renaissance (Figure 7.1).

Because the southern tip of the Iberian Peninsula is so close to the north of Africa, North African followers of Islam (known as Moors or Saracens) invaded during the eighth century and occupied some parts of what is now Spain for the next seven hundred years. Though occupied by conquest, these areas were ruled in relative peace where Christians, Moslems, and Jews were all allowed to flourish. Thus Moorish-ruled areas, particularly the urban centers of Seville, Cordoba, and Granada, became cultural centers where artists, musicians, and scholars abounded. Christian-ruled areas, while less tolerant of non-Christians, also had rulers who heavily patronized the arts and became musically sophisticated.

Within all these factions, musicians lived and plied their trade. They sang and played in the courts, for their various religions, and in festivals and milestones in their secular lives. Over the Middle Ages, musical styles and instruments crossed

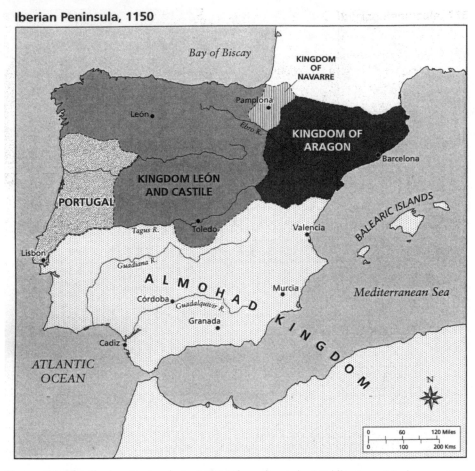

Figure 7.1 The Iberian Peninsula in 1150. Throughout the Middle Ages, Moslem territory shrank until the Moslems were ousted from Spain completely in 1492. Courtesy of Facts on File, Inc. Historical Maps I, Revised Edition © 2002.

these cultural borders, eventually to form the unique musical blend known today as Spanish and Portuguese music.

THE MUSIC OF CHRISTIAN IBERIA

The earliest Iberian music reaches back into the seventh century and the writings of the musically minded Archbishop of Seville, St. Isidore of Seville (c. 559–636). He was responsible for codifying the order of Mass for the Visigothic Rite, including its extensive body of non-Gregorian chants. The surviving chants are now known as Mozarabic (see Chapter 2). In a strange twist of fate, these chants' survival owes much to the Moorish occupation, which allowed Christians to continue their accustomed practices. When Toledo was retaken by Christian forces, they imposed Gregorian rites and chant on this area in 1080. But a few areas quietly continued their masses and music as usual, and the Visigothic Rite not only survived but may still be seen today in some regions of Toledo.

THE FEAST OF ST. JAMES DE COMPOSTELA

During the Middle Ages, a prime source of worship music involved the area of Galicia, which is now the northwestern tip of Spain, and particularly the Cathedral of Santiago (St. James), in which parts of the body of St. James (the Apostle, son of Zebedee) are supposedly housed. At that time, this area drew as many pilgrims as the Holy City of Jerusalem, and the service of the Vigil and Feast of St. James was codified as early as the mid-1100s. Mono- and polyphonic church music (original chants, tropes, sequences, and conductus) pertaining to this celebration are precious, as the collection gathered and copied over many years includes both music of Iberia and also music from other parts of Europe, including the Christian-held Jerusalem.

The music and the order of service was preserved in a collection called the Codex Calixtinus, named for Pope Callistus (or Calixtus) II (d. 1124), who is credited with writing the Offices and Masses for the Feast of St. James. In fact, although the cathedral and its feast were both in Spain, much of the music seems to have had a great French influence. A note found among the Codex's pages says that most of the polyphonic works were written at a Benedictine Abbey in Cluny, France. Although scholars do not entirely trust this note, since it is unknown when it was included, they do concede that, for instance, the style of notation used is the type that was in use in central France during the Middle Ages.

One of the entranceways to the church is also of great interest to people curious about instrumental performance during the Middle Ages. Surrounding those particular entrance doors are stone carvings depicting the twenty-four elders of the Apocalypse, all playing instruments of the Middle Ages. They are depicted in such detail that scholars can see the placement of fingers on wind instruments and the number of strings on stringed instruments. As if that were not enough, the Cathedral library still holds a book entitled *Liber Sancti Jacobi* (The Book of St. James), which was a sort of travel brochure guide to Compostela. From the point of view of the Middle Ages, it outlines important buildings, shrines, and other places recommended for visitors to see, and even what kind of people lived in outlying areas through which pilgrims were likely to travel, with recommendations as to which people were hospitable and which were likely to be dangerous.

CANTIGAS

During the Middle Ages, monophonic songs were popular on the Iberian peninsula. Called *cantigas* to distinguish them from spoken poetry, known as *decir*, these songs were collected in Christian areas, and some of those collections survive today. Although the lyrics of many cantigas are religious in nature, the songs themselves were considered secular. Some cantigas remain with only their lyrics left, but present-day scholars and music lovers are fortunate that in other instances the music has also survived. Cantigas were sung on the Iberian peninsula until the 1450s, when they began to give way to other, Renaissance, song forms.

In the Christian areas, one of the earliest Iberian collections of cantigas is by Martin Codex. These are seven love songs (*Siete canciones de amor*) of which six melodies have survived (the seventh has only the text). The words are in Galician-Portuguese, which was considered the best Iberian language for poetry. They were monophonic, with simple but elegant melodies and a simple repetitive rhyme scheme. Each verse has only three lines. The first and third lines are identical every time, and only the middle line is changed. The effect is hypnotic and quite lovely. The following is a translation of one of the songs entitled "Ondas do Mar de Vigo" (O waves of the sea of Vigo):

I.   O waves of the sea of Vigo,
       If you have seen my friend,
       O God, let him come back quickly.

II.   O waves of the sea of Vigo,
       If you have seen my lover
       O God, let him come back quickly.

III.   O waves of the sea of Vigo,
       Him for whom I sigh
       O God, let him come back quickly.

IV.   O waves of the sea of Vigo,
       For whom I have great concern
       O God, let him come back quickly.

It is interesting to note that until 1914, scholars had only the text for all of the Vigo songs. It wasn't until then that another book binding revealed the notation for all the songs except one![1]

ALFONSO THE WISE AND THE CULT OF THE VIRGIN MARY

In the 1200s, a popular religious conceit spread throughout Christian Iberia. Inspired by the French troubadour tradition of courtly love, Iberia took the concept of an unattainable female object of adoration and applied it to the Virgin Mary. This satisfied both Church leaders and the secular population, and the cult of (meaning the practice of reverence toward) the Virgin Mary had a lot of punch in the thirteenth century. After all, God seemed far away, and although Jesus the Son was more approachable, Mary his Mother had lived on earth, borne a Child, and lost him, just as earthly mothers had. Thus, she was immediately approachable, and available especially to women—particularly fallen women who needed a second chance. But she would also help men, as long as their sins did not include adultery against their wives!

From this adoration sprang a series of stories and songs about miracles brought about by the Virgin Mary. A huge collection was put together by one of Spain's greatest leaders, Alfonso the Wise (1221–1284). Alfonso's father, Ferdinand III, had successfully put together the kingdoms of Castile and Leon, which made Alfonso's territory as large as the biggest Moorish territory in the Iberian south. Even though his rule (1252–1284) was marked by many wars, including civil war with his own sons, Alfonso's court became a center of Christian cultural development.

Besides the fact that Alfonso may have written some literature and music on his own, his historical and artistic calling card was collecting. Alfonso collected everything: legal documents, scientific tracts, treatises on a variety of topics, histories, art and artists, music and musicians. Unusual for his time, he admitted both scholarly and artistic works of Jewish and Moorish scholars. He also gathered styles and works from French musicians traveling through his lands, took note of local traditions, and even gave safe haven to some of the last troubadours who were fleeing the Albigensian Crusade (see Chapter 3).

The Cantigas de Santa Maria is one such collection, of about 400 songs with texts written in the Galician-Portuguese language. Not only is it one of the largest collections of songs from the Middle Ages, it is also one of the best arranged. Beginning with a song of praise about the Virgin Mary, the next nine songs outline various miracles through her intervention. The tenth song is always another one of praise on her behalf. Each song is numbered and given an indication as to what it will be about, and the book is impeccably written and decorated with many beautiful miniature paintings of musicians playing various instruments. There are four copies of the *Cantigas*, made at various times. Three are almost identical, except for the miniatures. The fourth contains only empty staves. One of the rarest parts of this extraordinary collection is that not only are these monophonic (single melody) songs on staff lines—so that later generations can reproduce the pitches—but they are written in mensural notation (see Chapter 3), so that their rhythmic values were also preserved.

As far as the text, the miracles happened to all types of people known at that time, for instance: "men and women, knights and nuns, merchants, robbers, an incestuous widow, a pregnant abbess."[2] A sample story is that of a pilgrim who is persuaded by the Devil into the sin of sleeping with a prostitute. Then, overcome by guilt, he compounds his errant ways by committing suicide, which was considered a grave sin in the Middle Ages. When the Devil comes to claim the man's soul, the Virgin Mary takes pity on him and gives him back his life, which he wisely uses to do penance and reclaim his soul.

The variety of sins and salvation situations resembles the kind of fascination with which people today watch soap operas, or slow down in traffic to crane their necks at an automobile wreck. As one scholar put it, people seemed to love knowing about all the bad things people did, almost as much as they enjoyed the miracles!

KING JOHN OF ARAGON

In the second half of the 1300s, King John of Aragon became a huge patron of the arts and sparked off a musical spurt in the Catalonia/Aragon region. He collected musical instruments, wrote music himself, and sent scouts out all over Europe to find the best musicians and bring them to his court.

One historian wrote, "Even though Catalonia could at that time supply numerous and good performers, John was not content but scoured Europe for others, bombarding kings and courts with requests for musicians, instruments, and exchanges of the same. He desired to possess every new instrument that was invented and sent his musicians all over Europe in quest of them and of people to play them."[3]

King John reigned from 1350 to 1396, and court records show the names of hundreds of musicians who were paid for their services at his court. John had a special weakness for French forms and music. In fact, music supposedly written by himself used the French forms of his day such as lais, virelais, and rondeaux, and apparently the French language as well. During the Great Schism (1378–1409) (see Chapter 1), John seems to have sided with the French Pope instead of the Pope in Rome, and the musical developments in Avignon found their way into his court. A French collection of Ars Subtilior works (see Chapter 3), known as the *Chantilly Manuscript*, contains the names of many of Avignon's top Schism-era musicians. The names of these same musicians also show up on the payrolls of King John.

Apparently not only French influence found its way into Catalonia, also ruled by King John, but Italian music and literature as well. The library of Monserrat Monastery near Barcelona contains a collection of songs from the 1300s called *The Red Book,* showing Italian influence. It contains the Pilgrim Songs (*Cants dels Romeus*), a collection of songs either sung or danced to by pilgrims either on the way to shrines to celebrate feast days or on the feast days themselves. Because the songs would have been remembered by the pilgrims and taken back to wherever they had come from, they were spread far and wide. The pilgrim songs were short and used either two or three voices. Scholars believe that they started as older folk songs, and were adapted to later use at festivals with religious words substituted for their older secular texts. One type of work looks like the Italian caccia. Known as a *cacha*, it lacks the instrumental tenor line of the Italian form.

The monastery library also contains a Dance of Death. An outgrowth of the plague years of 1347–1348, this Spanish form seems to have been a native product of Spain and not influenced by any outside source. Translated into English, its text is:

We hurry towards death, let us desist from sin.
I have resolved to write concerning contempt of the earth,
So that the living of the world may not be crushed in vain.
Now is the hour to rise from the evil sleep of death.[4]

ALFONSO V (THE MAGNANIMOUS)

Near the end of the Middle Ages, another Alfonso became a great patron of the arts in Iberia. Alfonso V (1394–1458) ruled from two places. From his accession in 1416 to 1433, he was living in Aragon on the Iberian peninsula. After that, he lived in Naples—now in Italy, but at that time under Spanish rule. While he was in Iberia, his royal chapel was filled with some of the finest musicians of his day, including not only singers but instrumentalists. They came from Iberian areas, France, Italian areas, and even Germanic lands. In fact, he was responsible for bringing northern European styles from the Franco-Flemish Burgundian areas (see Chapter 8) into Spanish territory, which effectively jump-started those areas into the Renaissance styles of music.

MOORISH MUSIC ON THE IBERIAN PENINSULA

At the first rush of the Islamic invasion, most of the Iberian peninsula was conquered. But over many years and many battles, much of the area was retaken by Christian forces until only the southern part of Spain, known as Andalusia, remained in Moorish hands. Several Andalusian cities such as Seville, Cordoba, and Granada became important cultural centers. Because most Iberian Muslims were not actually Arabs but were either of Berber stock or were converts from Christianity or Judaism, they will be referred to here as Moors.

Although Moorish music theory texts remained largely untranslated during the Middle Ages and thus unavailable to Europeans, other Moorish musical ideas and instruments did infiltrate Europe, either by Crusaders returning from the Middle East or by cross-pollination bred of the close proximity of Christians, Jews, and Moors on the Iberian peninsula.

For one thing, the cantigas of the Christians used some Moorish poetic forms for their own texts. For instance, the *zajal* was a type of poetry used by Spanish Christians and sometimes set to music. Later, during the Renaissance, a blind monk named Salinas was inspired to collect and preserve as many old Iberian tunes as he could, in a collection known as *De Musica Libri Septem* (The Seven Books of Music). His collection contains samples of native songs, some of which were already hundreds of years old. And some of those old songs clearly show Moorish roots. One for instance, has the title "Calvi vi calvi, calvi arabi," which turns out to be a phonetic rendering of Arabic *Qalbi bi qalbi, qalbi 'arabi*, translated as "Heart, oh my heart, it is the heart of an Arab."[5]

Instruments also crossed cultural divides, bringing the lute, rebec, and the small kettledrums known as nakers to Europe (see Chapter 10). The *oud*, a plucked stringed instrument still in use today in Arabic lands (we get the word "lute" from *al-'oud* "the oud"), was particularly pertinent to Iberia, as it was the wellspring from which the modern guitar developed. Even some of the miniature paintings in Alfonso's cantiga collection show musicians in Islamic clothing playing Islamic instruments.

Iberian Moorish areas had a tolerant attitude toward other religions, and thus Islamic, Jewish, and Christian musicians all practiced within those realms. Several Moorish writer/philosopher/musicians wrote texts about music theory and the science of acoustics. Some attempted, with more or less success, to meld the Christian and Moorish musical styles into a greater whole.

AL-FARABI

One such writer was Al-Farabi (d. 950). His monumental work, The *Great Book of Music,* survives only in part, but because it was written about, we know that it was a three-volume work and was systematically divided into subject areas. Book One included the physics of sound, Pythagoras's interval studies (see Chapter 1), and ancient Greek music theory. Book Two concerned musical instruments, their scale systems and tunings, studies of the placement of their frets, and the plucking and bowing of various types of stringed instruments. (Unfortunately, actual physical descriptions were not included.) Book Three delved into rhythms, melodic patterns, and combinations of note patterns. Al-Farabi is also known for two smaller books dealing with rhythms—*Book of Rhythms* and *Book of the Comprehension of Rhythms.*

Unfortunately for Western music, his *Great Book* never became available to the West. But another one of his books was translated into Latin in the twelfth century. Known as *De Scientüs,* its section on music theory was used as a reference to Western music theorists, and parts of it even found its way into other, later books.

IBN BAJJA (AVENPACE)

Ibn Bajja (d. 1139) was a government administrator but also a philosopher and composer. Some of his writings have been lost, but one, titled *Book on the Soul,* includes studies on acoustics. Ibn Bajja is known for his attempt to find areas in which the various musical cultures by which he was surrounded could meld into a beautiful, if different, style. Because of his success, he was a major contributor to the future of Iberian music, as his songs are said to have blended the Christian and "Eastern" styles of music so well that his new way laid the ground for the future of Spanish-flavored sounds.

IBN RUSHD (AVERROES)

Ibn Rushd lived from approximately 1126 to 1198 and wrote a commentary about the writings of the ancient Greek philosopher Aristotle, which included studies of the theory of sound. His work was translated into Latin and became so popular during the Renaissance that by 1600 there were about 100 printed editions.

THE MOORISH EXPULSION

Moorish occupation of the Andalusian area continued until the early Renaissance. Then, in 1492, under the reign of King Ferdinand and Queen Isabella, the last Moorish strongholds were overcome. The Iberian peninsula at that point became a Christian stronghold. Followers of Islam and Judaism were given four months to vacate, convert, or die.

A later song of a secular type called a *villancico*, brings these mass conversions to mind—as well as the idea that, even though the people converted, their new Christian faith was considered only a gloss put on for survival. Diego Fernandez wrote this work, entitled *Tres Moricas M'enamoran*. The words in translation are:

> Three Moorish Girls made me fall in love in Jaen [pronounced hi-YEN],
> Axa [pronounced AH-sha], Fatima, and Marien.
> I asked them, "Who are you, ladies, who have robbed me of my life?"
> "We are Christians who were Moors in Jaen.
> Axa, Fatima, and Marien."
> "I swear by the Koran in which, ladies, you believe,
> That one and all three of you have caused me great anxiety;
> Where can my sorrowful eyes see at last
> Axa, Fatima, and Marien?"[6]

JEWISH MUSIC

Alfonso's court aside, most of the Iberian Jewish community was centered in Moorish areas, which had a more tolerant attitude toward religious variety. These communities, as well as those found in farther Eastern areas, became known as Sephardic. (European Jewry became known as Ashkenazi.)

While the Jewish community already had its own music, its close proximity to Arabian styles found inroads that made Iberian Jewish poetry and musical forms distinct, even in synagogue worship. Although much information has been lost due to the expulsion of 1492, there is a record of a rabbi's complaint during the second half of the thirteenth century that Jewish cantors were being selected not for their religiosity, but solely based on their beautiful singing voices. Although a bit lopsided, this observation indicates the importance of musical beauty to the Sephardic community.

The scarcity of Sephardic music from the Iberian Middle Ages is a blot on history. However, many Jewish converts to Christianity held onto certain habits, customs, and songs, which preserved at least some of their Jewish roots. Passover songs, wedding songs, and traditional ballads survived despite overwhelming odds. Jews of this Diaspora continued to sing their songs—in Spanish—in North Africa and the Eastern Mediterranean, areas that afforded them some measure of protection. One traditional ballad is still sung today in the Marmara region of Turkey, instead of its original Iberian home. Entitled *El Paso del Mar Rojo* (Crossing the Red Sea), its words in translation are:

> When the people of Israel fled from Egypt singing,
> The women and the children left singing the Song of Songs:
> Moses saw Pharaoh pursuing them, waving a red flag.
> "Where have you brought us, Moses to die in these sands,
> To die with no graves, or to be drowned in the sea?
> "Do not be afraid, my people, do not despair . . ."
> Let us remember the miracles of God on high.
> He is One, there is no other,
> He is Master of all the world.[7]

Another pre-expulsion song celebrates a happy wedding day. This work is still sung worldwide today by many choruses, because of its rousing melody and cheerful words. Entitled *¡Ah, el novia no quere dinero!* (Oh, the groom wants no money!) its text in translation is:

> Oh, the groom wants no money,
> He wants only his bride of good fortune.
> I have come to see that they should be
> Happy and prosper and have all the best.
> Oh, the groom wants no money,
> He wants only his bride of good fortune.
> The groom wants no bracelets,
> He wants only his bride to have a happy face.
> Oh, the groom wants no money,
> He wants only his bride of good fortune.[8]

FLAMENCO MUSIC

It seems odd to have left out a kind of music for which the Iberian peninsula is justly famous. However, this style of music came to the Iberian peninsula during the Renaissance, not the Middle Ages, and thus has not been included in this book.

NOTES

1. Jeremy Yudkin, *Music in Medieval Europe. Prentice Hall History of Music Series*, edited by H. Wiley Hitchcock (Englewood Cliffs, NJ: Prentice Hall, 1989), p. 302–303.

2. Ibid., p. 305.

3. Gustav Reese, *Music in the Middle Ages with an Introduction on the Music of Ancient Times* (New York: W. W. Norton & Company, 1940), p. 376.

4. Ibid., p. 375.

5. Ibid.

6. Eugene Enrico, prod., dir., *1492: A Portrait in Music* (University of Oklahoma, 1992) [VHS].

7. Ibid.

8. Ibid.

CHAPTER 8

MUSIC OF BURGUNDY AND THE LOW COUNTRIES IN THE MIDDLE AGES

Although Burgundy is an area of France, in the last quarter of the Middle Ages the Low Countries such as Flanders, Brabant, Hainault, and Holland were a part of that area. Thus, Burgundy and the Low Countries are inextricably linked together and must be taken as such.

The area of Burgundy was a duchy, ruled by a duke instead of a prince or a king. During much of the Middle Ages it was a relatively quiet fiefdom. Then in 1364, it became vacant due to lack of an heir, and King John II of France gave it to one of his younger sons, Philip the Bold, for having saved the King's life during the Hundred Years' War. Philip ruled from 1364 to 1404, and one of his hallmarks was managing to keep his own territories intact while France "proper" was being torn apart by the ever-continuing Hundred Years' War (see Chapter 1).

In fact, while his older brother became Charles V of France, Philip did not do too badly either. He married the richest woman in Europe: Margaret, heiress of Flanders. Since the English King Edward III had wanted this territory for his own, it was a great relief for France to have Flanders under the French flag. The Flemish did not go peacefully; there was a rebellion. When it was put down, however, Philip actually ended up with more territory than he had inherited.

When Charles V died, his son, Philip's nephew (also named Charles), became heir to the throne of France while still a minor. Philip filled the gap. For all intents and purposes, Philip ruled France as well as his Burgundian territory. He also managed to drain most of France's treasury. When Charles came of age and became Charles VI, he stopped taking advice from his uncle and listened only to his own brother, Louis of Orléans. But then, after 1392, Charles became increasingly insane until he was incapable of governing. Philip tried to move back in, but Louis fought for his own power over the throne, and the two engaged in a civil war that did no one much good. The houses of Burgundy and Orléans split and looked for support in some strange places.

Louis of Orléans went to the Avignon Pope, Benedict XIII, for support. Philip turned to the Holy Roman Emperor, the Pope in Rome, and also to Henry IV, the King of England. It seems extremely odd for the French-speaking Philip to look for support from France's most bitter enemy. But in Philip's territory, Flanders was a major cloth manufacturer, and one of their main raw materials was wool from England. Philip's siding with the Roman Pope also had a practical reason. Flanders did a lot of trading with Italy, and so during the Great Schism they had always sided with the Pope in Rome, not the French Pope in Avignon.

The Burgundian forces and their allies eventually won control of France. Philip entered Paris, excommunicated everyone who had followed the Avignon Pope, and put his own patron saint, St. Andrew, over Paris' own holy images.

When Philip died, his son, John the Fearless, inherited all the Burgundian territory. John ruled for 15 years, from 1404 to 1419. One of John's less admirable moments was engineering the assassination of his father's formal rival, Louis of Orléans, in 1407. This act set off a series of conflicts that lasted throughout his reign.

John had the daunting job of fending off his French enemies, keeping England at bay, and consolidating his own disparate dukedom. His territory's language barrier was a problem that he worked to smooth over. Although still undeniably French, John as a youth had had Flemish tutors as well as French, ensuring that he would know something of the language and character of all the people in his future realm. Now, under his rule, the official language of the court was French, as was the language of the highest legal and religious entities. But lower legal courts, parish priests, and ordinary soldiers in the army could speak the language of their choice. The wisdom of this was priceless. During the reign of John's father, some important petitioners had wasted a week having documents that had been written in Netherlandish translated so that the French could read them. John had no such problems.

John also made the most of his area's mercantile possibilities. He knew what Burgundy and his Netherlandish lands made and what would sell. He also made it his business to know what other countries had that Burgundians wanted to buy. Soon the Burgundian territory was famous for its industry and wealth. The relative fluidity among languages spilled over into other areas as well. Whenever a good idea pertaining to laws or customs came up on one side, the other might also adopt it. The French accepted Netherlandish (also known as "Low German") as an official language, and the Flemish understood that Burgundy and France were not the same entity at all. In fact, John was as close to being an English ally as a French nobleman could be.

Then John the Fearless was murdered on a bridge in France in 1419, with the tacit consent of (and it was rumored, in the sight of) the soon-to-be French monarch Charles VII, son of Charles VI.

After John's death, Philip the Good (1396–1467) inherited the duchy, with all the territory won by both Philip the Bold and John the Fearless. And it was under Philip that the Burgundian territory reached its height. In the early part of his reign, Philip had been allied with England, since the future king of France had been complicit in the murder of Philip's father. In fact, it was Philip who captured Joan of Arc and sold her to the British. But in 1429, Philip and Charles made an uneasy peace when the latter was crowned Charles VII. Still, Charles never let Philip forget that he himself was a King, whereas Philip was "only" a Duke. And Philip in his turn never pledged himself as a vassal to the King, considered himself a king in everything but name, and acted accordingly.

Under Philip the Good, Holland, Brabant, and Luxembourg were added to the territories of his predecessors. And despite occasional uprisings, Philip managed to keep his Duchy out of other people's wars for 30 years. Plus, he ruled for almost 50 years (1419–1467) and that stability alone provided a launch pad for his area's successes.

For awhile, Philip tried to upgrade his position into a kingship, and there was a flurry of negotiation with the Holy Roman Emperor (Frederick III) that eventually came to nothing. Failing that, however, Philip decided to turn his energies into having the richest, most powerful and influential court in Europe. One of the things he did, while marrying Isabel of Portugal at Bruges in 1430, was to initiate his own order—something only kings and emperors usually did. The Order of the Golden Fleece was supposedly put together to launch a Crusade, and thirty-one knights were in the first oath-taking. The Crusade failed to materialize, but this Order made Philip the head of his own fiefdom. It also encouraged and supported musical endeavors, and the song "L'Homme Armé," came from this quasi-military organization and eventually kicked off a fad of composing Masses based on its melody.

More of a confederation than a solid state, the Burgundian/Low Countries mix was still a win-win situation. The Low Countries got all the protection that their sea routes needed for their trading ventures, and the Burgundians got the world's best shipbuilders, first claim on their fishing, plus "iron, lead, coal, marble and chalk, saltpeter and vitriol, sulfur, and gold" as raw materials, and some of the best cloth products in Europe.[1]

LIFE IN THE BURGUNDIAN TERRITORY

The Dukes of Burgundy had the means and power to indulge their tastes, and because of the mercantile nature of their territory, others shared in the general wealth. Of course nobles attached to the Court did well, but the Burgundian territories had an unusually large and well-to-do middle class. Ghent, Bruges, and Ypres were the major areas of trade. The Cloth Hall in Ypres was famous, and its building was considered the equal of any other in the world, including Paris and Constantinople. In Ghent, merchants used official seals on shipments of goods leaving their ports, and records show that in one year 92,000 seals were used. Also a cloth center, Ghent at one time had over 2,000 active looms turning out cloth sold all over the known world.

Bruges not only traded goods but also became the brokers, bankers, and money-changers for the Franco-Flemish territory. As a result, Bruges became an international center, with various countries keeping permanent representatives there (a more convenient arrangement than constant travel) and these foreigners bought properties and sometimes entire streets for their own use. At its height, forty-four nations were sending produce to Bruges and returning with goods from Franco-Flemish territory to be sold in their own countries.

Because of the trade and banking interests, by the end of the Middle Ages, Burgundian territory was pulling in as much money as Venice, four times as much as Florence, and twice as much as the Vatican! Because currencies could fluctuate wildly, the Burgundian Dukes tended to fill their coffers with goods—*lots* of goods.

Burgundians of all classes were not only selling, they were buying. And they had, for the Middle Ages, a mind-bending array of things from which to choose! If a person had the means, they could find "groceries and luxury-wares from the Orient . . . English wool and coal, precious metals from Bohemia and Hungary, Russian pelts, sailcloth from Navarre, gold brocade from Tartary, and costly silks, sugar from Morocco, and fruits from Granada and Andalusia."[2]

One item of conspicuous consumption in which Burgundians indulged was clothing; after all, they were the cloth center of Europe. Even in Philip the Bold's time, when he visited Paris in 1389 to meet Charles VI's new wife, he wore "a scarlet doublet on which were embroidered forty lambs and swans in pearls. From the necks of the lambs and the swans hung little gold bells."[3] (Remember, in the Middle Ages there were no cultured pearls!) When Philip's daughter, Margaret, was married, the officiating bishop received not only "fine Brussels cloth" for a coat, but the skins of 1,250 squirrels for its lining![4]

Women were just as lavish. One way they showed their wealth was with their hats. These are the hats of legend, the long cone-shaped ones with a piece of fine linen flowing from the top. Called "hennins," these were higher or lower according to a lady's status. A noble lady might have a two-foot hennin, but a princess could have a cone reaching a yard or more. Some hats had two cones instead of one, which looked rather like horns. Critics of the time sneered that women looked more like sailing ships than human beings.

While women sailed by in their dresses with long trains and wearing their hennins, men wore their tunics so short, and their hose so tight, that little if anything was left to the imagination (in fact, men would sometimes pad their not-quite-so private parts to make them appear larger). To show off their shapely legs further, men's shoes sported long pointed toes, turned up at the end. The shoe toes became longer and longer until they were several inches long and had to be held up by a golden chain attached to the wearer's knees, so that he would not trip over his own shoes.

While everyone else was on display in a dizzying array of color, Philip the Good wore black. Why? There are two theories. One reason may have been to remind others of his father's death and its circumstances. The other was that the embroidery and jewels bedecking the cloth stood out even more brilliantly from its black background.

Besides clothes, another clothlike work favored by Burgundian dukes and their nobles was tapestry. Even the finest castle tended to be drafty and cold. Wall-hangings of thick cloth helped alleviate the chill. These were not just cloth— they were entire tales and intricate scenes woven into the cloth. Hundreds of man-hours and colors went into these elaborate weavings. The subjects were generally heroic, such rulers of ancient Greek and Roman times and their deeds, scenes from the Trojan War, and historic battles. Unlike frescoes (art works painted on walls), tapestry art works were portable, an advantage when the court moved around its vast territory from time to time and the Dukes were ensured comfortable accommodations and a homelike atmosphere. When Philip the Good married Isabel of Portugal in Bruges in January of 1430, fifteen cartloads of tapestries were sent ahead to make sure of their comfort.

The dukes were also avid book collectors. Philip the Bold had about 200 books in his personal library, and his son John the Fearless added about 250 more, but Philip the Good outdid them all. By the time he died, the Burgundian court library held over 900 volumes. It was one of the best libraries in Europe. Taking the dukes' lead, other nobles began collecting books, and libraries all over the duchy started springing up. Happily, a number of volumes survive to the present day in various collections and museums. Women as well as men had books, although they would be mostly of a religious nature. Noble women would have a Book of Hours, which they would use during Church services. One literary source wrote sarcastically that a really fine Book of Hours with richly illustrated miniature paintings and gold print inside, and a cover of fine velvet encrusted with jewels outside, was one way that a vindictive wife could bankrupt her husband!

With all the fashion, wealth, and pomp, it is not surprising that the Burgundian court observed a strict code of ceremony. Everyone from the dukes to their lowliest servant knew what they were supposed to do, and exactly how to do it. It didn't matter whether one was signing a peace treaty or holding the salt-cellar at dinner— there was a right way to do it.

For instance, when the duke ate, a parade of dishes was brought in, and each dish was carried by a different person. Every dish was tasted before it got to the duke, and six physicians also advised him what he should or should not eat on that day. There was even a "unicorn's horn" provided to test liquids for poison. After the duke had approved the wine for his meal, the steward filled the duke's personal goblet. Then the steward held that goblet over his own head so that his breath would not sully the cup and, bowing low, presented it to the duke.

The dukes each had their own knights, and, especially during Philip the Good's reign, they were an integral part of all the feasts, hunting expeditions, tournaments, and pageants. Sixteen of Philip's favorites accompanied him everywhere and attended to his needs. They even slept near him as his personal guard. When the day's duties were over, these men kept him entertained. "Some sang, others read romances or tales aloud, others spoke of love and military glory."[5] During peacetime the duke kept his knights busy by reviving as many of the chivalric ideas as possible from past days. Naturally they were supposed to be experts in martial pursuits, but they were also expected to cultivate some knowledge of literature, art, and music.

BURGUNDIANS AND THE ARTS

All of the fine arts were present and accounted for in the Burgundian territory. It had authors of the stature of Christine de Pisan (1364–1430), considered Europe's first female professional writer, and artists of the stature of the Van Eyck brothers, Hubert (1370–1426) and Jan (1390–1441). But music was dear to their hearts. The Low Countries had always had an interest in musical excellence, and the power and riches brought about by trade and the powerful dukes who made it possible gave its nobles and city governments the means to train and support the finest musicians in Europe. Moreover, the political realm in which the Burgundian dukes were enmeshed had two curiously positive effects. First, their relationship with England put them in the position of hearing what the English had been doing musically, which they added to their own musical styles. Second, as the Council of Constance (1414–1418) knitted together the Great Schism (see Chapter 1), musicians from all over Europe gathered into one area to entertain the council fathers. These musicians and composers, too, heard regional styles and brought those styles (and copies of the music) back to their home countries. Thus Burgundy was able, because of the first factor, to develop its own unique style and, through the second factor, to disseminate it all over Europe. The two points are also the reason why, in an age before printing was common and before any sort of mass communications had developed, manuscripts of French music show up in collections such as the *Old Hall Manuscript* in England (which was put together between 1413 and 1420). And finally, because of the enormous range of trade that Burgundy and the Low Countries enjoyed, people of many lands were aware of this area and its very musical court. As mentioned before, Italians were major trading partners, and as their own fortunes began to rise, they began hiring Franco-Flemish composers to work in major Italian areas such as St. Mark's Cathedral in Venice.

The Burgundian dukes were hands-on music lovers. In the late 1300s Philip the Bold was part of a society called the *Court of Love* (Cour d'Amour), where nobles gathered to express their artistic leanings. This could be someone hired to read poetry, or a minstrel hired to play and sing music, or it could even involve personal participation from its members. The head of this "fraternity" was called the "Prince of Love," and this person was not necessarily the duke. Its principal holiday was St. Valentine's Day, and at that time only soft-sounding (*bas*) instruments could be played. The Court of Love's assemblies were held periodically until the mid-fifteenth century, through the reigns of John the Fearless and Philip the Good. At one time it had over 700 members.

Music was an integral part of Burgundian worship services. Philip the Bold formed his private chapel in 1384. By the time of his death in 1404, it had 28 members—more than either that of the King of France or that of the Avignon Pope. Under John the Fearless, those numbers went down, but Philip the Good brought the Burgundian chapel to its zenith. In 1445 it had seventeen chaplains, two clerks, four porters, and composer/singers of the stature of Hayne van Ghizeghem, Guillaume Dufay, and the English musician Robert Morton. Philip the Good personally auditioned singers for his chapel and turned down candidates who did not meet his standards. He also founded choir schools in various areas of his realm to teach talented young boys singing and Latin, in addition to the more usual school subjects.

Since men and women did not sing together in chapel choirs, the boys provided its top voices. All the choristers worked hard. Most of the grown men were in the service of the church (usually as priests), but at any time they might be used as "priest, performer, composer, teacher, and scribe, [or] assisting at the daily celebration of the Mass and canonical hours."[6] The music for a normal daily Mass would be monophonic chant. But for special services on major feast days and saints' days, the music would use polyphonic Mass movements and might also add polyphonic hymns or motets from the collections in the chapel library as well.

Burgundian choristers—particularly the Flemish ones—were renowned for their excellent bass voices. One ear witness wrote, "you would say on hearing him that he must be a Fleming, for his gullet is disposed as [if] it were a great organ pipe . . ."[7] These choristers were renowned for another trait, too. They loved to wet their whistles. Happy drinkers, they seemed to perform with even more gusto after a few quaffs. One Italian wrote, "having drunk good wine, [the choristers] begin to sing with vibrant voices, the which their throats may very easily send forth as they are all strong and robust in the chest."[8]

The dukes of Burgundy did hardly anything without music. They were entertained at table. Music marked the occasion when food came and went. There was music at jousts, at feasts, at balls, and at state occasions. There was music at baptisms, banquets, and weddings. They even took musicians with them to battle. Any soldier knows the axiom "hurry up and wait," and musicians helped to relieve long tense hours of waiting. Besides, music was a morale-booster and gave soldiers a more positive outlook as they headed into battle.

Trumpet players were especially valued by the Burgundian dukes and were highly paid. They played signals on one of the few instruments that could be heard above the din of battle. Knowing which tune was which could mean the difference between life or death. Also, whenever one of the dukes entered a town, he was announced by a flurry of trumpets. And while the duke was in a particular town, trumpets sounded throughout the night to remind the people living there of the honor that their town had received. Visitors to the Burgundian court were suitably impressed with the wall of sound provided by these trumpeters. One wrote, "these minstrels sounded so loud that one could not have heard the thunder of God!"[9]

FEAST OF THE PHEASANT

Although its date should put this feast outside the boundaries of this book, the Feast of the Pheasant on February 17, 1454, is an outstanding example of the kind of excess to which Burgundian dukes were capable. The Feast took place on the cusp between the Middle Ages and the Renaissance. The Ottoman Turks had just captured the capital city of the Byzantine Empire, Constantinople, and Philip the Good's Order of the Golden Fleece gathered to swear an oath to take it back for Christendom. Various eyewitnesses wrote about what they saw and heard, and one thing shining through is how important music was to this entire affair.

It took place in a large, tapestry-hung hall. Inside were huge tables. One held a miniature church with four singers inside who sang, rang the church bell, and played an organ at various times. Another table held a huge pastry, inside which twenty-eight musicians played instruments, taking turns so that the music continued uninterrupted by human fatigue. (Anyone familiar with nursery rhymes will recognize the "four and twenty blackbirds baked in a pie; when the pie was opened the birds began to sing.")

Then a horse came into the hall, trotting backwards, while two trumpeters seated on this animal played a fanfare. Afterwards, the church musicians and the pastry musicians took turns making more music. Then an artificial white stag (male deer) came in, with a boy of twelve riding it. The boy sang the high part of a song (which may have been written by Guillaume Dufay) while the "stag" sang a harmonizing lower part. Then the church singers sang again, and the pastry musicians played a chasse (a song like a round, generally about hunting, like the Italian caccia discussed in Chapter 4) that imitated hunting sounds right down to the barking of the dogs.

Afterwards, there was the appearance of a fiery dragon flying through the hall, and also a live heron was let loose up in the ceiling and hunted by falcons. Then there was a series of play scenes about Jason and the Golden Fleece. And after that came the main attraction. "A huge giant, dressed in green and striped silk, now appeared who represented a Saracen. In his left hand he held an ancient battle-axe, and with his right hand he led an elephant. On its back it carried a tower resting on a silken saddle-cloth, and in the tower a personage was seated wearing female attire."[10]

The giant represented the Turks, the elephant represented faraway lands, and the lady in the tower represented the captive Church. The lady (played by a man) sang a sad song about her fate, followed by four singers singing a four-part motet (probably composed by Gilles Binchois) lamenting the fate of Constantinople. At the proper moment, the Duke stepped forward and made a declaration to rescue Constantinople and its Christian church. The "lady" thanked him in verse form, and then the giant led the elephant out of the hall.

The duke's followers also swore to go on to Crusade and rescue the church. And they sealed that oath by eating a piece of meat from a bird—but, despite the name of the feast, not from a pheasant but from a peacock. The hall doors opened and torchbearers led in musicians playing various instruments, followed by a nun-like woman and twelve other women. The first woman represented "God's Grace." The others were the twelve virtues: Faith, Love, Hope, Truth, Justice, Understanding, Prudence, Courage, Temperance, Strength, Ardor, and Generosity. Each was lead to the duke and introduced with poetic verses. When they left, the general party started. Now there was dancing, entertainments, and lots to eat and drink. The duke and his courtiers broke the party up at around 3 A.M.

"THE ENGLISH FACE"

As discussed in Chapter 6, the encounter between English and French music is something that propelled music from the Middle Ages into the Renaissance, and it is something that could not have happened anywhere else during the early fifteenth century except in the Burgundian territories. Because of the temporary alliance with England against the King of France, French and English ideas were able to cross-pollinate. Thus, for a brief period, the musicians of France, who felt that only the perfect fourth, fifth, and octave of Pythagoras were consonant and all other intervals were dissonant, came into contact with the musicians of England, who favored the more folk-like flavors of thirds and sixths. The English preferred four-voiced layering for their music and put a bassus line underneath their tenor line as a matter of custom. And although their tenor line might still be based on a chant melody (Sarum, not Gregorian for them!) or a secular tune, the real melody for them was in the top voice. But British music of the time lacked the subtlety and complexity of French music.

Burgundian musicians were stunned by the beauty of the English music and gave it the name "the English face" (*la contenance angloise*). The music of John Dunstable (see Chapter 6), in particular, came to the attention of Burgundian musicians Dufay and Binchois, who began to fuse English and French music styles together. What happened was a third style of music, known as Burgundian or Franco-Flemish style, and a great leap forward for music happened.

From this point on, music would sound different. To present-day listeners, it sounds more "normal." This is because the four standard voices—soprano, alto, tenor, and bass—were now in place, and the melody line would more usually be in the top voice, not the tenor. Also, all intervals were now considered consonant except the second, the seventh, and the ever-despised "Devil's interval" of the diminished fifth/augmented fourth—a situation that held true until the mid-twentieth century. Music did not yet look the same on paper, and its theory was still based on the six notes of the scale described by Guido (see Chapter 4). But it now had the basic setup for the major-minor scale system and chord-based composition of the future.

The Franco-Flemish style outlived its Burgundian roots. Long after the Burgundian territory had ceased to exist, Franco-Flemish musicians were considered the best in Europe. Because of the mercantile trade, Italians were some of the first to begin hiring those musicians outside of French territory. As the Renaissance took hold, it was the Franco-Flemish composers working in Italian areas who composed its early music and taught their Italian pupils how to bring music of the Renaissance to its highest point.

TWO BURGUNDIAN MUSICIANS

GILLES BINCHOIS

Binchois (c. 1400–1460) was born in Flanders, but he is usually incorporated into French music history. As with most names in the Middle Ages, *Binchois* is also variously spelled: Binchoys, Binch, Bins, or Binche. Most of what is known about his early life comes from a "deploration"—a musical obituary—written by a contemporary. According to that source, Binchois was a soldier before coming to sing in the Burgundian court chapel. Apparently he was not a priest, as were most other court musicians, although he held Church properties and was closely connected with the Church as a subdeacon. He and Dufay (discussed in the next section) knew one another and had at least one meeting, although more are certainly possible. But Binchois mostly stayed within Burgundian territory, retiring with a generous pension until his death.

Binchois's music was well-respected in his time, but it is his later influence that is more important. He was known for his beautiful melody lines, and his secular tunes (rondeaux in particular) were used as a basis (cantus firmus) for a host of other, later works. One in particular, "De plus en plus," became the basis for future Masses, instrumental works, and contrafacta secular songs by later composers who lived in German territories, England, France, and Burgundian lands. "Nobody's music, not even Dufay's engendered as many imitations, paraphrases, and allusions in the world of other composers."[11]

GUILLAUME DUFAY

Dufay (c. 1397–1474) was born in Brussels. As the illegitimate son of a single woman and an unnamed priest, Dufay might have had a brutal life had he not been an exceptionally bright and talented youth. He entered Church service, and his long career was divided among secular chapels and the papal chapel in Rome. In fact, he was caught in papal tensions of his day and at one time two rival claimants to the papacy—Eugene IV (counted as legitimate) and Felix V (who was elected by a council at Basle and who was also the duke of Savoy)—wanted him for their respective papal courts. Dufay traveled widely in Italy, France, and all around the Burgundian territories (where he spent his last years), and there is even evidence that he visited England at one time.

Dufay is revered for the excellence and amount of his surviving music. Possibly because of his travels, more of his music survives from the early-to-mid fifteenth century than of any other contemporary composer's works. Moreover, because Dufay wrote in a wide variety of styles, his music may be found in many present-day music history texts and anthologies. In addition, Dufay took *la contenance angloise* to heart, which makes his music more palatable to modern ears. Many of his Masses use secular tunes for their cantus firmi and are named for them, such as *Missa "Se la face ay pale"* (Mass "If My Face is Pale") from a love song, and *Missa "L'homme armé"* (Mass "The Armed Man") from a popular martial tune. Thus it is easy to trace the original tunes of Dufay's Mass tenors—a real plus for music historians.

L'Homme Armé

The original text of *"L'Homme Armé"* was distinctly un-churchlike—translated in part, "The armed man is to be feared"—and those words were replaced for sacred use. But the tune caught on and became a fad for Mass settings during the Renaissance era. At least 100 composers from roughly 1450 to 1550 set Masses based on this melody. In fact, some Renaissance composers were distinguished by their *not* having ever written a *"L'Homme Armé"* Mass.

Nuper Rosarum Flores

One of Dufay's most famous works was a motet, *Nuper rosarum flores,* which was written for the completion of Santa Maria del Fiore Cathedral, the cathedral in Florence that still dominates its landscape with its brick-red dome (and that contains many of the works of Michaelangelo). The cathedral's dome was a masterpiece of architecture, and Dufay's work tried to represent it musically.

This motet was conservative in style, which meant that it contained isorhythm (see Chapter 3), which was by this time considered passé. Its cantus firmus was *Terribilis est locus iste* ("awesome is this place"), a chant from the liturgy for the dedication of a church (it comes from Jacob's words after he had the vision of the ladder, Genesis 28:17). There are two tenor lines carrying its melody, because the church dome was actually a double dome, one under the other. So the tenor lines are one under the other as well—tenor 1 sings five tones below tenor 2. Each color (melody line; see Chapter 3) of the tenors is stated four times—the four points of a cross. The tenor's taleas (rhythms) are proportionally the same each time, but in different mensurations (see Chapter 3). These differences correspond to the Biblical proportions of Solomon's temple—6:4:2:3. Each of Dufay's four stanzas begin with a duet, and then the double tenor lines come in to signify that the church (first voices) had added the dome (the double tenor lines). The church was 72 *braccia* high, and its dome was also a further 72 braccia high, adding up to 144 braccia for the entire structure. The numbers in Dufay's mensural scheme of 6:4:2:3 (reflecting Solomon's temple), when multiplied, also equal 144! ($6 \times 4 = 24 \times 2 = 48 \times 3 = 144$.)

The number 28 is also key to this work. Why? Because in the Middle Ages this was considered a perfect number, and the cathedral dedicated to the Virgin Mary represented the perfect union of earthly need to divine providence. The formula for this perfection was: $1 \times 28 = 2 \times 14 = 4 \times 7$, and taking all the smaller numbers, $1 + 2 + 4 + 14 + 7$ also $= 28$. In Dufay's motet, each of his stanzas has seven lines and there are four stanzas, and $4 \times 7 = 28$.

Even a cursory look at the symbolic thinking involved in this endeavor is mind-boggling. And to have all this emerge as a viable piece of music is even more incredible.

THE END OF BURGUNDIAN RULE

When Philip the Good died in 1467, he passed the dukedom to his son, Charles the Bold (1433–1477). Charles showed all the earmarks of following his father's footsteps. He was himself an amateur musician. He not only played the harp, but composed music. A contemporary wrote of him that he "brought together the most famous musicians in the world and maintained a Chapel graced with such harmonious and delectable voices that next to celestial glory, there was nothing as blissful."[12]

Unfortunately, Charles was killed in battle. He left no son, only a daughter. When she was old enough, she married Maximilian I, the Holy Roman Emperor. Part of her lands reverted to the French crown, and the rest were absorbed into Maximilian's territory. Thus, the Burgundian territory was ended, and its composers would afterwards be known as Franco-Flemish.

NOTES

1. Otto Cartellieri, *The Court of Burgundy* (New York: Haskell House Publishers, 1925), p. 13.

2. Ibid., p. 4.

3. William R. Tyler, *Dijon and the Valois Dukes of Burgundy* (Norman: University of Oklahoma Press, 1971), pp. 65–66.

4. Ibid.

5. Otto Cartellieri, *The Court of Burgundy* (New York: Haskell House Publishers, 1925), p. 67.

6. Craig Wright and David Fallows, "Burgundy" *The New Grove Dictionary of Music and Musicians* (2nd edition), edited by Stanley Sadie (New York: Oxford University Press, 2001), Vol. 4, p. 621.

7. William R. Tyler, *Dijon and the Valois Dukes of Burgundy* (Norman: University of Oklahoma Press, 1971), p. 104.

8. Ibid.

9. Ibid., p. 107.

10. Otto Cartellieri, *The Court of Burgundy* (New York: Haskell House Publishers, 1925), p. 147.

11. James McKinnon, ed., *Music and Society: Antiquity and the Middle Ages from Ancient Greece to the 15th Century* (Englewood Cliffs, NJ: Prentice Hall, 1991), p. 290.

12. William R. Tyler, *Dijon and the Valois Dukes of Burgundy* (Norman: University of Oklahoma Press, 1971), p. 110.

CHAPTER 9

THE MUSIC OF OTHER EUROPEAN AREAS IN THE MIDDLE AGES

There is an old saying that goes, "Europe is divided into two parts: the Western, where the shirt is worn inside the trousers, and the Eastern, where it is worn over the trousers."[1] Although the main focus of this book is the music of Western Europe, other areas were also under its influence. These included the areas of present-day Slovenia, the Czech Republic and Slovakia, Hungary, Poland, and Croatia. All of these areas, though situated in more easterly areas, remained within the Roman Catholic Church, and while they may have been influenced by other cultures such as Byzantium or Turkish Islam, they tended to blend their older, pagan cultures into something acceptable to the Church in Rome.

Unfortunately many of the folk elements of these countries have been lost as the chain of oral transmission was broken by conquest, suppression, and simple neglect. But certain elements were retained in later music, and scholars have also gleaned information from written sources, carvings, and paintings. Church music has fared better, however, and a number of manuscripts survive in monasteries and museums worldwide.

The author regrets the brevity of these accounts, but hopes that the reader will be moved to take further interest in the music of these areas.

CZECH LANDS

The area of the present-day Czech Republic was once part of the Great Moravian Empire, which tried to resist invasion by the Franks, and even sought help to that end by asking for help from the Byzantine Empire. The Byzantine envoys who responded brought with them a Slavonian church liturgy and Glagolitic script. The script and liturgy helped the Czechs to understand important liturgical texts, and the Glagolitic script fitted their language. However, the Franks prevailed, and by the start of the tenth century the Roman liturgy, complete with Gregorian chant and Latin text, became the official religion. It was also during this time that the governmental power base shifted from the Moravian area to the Bohemian.

Slavic-language services were suppressed, but a few older sacred-texted folk songs—four in particular—survived. Happily, these continued to be sung in the vernacular Czech language, with permission from the Roman Church. One praised King Wenceslas (yes, the same king in the Christmas carol "Good King Wenceslas"). Two others, "God Almighty" and "Jesus Christ, Thou Bounteous Prince," come from the beginning of the fourteenth century. The oldest, surviving from around 1000, became a sort of national anthem. "Lord, Have Mercy Upon Us" was used both as a battle anthem and during the crowning of Czech kings. Other songs, sung in Latin but locally composed, were connected with Church plays and usually performed at Easter time.

Many secular songs came in from outside Czech lands. Germanic Minnesingers and Meistersingers came first, followed by French trouvères who had been invited to perform at the Czech royal court. The French connection came through the Luxembourg dynasty of rulers (1310–1437). The French composer Guillaume de Machaut was a musician in the court of King John of Luxembourg, but neither the composer nor the king spent much actual time in Bohemia.

During the reign of Charles IV (from 1345–1378), Prague became the capital of the Holy Roman Empire, and this cultural upswing had a definite effect on music. The Czech School of Composition was founded in 1348 and its founders—Zavis of Zapy and (Archbishop) Jan (John) of Janstejn are the first two Czech composers whose names have survived. All forms of music, secular and sacred, vocal and instrumental, flourished. But troubled times were coming.

The end of the fourteenth century saw the rise of Jan Hus, a radical religious reformer who has also been described as a "champion of the oppressed people, learned writer, preacher, Master and Rector of Prague University" and a musician himself.[2] His followers, known as Hussites, rose up against the government and religious institutions and used music as a recruitment tool and morale booster. Hus himself was burned at the stake in 1415, a sentence passed during the Council of Constance (1414–1418).

Works such as "Rise, Oh Rise, Thou Great City of Prague" from 1419, and "Children, Let Us Meet Together" kept the Hussite movement going. One work,

"Ye Warriors of God," became legendary as it had the reputation of causing enemies to scatter in fright just from hearing the sound of it coming their way. The Hussite army was defeated in 1434. After that there were still Hussites, but their revolutionary fervor was gone. The rebellion, however, was a blueprint for the later Protestant Reformation movement and also future revolutionary movements.

By the end of the Middle Ages, Czech music was trying to catch up with the rest of Europe, having been left behind during their internal struggles. Not only were Czech composers encouraged to create new polyphonic works, but various guilds organized "literary fraternities," and one of the requirements for membership was some musical knowledge. From this time, and on into the Renaissance era, one way of keeping native songs alive was to use them as a cantus firmus (see Chapter 2) for a newly composed sacred or secular polyphonic work.

HUNGARY

Western Hungary had been part of the ancient Roman Empire and was called Pannonia. Musical relics such as a Roman water organ (*hydraulis*) from the third century A.D. have been found. When the Romans withdrew, Huns, Avars, Slavs, and Germanic tribes variously occupied the area until it became part of the Frankish empire. But the origin of the Magyar (as the Hungarians call themselves) tribes who invaded and settled the country in the tenth century is one of history's mysteries. Musicologists have studied features of some of the oldest surviving folk music to trace ancestral culture, and this source maintains that "Asian memories slumber in the depths of Hungarian folk music."[3] As tribal ties disintegrated, a class society gradually emerged. Affluent classes had more contact with Western Europe and their musical forms, while the more isolated lower classes both held onto their ancient songs and independently developed new ones.

The pagan Magyars certainly had their own music. A Byzantine historian wrote that they "honored the soil with songs,"[4] and another wrote in 926 that they "cried to their gods in a peculiar way."[5] In the eleventh century, the Hungarian kings became Christians, and Gregorian chant came to the churches, cathedrals, monasteries, and church schools. Written sources indicate that Hungarians used Guido's solmization techniques, and many church music manuscripts of the time are filled with Gregorian chants.

Sometimes scholars find that Hungarians "Magyarized" some tunes to fit their language, and there is even evidence of some independent melodies. However, the use of vernacular language was resisted by Rome, and the Synod of Esztergom in 1114 denounced songs that were not "approved"—meaning, among other things, not in Latin. Still, in the *Pray Codex*, a collection of church music copied out between the years of 1192 and 1216, a Funeral Oration is the "earliest written extant of the Hungarian language."[6] This collection, named after a Hungarian researcher, also contains notation that is different from the Roman neumes.

Not much is known about Hungarian secular music of the Middle Ages. Stories tell of the year 1061, when pagan priests used songs to get people to kill the new Christian priests and bishops and burn down their churches. Later minstrels and joculators who sang old songs were condemned as keeping pagan memories alive, and the Church tended to target them along with condemning secular song in general. Minstrels continued to sing, attached to particular courts and even given land by their noble patrons. Joculators also entertained at court, both singing and playing instruments, but they were lower in social status and also tended to wander and entertain in other places such as taverns and market fairs.

Thus it was that the joculators were more roundly condemned. The Synod of Buda in 1279 warned congregations not to listen to the joculators. Partly possibly because of the ban on singing, instrumental music eventually took an upswing. Instrumental players began showing up on court records more frequently, and by 1420 lutenists and fiddlers had pretty much taken over the role of the joculators and even that of the old court minstrels.

Instruments were mentioned in written records from the early twelfth century on, and these court records show the variety of instruments. From the thirteenth to the mid-fifteenth century, records show whistle-players, buglers, trumpeters, lutenists, fiddlers, bagpipe players, and (after 1437) organists. Their tunes have largely been lost, because nothing was written down. One monk from around 1520 wrote down a fragment of an old song, and that is apparently the earliest written record of Hungarian music. All other evidence must be taken from oral traditions that were eventually written down.

POLAND

By the tenth century Poland was already a strong state, and always Western-oriented. Through writings of early travelers, scholars know that there was a thriving musical culture by the time Christianity became the official religion in 966. Unfortunately, none of that music has survived.

When Christianity came to Poland, its Gregorian chant and neumatic plainsong came into collision with native music making. This cultural tug-of-war hindered the development of music in Poland, and Polish music did not really hit its stride until the Renaissance.

However, the first composition with a Polish (not Latin) text is from the thirteenth century: an anonymous composition titled *Bogurodzica* ("The Mother of God"). It was a favorite song among Polish knights, and if there had been a national anthem in those days, this song would have been it. Krakow University was founded in 1364, and music was one of its important subjects. As far as secular music, there were musicians' guilds from the beginning of the fourteenth century, and among their preserved works are a comic song from Krakow students titled *Breve Regnum* and a hymn titled *Cracovia civitas* ("City of Krakow").

By the beginning of the fifteenth century, a Polish composer named Mikolaj of Radom wrote some very fine polyphonic works. As Poland entered the Renaissance era, Polish and foreign musicians began to flourish and fill the area with works written by native composers, and also imported from all over Western Europe.

SLOVENIA

This area, between the Danube and the Adriatic, was called Noricum, and the natives were known by their tribal name, the Sclaveni. This area was Christianized earlier than some of its neighbors—in a first wave from 600 to 625 and a second wave from 690 to 739. The first wave came from Ireland. The Irish missionaries learned and used the vernacular language for preaching, and their extreme asceticism was admired even by the pagans. The second wave came from Charlemagne, and the Irish monasteries were replaced. The second wave was not as understanding as their Irish predecessors and suppressed any Slavic liturgy, replacing it with Latin. This effectively "robbed the main Slavonic tribes in Central Europe of their national life and identity."[7]

However, vernacular liturgy and Glagolitic script continued to be used in some areas, and manuscripts and books using Glagolitic script were still being found in parish houses as late as the twentieth century. And scholars believe that older songs were also reworked into Christian versions and passed down along with other pre-Christian customs such as investiture ceremonies. During the thirteenth and fourteenth centuries, the area—by then known as Karantania—was governed by dukes. These dukes were apparently elected. The investiture ceremony for a duke made it perfectly clear that, far from being a tyrant over the lower classes, he was there to *serve* his people. Without them, he was nothing.

The ceremony itself was conducted in the Slovene language. The new Duke, dressed in peasant clothes, surrounded by a crowd of people who included his court nobility, lead a horse and an ox up a hill. At the top of the hill a free peasant sat on a stone table and asked, "Who is he that is approaching?" The crowd answered, "He is the Duke of the land." The peasant asked, "Is he a just judge? Will he care for the welfare of the land? Is he of free birth? Is he a faithful of the Christian faith and a protector of that faith?" The crowd answered, "He is and always will be." The peasant then asked, "By what right can he displace me from this my seat?" The people answered, "He will pay you fifty denarii and give you his garments as well as both animals, and thy family and thy property will remain free of every kind of tax."

At that the peasant would rise and give the duke a stroke on the cheek. The duke then stood on the table, raised his sword to all four corners of the world and swore that he would be a good judge to the people. Then the peasant gave the duke some fresh water, held in a peasant hat, which the duke drank. The entire crowd went to church, where they had a Mass followed by a feast and a final ceremony in which the duke received oaths of fealty from various subjects. Meanwhile, two peasants had been allowed, without punishment of any kind, to trespass on other peasants' property and create general mayhem. They even burnt some sheds. The reason for this was to show what could happen if the people did *not* have a protector. During the entire ceremony the people sang old songs in the Slovene language. All of those songs have been lost, and only the description of the ceremony remains.[8]

CROATIA

Parts of Croatia were Roman territory, and its southern tip had once even been a colony of ancient Greece. During the early seventh century, Slavic tribes migrated from Carpathian regions toward the Adriatic coast, settling along the way and eventually intermingling with the Italianate populations along the shoreline of the Adriatic. In the ninth century, Croatia was a kingdom under King Tomislav and his successors, but as a small and rather fragmented territory, it made an alliance with Hungary in the twelfth century, and in 1102, Koloman from the Hungarian Arpad dynasty became king of Croatia and Dalmatia. As a subject nation, Croatia was subjected to abuses, such as the sale of its coastal area to Venice in 1409 for 100,000 ducats. Also in the fifteenth century, Ottoman Turks attacked, and Croatia became a "big battlefield." By the Renaissance, it was referred to as "the remains of the remains of the once-famous Croatian kingdom." On the other hand, because of its history, it was brought into contact with a wide variety of cultures.

Croatia's religious music during the Middle Ages came from two "streams": Gregorian chants and Glagolitic chants, which were both linguistically and melodically different. Glagolitic chants were sung in Old Church Slavonic and transmitted by oral tradition. Parts of that tradition have miraculously continued in some areas such as Krk, Senj, Zadar, and Šibenik "although certainly not in the same way as before."[9] Unlike Gregorian monophonic chant, Glagolitic was multipart and may have also included heterophony. It was hard to notate, because the pitches were not in tempered tuning. But, fortunately, some of this traditional singing has now been recorded.

The Croatian Catholic Church retained the right to use its vernacular language, and thus avoided much of the angst of other areas. There are instances in which scholars have found Gregorian chants altered to fit the Croatian language. Codices either imported from other countries or copied by Croatian scribes are scattered throughout parish churches and monasteries, and many date back to the eleventh century. Roman Catholic influence spread from the northern areas, right down the Adriatic coast, and reached as far as the then-Dalmatian province of Kotor (now in present-day Montenegro). During the Middle Ages scriptoria were located in the Zagreb area in the north, and the coastal areas of Zadar, Split, Osor, Trogir, Kotor, and Dubrovnik. Sources for notation came mainly from the monastery of St. Gall, but they sometimes also used Beneventan notation from Italy.

Franciscan monks came to Croatian areas relatively early in its own history. The Franciscan monastery in Dubrovnik dates from 1317 and is still standing. A codex found in a Franciscan monastery in Šibenik is in the neumatic script common in St. Gall and is devoted mainly to the praise of St. Nicholas, the patron saint of sailors—an important figure to Croatia's coastal areas. Also, an early example of polyphony (a two-part *Sanctus*) was found among legal papers in a monastery in Zadar.

In addition to manuscripts, the country has many surviving carvings, mural paintings, sculptures, and engravings from the Middle Ages, showing instruments of the time. Instrumental objects include "the horn, the trumpet, the busine, the flute, the shawm, the bagpipe, the portative organ, the organ, the viella, the rebec, the viola da gamba, the hurdy-gurdy, the lute, the psaltery, the harp, the cymbal, the harpsichord, the clavichord, the drums, the kettledrums, the rattle, the turning wheel with bells, the triangle, and the tambourine."[10]

An area that broke away from Venetian rule in 1358 and functioned as a Republic was the territory of Dubrovnik. Governed by a rotating set of patrician families, this city was known for its music and festivals. The yearly festival of its patron saint, Sveti Vlaho (St. Blaise) has been held for almost 1,000 years and continues to this day. Records of these festivities go back into the late twelfth century and include part-singing, a procession, and folk music groups playing flutes, reed-pipes, trumpets, and native instruments. Foreign musicians were also welcome, along with actors, traveling comedians, and other entertainers. These came from all over Croatia, from nearby areas such as Bosnia and Serbia, and also from Italy, Germany, Greece, and Albania. These musicians' names are recorded as far back as the fourteenth century.

NOTES

1. Aloysius L. Kuhar, *Slovene Medieval History* (New York and Washington: Studia Slovenice, 1962), p. 131.

2. Vladimir Stepanek and Bohumil Karasek, *Outline of Czech and Slovak Music* (Prague: Orbis, 1964), p. 13.

3. Bence Szabolcsi, *A Concise History of Hungarian Music* (London: Barrie and Rockliff, 1964), p. 8.

4. Ibid., p. 12.

5. Ibid.

6. Ibid., p. 14.

7. Aloysius L. Kuhar, *Slovene Medieval History* (New York and Washington: Studia Slovenice, 1962), p. 84.

8. Ibid., p. 52.

9. Josep Andreis, *Music in Croatia*, translated by Vladimir Ivir (Zagreb: Zagreb Institute of Musicology, Academy of Music, 1974), p. 5.

10. Ibid., p. 21.

CHAPTER 10

MUSICAL INSTRUMENTS OF THE MIDDLE AGES

Instrumental music was a poor second to the dominance of vocal music in the Middle Ages. But despite the fact that very little purely instrumental music remains, since much of it was never written down, a surprising variety of instruments found their way into medieval society.

The playing of many instruments was tied to vocal music. As the use of polyphony grew and music became more complicated, instruments could take one or more vocal parts. When scholars see, for instance, a three-part chanson with words under only one or two of the parts, they believe that the musical line(s) without text might have been played on an instrument. Which instrument? Nobody really knows. In the Middle Ages, specific instruments were seldom called for. Any instrument that could play in the required range could be used.

Instruments were categorized differently than they are today. Nowadays we classify instruments according to their "family" (how they make their sounds, how they are played), which is how this chapter will also present them, in a tradition going back to Cassiodorus (see Chapter 1). But in the Middle Ages and Renaissance, instruments were known as *haut* or *bas* instruments. Literally these terms mean "high" and "low," but they referred to the instruments' volume instead of their pitch range. A *haut* instrument would be one more suited to outdoor use (high volume), while a *bas* instrument would be used indoors (low volume).

Most larger courts had at least one minstrel: a professional musician who played one or more instruments and made his or her living entertaining nobles. Some minstrels went from place to place earning their living by singing long, involved stories of famous events such as the deeds of heroes or long-ago legends and famous battles. They normally used an instrument such as a harp or psaltery to accompany themselves. Troubadours and trouvères sometimes played an instrument such as a lute when they sang, although they often hired a jongleur to do it for them.

Most of what scholars know about instruments of the Middle Ages and their uses in society comes from paintings, sculptures, and contemporary writing. Monks in medieval scriptoria, where manuscripts were copied out, put beautiful paintings in the margins or capital letters of the pages. These paintings sometimes showed instruments being played. Psalters—the Biblical book of Psalms put into book form—often included beautiful miniature paintings of instruments and musicians, since Psalms mentions them. Stained glass windows are another source of knowledge, as are carvings inside churches and on their porticos. People wrote accounts of great feasts and celebrations, tournaments, the crowning of royalty, investitures of Popes and bishops, and other great occasions. Most of these occasions had instrumental music, and scholars learn what instruments were played, when the players performed, and sometimes even the name of the work.

Churches needed some kind of instrument to keep singers on tune, and during the Middle Ages churches began building larger and more elaborate organs. For variety and color, instruments such as bells, plucked or bowed stringed instruments, wind instruments, or some brass instruments could play along with the organ, although the extra instruments did not play all at the same time, or play definite roles. Large ensembles and orchestration would have to wait until a later era.

Of course instruments were played in a variety of secular settings such as fairs, market days, and holidays such as saints' days. The music that ordinary people played and danced to has largely been lost, but scholars have made considerable progress in ascertaining what instruments they used.

The majority of instruments came from Eastern lands. Through adversary contact during the Crusades, on trade routes in search of Eastern spices, from diplomatic ties to the Byzantine Empire, and because of the Islamic presence on the Iberian peninsula, Eastern instruments began to trickle into Europe. Once in Europe, they developed into the forerunners of our modern instruments.

STRINGED INSTRUMENTS

There were a wide variety of stringed instruments in the Middle Ages. Most of them were either brought back by Crusaders or acquired from trade routes. In general, stringed instruments were tuned as the player preferred. The interval between strings was whatever the player was comfortable using. Also, it was not important to the performer of a stringed instrument during the Middle Ages that an instrument be in any specific "key" area. If used with a singer, the instrument would be tuned to whatever range the performer was comfortable singing in. For instruments such as harps or lyres, strings would be arranged diatonically, with one exception: the note B, which could be altered as a "hard" (natural) or "soft" (flat) note (see Chapter 2).

LYRE

The lyre of the Middle Ages may have come to Europe from Byzantium, possibly through Germanic mercenaries hired as part of the Byzantine Imperial Guard. At any rate, it seems to have been in Europe as far back as 600 A.D. Several lyres have been found over the years. One complete lyre from the Dark Ages was in the Berlin Museum für Volkerkunde, but the museum and its contents were destroyed during World War II. A royal Anglo-Saxon burial site in Britain, known as Sutton Hoo, included fragments of something scholars believed to be an instrument. After several attempts at reconstruction the instrument was found to be a lyre from around 670 A.D. It has a wooden soundbox, with an arch extending up from the two sides and crossing over at the top. The strings are attached to the top of the arch and run over a bridge on the soundbox.

CRWTH

The spelling and pronunciation of the name of this six-stringed instrument have confounded generations of speakers. It is pronounced "crooth" and was especially favored in Wales by bards: performers who, like the old English scops, sang long heroic sagas at various courts. Also known as the criut, croud, and chrotta, some sources say that an instrument known as a "rotta" was simply the bowed crwth. The instrument is somewhat similar to the lyre found at Sutton Hoo except that it has a neck extending from the middle of the arch to the soundbox, and the strings run over the neck and therefore can be fingered as on a fiddle. Four strings were tuned in octaves, but two were "drones" and always played the same note. Scholars have deduced that the crwth was originally plucked with fingers or a plectrum. It fell out of favor, but returned during the late Middle Ages as a bowed instrument. It is still played by Welsh traditional musicians today.

HARP

Known also as the *Harfe* (Germany), *arpa* (Italy), and *harpe* (French), the harp is believed to have hailed from Syria. Throughout the Middle Ages, there were a variety of harps that came in various shapes and sizes, But two stood out from the rest. The first was a small, triangular harp, highly identified with Ireland. The first depiction of this harp is on a reliquary (a container holding a bone or body part of a saint) in Dublin, dating from the ninth century.

The Irish harp took the place of the crwth or rotta as the instrument of choice to accompany bards singing stories of heroism at noble courts. This harp was tuned diatonically, with seven notes before coming to the next octave, but each player tuned his strings to suit his voice range. It had various numbers of strings, but not more than 12. The harp enhanced the performance of a song sung with no harmony, it helped the bard remember what came next, and if the bard had a memory slip he could play the harp alone to cover the problem and give himself time to recover his thoughts!

In the second half of the thirteenth century, a really large harp emerged. It looked more like the modern harp, with a sounding box and front pillar. This instrument was much too large for a player to hold on his lap. Instead, it leaned on the player's shoulder in the same manner as the concert harp does today. It gave a great deal more sound than its tiny cousin, as the sounding board was huge for its day. And because there was literally more room, it had more strings and a larger range.

This larger harp had an additional feature called "brays." Brays were L-shaped pegs built into the harp's belly that not only kept the strings pinned in, but also touched the strings lightly, to give the harp a slight "buzzing" sound. This effect helped the harp's sound carry even further, and also sustained the sound. Over time, the use of brays spread to harps all through Europe. The earliest depiction of this harp is a carving in England's Lincoln Cathedral, from around 1270. One actual harp from fourteenth-century Ireland, known as the Trinity College harp, has survived. Its strings were brass wire, and the player plucked them with his fingernails. When an exact replica of the instrument was made and played, listeners said the sound was extraordinarily sweet—something between the sounds of a bell and a guitar.

FIDDLE (VIELLE)

This was one of the main instruments of its age, and had many names. Known as the *vielle* (French), *videle* (Middle High German), *fithel* (England), *fidel* (German), *viola* (Italian), or *vihuela de arco* (Spain), it most likely came to Europe from the Middle East around the ninth or tenth century. The early fiddle was shaped like a small spade, with the strings attached at the bottom and stretched over a bridge and up the neck to tuning pegs, and was bowed. The bow actually looked like something that could shoot an arrow, and the tension of the bow hairs was controlled by pressure from the player's finger. The early fiddle was held upright on the player's knee, facing outward and bowed from there. As the instrument moved north from Spain, players held it either on the shoulder or across the chest—but *not* under the chin in the manner of present-day violins. The player was not required to play as many fast notes either, so part of their hand could also support the instrument. And, as with many medieval instruments, it could be played either right- or left-handed. Some early fiddles had sound holes, but not all. Some fiddles had frets.

Another fiddle-like instrument being played at the same time was shaped more like a pear, and its back and neck was carved from a single piece of wood, hollowed out to look something like a big spoon. The facing put over it was sometimes made of skin, which tended to stretch and dull the sound, so wood facing soon became the norm. The bridges of medieval fiddles were quite low. So when organum began to replace monophony, it was quite easy to play the two lines of parallel organum simultaneously.

Around 1250, a writer named Heironymus of Moravia described the fiddle of his day. He said it had five strings: four on which the player could change pitches, and a drone string on which the pitch could not change. The drone string could be plucked by the player's thumb if needed. There were other fiddles strung without a drone, he wrote, and these four-stringed fiddles were tuned in intervals of perfect fourths and fifths.

In the fourteenth and fifteenth centuries, the fiddle went through some big changes. It acquired a "waist," which made it look more like today's violins. Its back was either flat or slightly curved outward, and it had side walls connecting the top and back of the instrument. The entire soundboard became lighter and more resonant. Its bridge was higher, making it easier for a musician to hit a single string instead of two or even three at a time (the waist made room for the bow to be held at the necessary angle), and now it had a pair of sound holes, shaped like the letter "C" rather than the letter "f" as on the modern violin.

With the revival of period instruments, musicians are able to play music of the Middle Ages on reproduction fiddles. While the sound of the Middle Ages' fiddle is less full and warm than a modern violin's, the medieval fiddle has a charm all its own when used to perform the music it was made to play.

CITTERN

This instrument is similar to an older fiddle, but it was plucked rather than bowed. Players used a plectrum (like a guitar pick) to pluck the strings. The cittern's shape, like the fiddle's, changed from a spade shape to a pear shape, and in the latter shape it was much preferred by French troubadours. By the fourteenth or fifteenth century the strings were tuned in pairs, called "courses." A course is two strings tuned to the same pitch an octave apart, to make the sound stronger. Musicians came to give up the plectrum, plucking the strings with their fingers instead.

GITTERN

This stringed instrument looks like a cross between a vielle and a guitar. Its most outstanding characteristic is a neck that doubles back on itself, enabling the player to put the thumb of the fingering hand through the opening. It was also famous for being covered in elaborate carvings. It usually had four strings. Not only was the instrument rather thick, but the plectrum that played it was also thicker than usual. The gittern survived into the Renaissance, where it had its heyday.

ORGANISTRUM (HURDY-GURDY)

This instrument was also known as a Symphonia, or Symphony. Sculptures of it go back to the twelfth century, but descriptions of how to set one up go back to the 950s. The early instruments were rather large and took two people to play them. One player turned a crank that set a wooden wheel turning inside the instrument's body. Strings lowered to touch the wheel vibrated and created sound in the same way as the strings of the fiddle do when bowed. The other player worked wedges, called tangents, set at different distances along the instrument's strings to change the pitch, just as the fiddle player does with fingering, as the string touched the rotating wheel. Most depictions of the early organistrum show three strings. In use from the ninth to the late twelfth century, this instrument was highly regarded. In art works of the time, kings are often shown working the tangents. The Church, too, used it during the Middle Ages to help train choirs. As more and more churches acquired organs, the organistrum became more of a folk instrument.

In the late Middle Ages, the organistrum was reduced in size so that a single player could manage it. This instrument hung from the player's neck using a leather strap. The player worked the crank with one hand, while the other hand worked a "key bar" on the side of the instrument. When a key was depressed, that key raised a tangent to the string and produced the desired pitch. When the key was let go, gravity allowed the tangent to fall away from the string, and a stud kept the keys from falling out of the instrument. There were also drone strings, producing an effect remarkably like bagpipes. By this time, however, the organistrum had become a lower-class instrument used by peddlers and beggars, and it had picked up the name "hurdy-gurdy." In its single-player form, the hurdy-gurdy survived into the twentieth century, arriving in America via Italian immigrants. The author saw a hurdy-gurdy player, complete with monkey, at a street fair in New York City, in the 1970s.

LUTE

This plucked, stringed instrument may have come up through Spain through its Moorish territories, where it was known as al-'oud in Arabic, from which the instrument gained its European name.

Early lutes had a pear shape, with the neck made from a different piece of wood than the body, but seemingly growing from it. It had a tone hole on the wooden facing, and the cross-bar on the bottom of the "pear" was glued directly to the facing. Most distinctively, the tuning pegs on the neck were bent over a tuning box which was at right angles to the end of the neck. In other words, the neck looks like it is bent backwards. The lute of the Middle Ages had anywhere from three to five strings and was plucked with a small rod instead of a plectrum or fingers. The Spanish cantigas of Alfonso X (see Chapter 7) show miniatures of both the larger and smaller lutes. The larger one had a fingerboard and frets. The smaller one shows neither. But both are being played with a plectrum.

Around the thirteenth century, the lute changed. Its back ceased to be made of a single piece of wood; instead, it was built up from separate "ribs" bent outward and glued together, which enlarged and deepened the instrument's sound. The body and neck appeared as the two separate pieces that they in fact were. The original three to five strings became six to ten, tuned in pairs, or courses.

But it was not until the fifteenth century that the lute became more popular (Figure 10.1). This is when players realized that the lute could be used to play the much more complicated polyphony of that time. Also, it fit well with the human voice, which made it a good instrument to accompany solo singers. All sizes acquired frets, originally made of bands of gut wrapped around the neck. It had more strings—as many as 11—and they were made of various materials (gut and various metals) to vary the sound in the upper and lower registers of the

Figure 10.1 The lute, characterized by the sharp angle at the top of its neck, could be used to play several lines of polyphonic music. Facsimilie of *Musica Getutscht* (1511) by Sebastian Virdung. Paris, London, Basel: Barenreiter Kassel, 1970.

instrument. The older tone hole was replaced with the now-famous "rose." At first this was a series of holes put directly into the facing wood. But later, as the rose became more elaborate, it became a separate carved piece of wood inserted into the facing.

Although the lute receives a fair amount of attention in this chapter, it actually did not become popular until almost the end of the Middle Ages. It reached its peak in the Renaissance, when it was the dominant stringed instrument.

MANDOLA

As its other name, guitarra morisca (Moorish guitar), suggests, this instrument came from Islamic Spain. Some scholars believe that it was a descendant of an Arab instrument called the rebab. It arrived in Europe during the thirteenth century, later than most instruments of the Middle Ages. It was club-shaped, and its strings were attached to little buttons at the bottom of the instrument, went up over a bridge, and ended on a pegbox that was often carved to look like a little head. But by the fifteenth century, the mandola had changed drastically and became a poor imitation lute. Falling out of favor, scholars say that it eventually evolved into the Milanese mandolin.

CITOLE

This instrument was much like the mandola except it had a flat back, whereas the mandola's back was rounded. Eventually its design merged with the gittern (with which it is often confused) and produced the Cittern, an English guitar of the Renaissance.

REBEC

The rebec, sometimes known as a "gigue," was a club-shaped stringed instrument something like the lute and mandola, but its strings were bowed instead of plucked. This instrument, too, is said to have developed from the Middle Eastern rebab and came to Europe somewhere around the thirteenth century. Originally, the rebec had two strings, tuned to C and G. It sat on the player's knee when used, but later was held on the performer's shoulder and bowed from there. Sometimes it so resembled the shape of a mandola that it was called a "bowed mandola." Unlike other instruments of the Middle Ages, this one declined to change much. It fell out of favor because of its weak sound, but it had a revival in the late Middle Ages because it was smaller and lighter than a fiddle, and was able to play the top line—the line with the fastest-moving notes—of fifteenth-century polyphonic works. The bow used on the rebec was wood and had teeth, something like a saw blade. Sometimes jokes about the rebec showed it as a club-shaped bellows being played with a rake!

PSALTERY

The psaltery (Figure 10.2) was something like a harp, but with its strings lined up horizontally over its sounding board instead of in front of it. This instrument was in Europe by the twelfth century and came, as many others did, from an Arabic source. It was one of several similar types of instruments generically known as zithers, and it was sometimes called a canon, which came from the Arabic name for the instrument, *qanūn*. The Arabic instrument was plucked with several plectrums attached to the player's fingers. In Europe, players leaned the psaltery back and played it with both hands, using a plectrum made from a quill.

Psalteries came in several shapes, including triangular and rectangular, but the most common shape was the "pig's head." This shape had its shorter strings on either end of a "double-winged" shape and longer strings in the middle, forming the "snout." Italians eventually referred to the psaltery as *instromento de porco*.

During the fourteenth and fifteenth centuries, the psaltery's strings were paired in courses to increase its sound. It also used different materials, lengths, and tensions, to vary pitch and quality of sound in all registers. Many paintings of the Middle Ages show an angel playing a psaltery instead of the more traditional harp.

DULCIMER

A relative latecomer, the hammered dulcimer shows up in Europe around the fifteenth century. The dulcimer was constructed somewhat like a psaltery, but instead of being held upright it was laid flat, either on the player's lap or on a table. Shaped much like the older psalteries as a trapezoid or rectangle, it had strings that were made of metal and instead of being plucked or bowed, were hit with two padded sticks known as hammers. Although different pitched strings were set farther apart to lessen the chances of hitting their neighbors, strings tuned to the same pitch could be close together in "courses" of two or even three to increase the sound. Bridges for the dulcimer's strings were quite high, to prevent them from hitting the sounding board and stopping their sound. Some dulcimers had a separate bridge for each string, while others used alternating bridges on both ends, holding every other string up on one end and the alternate strings on the other end. The dulcimer's name came from the Latin *dulce melos*—sweet melody. It was also known as the doucemelle (France), dolcemela (Italy), and dulcema (Spain).

MONOCHORD

This instrument was known since the time of the ancient Greeks, and is attributed to Pythagoras (see Chapter 1). It was not a performing instrument. It was, instead, an educational tool to prove the science of acoustics. During the Middle Ages, church fathers used it as a means to teach young choristers to sing intervals correctly.

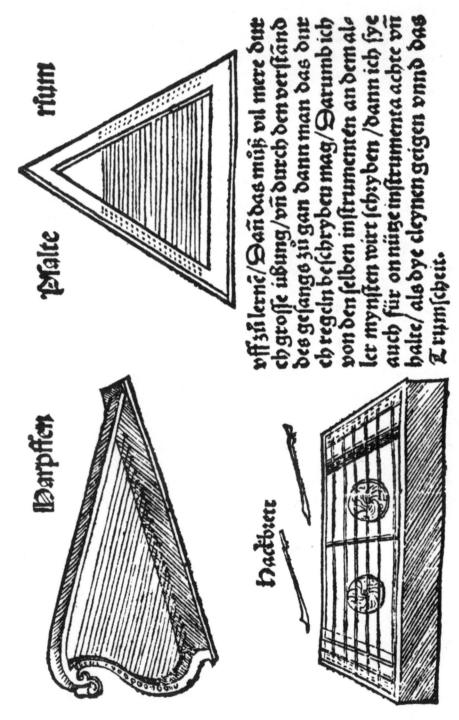

Figure 10.2 A harp at upper left, triangular shaped psaltery at upper right, and dulcimer at bottom. Facsimilie of *Musica Getutscht* (1511) by Sebastian Virdung. Paris, London, Basel: Barenreiter Kassel, 1970.

The monochord is simply a wooden box with a single string running along the top. A bridge at each end of the string holds it aloft, and the box has marks for where the string should be touched to arrive at the desired pitch. A teacher could stop the string at one of these marks with a rod (also known as a tangent) and pluck the desired pitch with a quill. An alternate method used a moveable bridge, which could be placed at the marks on the box so that the player could pluck the desired pitch.

TROMBA MARINA

This is one of the Middle Ages' stranger instruments (Figure 10.3). Although its name sounds as though it should belong to the brass wind family, it was a stringed instrument. Hard to miss, the tromba marina was triangle-shaped and could reach up to seven feet in length. It had one long string played with a bow, and sometimes there was a smaller, second string as well. But the performing position was its most unusual trait. Normally the player of a bowed stringed instrument bows the string farther down than the string is fingered, like a present-day stringed bass player. But on the tromba marina the strings were fingered farther down than they were bowed! Furthermore, the fingering hand did not press the string down to the fingerboard, as on a violin today, but touched the string lightly at precise fractions of its length, so, instead of the normal tones, the tromba marina instead produced sounds known as harmonic overtones, which sounded abnormally high and rather ethereal. As if that weren't enough, the bridge over which its string was stretched was left intentionally loose on one end so that when the string vibrated, the bridge would also vibrate against the instrument face and produce a rasping sound.

Its name is a reflection of several references. The "tromba" part may refer to the valveless trumpet of the Middle Ages, which also made use of music's harmonic series of pitches, or it is possible that its rasp sounded trumpet-like. The "marina" had nothing to do with the sea but referred instead to the Virgin Mary. Apparently this instrument was used in convents and played by nuns. For this reason, the many names for this instrument refer to these two items. It was known as the trumpet marine (England), trompette marine (France), tromba marina (Italy), Trumscheit, Nun-geige, or Marientrompete (Germany). Its one-stringed resemblance to the monochord earned it another name: monochord d'archet, or bowed monochord. Germanic areas and the Netherlands were the most partial to this instrument.

WOODWIND INSTRUMENTS

PANPIPES

The Panpipes of ancient Greece were different lengths of cane tubes stopped up at one end, but left open at the other end, and bound together with a leather strap. The player would blow over the open tops to produce sounds, and the length of each pipe determined its pitch. Panpipes of the Middle Ages (also known as a

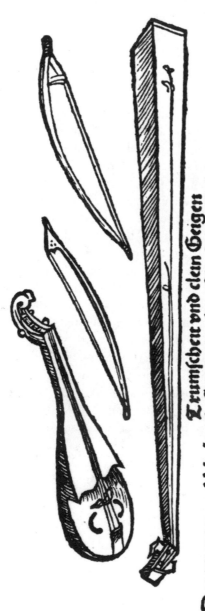

Figure 10.3 A pear-or club-shaped stringed instrument and sample bows on top, and a tromba marina on the bottom. Facsimile of *Musica Getutscht* (1511) by Sebastian Virdung. Paris, London, Basel: Barenreiter Kassel, 1970.

"syrinx") were a little different; Their cane tubes were enclosed in a wooden case. Sometimes they did not even use cane tubes, but bored holes of different lengths and diameters directly into a single piece of wood. But players still blew over the open tops, one note at a time, just as the ancient Greeks had.

TRANSVERSE FLUTE

Like the modern concert flute, this flute was held crosswise, across the player's face. Made of a single piece of hollowed-out wood, it had a long cylindrical tube stopped up at the end closest to the player's face and left open at the opposite end, six finger holes, and a mouth hole over which the player blew. Scholars believe that this type of flute came to Europe via Byzantium; by the twelfth century it was already heavily favored by Germanic peoples. This explains why, although German-speakers called it by the old Latin name *tibia*, others referred to this flute as the German flute (English), flute allemande (France), and flauta alemana (Spain).

Curiously, it became highly popular with Germanic soldiers. Then, as always, much military activity involved waiting, and soldiers would have various sized flutes at the ready, to while away the time. There are woodcuts showing brawny military men wearing large swords, playing their flutes together. Swiss mercenary soldiers liked them so much that the transverse flutes of the late Middle Ages became known as the Swiss pipe, or Schweizerpfeiff.

RECORDER

Players of this type of flute held the instrument up and down, like today's clarinet, and blew straight into the mouthpiece. The end of the mouthpiece was plugged with a block called a fipple that had a channel that sent the air across a sharp edge farther down the flute, which produced sound as in a police whistle. Holes below the mouthpiece were covered and uncovered by players' fingers to make various pitches.

Early recorders had three tone holes; later they had four or five tone holes. Finally, the recorder had six tone holes, three for each hand, a thumb hole in back, plus a double hole on the bottom. Because it had no keys, the recorder could be played with either the right hand or the left hand on the top holes. The only problem was the little finger. The double hole on the bottom was for either the right little finger or the left, depending on how the player decided to hold the instrument, and the other hole was plugged up with wax (Figure 10.4).

As the Middle Ages progressed, the recorder became a "family" of instruments that came in different sizes, roughly corresponding to soprano, alto, tenor, and bass. A recorder from the Middle Ages was found beneath the ruins of a house in Dordrecht, Holland. Cracked, missing its tailpiece, and warped into a slightly bent shape, it is a rare example of a surviving wooden instrument. Scientists have dated it at no later than 1450, but it could even be 100 years older than that.

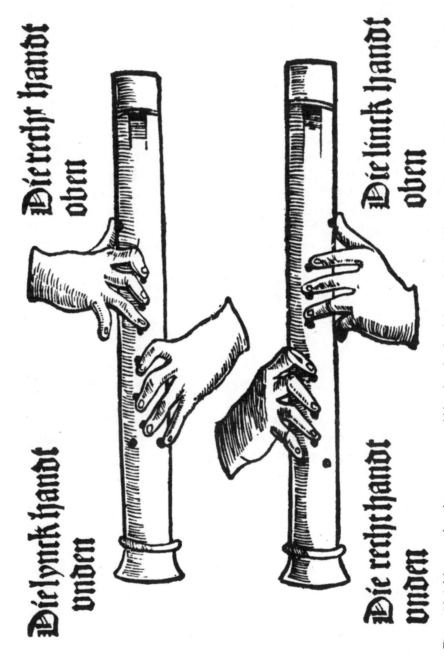

Figure 10.4 Most woodwind instruments could be played either left- or right-handed. One of the two little-finger holes would be plugged up, depending on which hand was on the bottom. Facsimilie of *Musica Getutscht* (1511) by Sebastian Virdung. Paris, London, Basel: Barenreiter Kassel, 1970.

There were also instances of a double recorder, two single-hand recorders put together. Sometimes the pipes were parallel, and sometimes they would flare out from one another. With the pipes parallel, the whole instrument could be made from one piece of wood.

PIPE AND TABOR

A staple of the Middle Ages, the pipe and tabor are two instruments played by one person. The pipe was a recorderlike instrument, but much shorter, with a more slender tube, and with only three tone holes drilled out close to the bottom end of the pipe. This arrangement made it possible for the player to play a fair amount of notes by blowing not only the three basic notes, but blowing harder to reach higher harmonic overtones. The tabor was a small cylindrical drum slung from the player's piping shoulder by a leather strap. While playing the pipe with one hand, the player could use the other hand to beat the drum. Beginning from around the thirteenth century, pipe and tabor players were in great demand at trade fairs, tournaments, and other festive occasions. In fact, there were still players working in parts of Britain as late as the nineteenth century. One scholar jokingly referred to the pipe and tabor as the basic dance band of the Middle Ages.

SHAWM

The shawm is a double-reed instrument, like the modern oboe, which is descended from it. This means that two pieces of thin reed are tied together so that when the player blows on them, they vibrate against one another and produce a sound. In the case of the shawm, it is a very loud sound. The shawm is a very old instrument, dating back to the time of the Etruscan tribes of pre-Roman Italy. From there it traveled throughout the Roman Empire, and when the Romans left, the shawm also vanished. But it reappeared from the Middle East and came back to Europe during the twelfth century via Sicily, which had a Moslem population at that time.

Also known as the shalmai (Germany), ciaramella (Italy), and chalemie (France), the shawm was made of wood and had the same finger hole arrangement as on the recorder, including the double holes for the little finger. Its shape was conical, smaller at the top end and progressively larger toward the bottom. Instead of manipulating the reed with the lips, as modern oboists do, shawm players shoved the entire reed into their mouths and blew like crazy. Many players used circular breathing, a technique in which air is forced from the mouth while the player simultaneously takes in more air through the nose, so as never to have to stop playing to take a breath.

The shawm sounded like a very large, very angry bee. It was definitely an outdoor instrument, and it was very popular for the kinds of festivities where a softer instrument would not be heard. It was also carried during the Middle Ages by some night watchmen, who knew that a warning blast from this instrument would wake up every citizen in town.

During the fifteenth century the shawm underwent some changes. Its reed acquired a pirouette, a mouthpiece extension that surrounded the reed but was separate from the rest of the instrument. The player still put the whole reed in the mouth, but the pirouette gave support. The shawm also had a thumb hole, enabling the player to more easily reach notes an octave higher. By then, shawms also came in two sizes. the normal soprano, and a larger contralto instrument which sounded a fifth lower. The larger instrument had another name: bombarde (in France) or pommer (in Germany). But the larger shawm had a problem. How could a human hand reach that bottom hole? The solution was a key—believed to be the first on a wind instrument. Now there was only one tone hole at the bottom of the instrument instead of two. It was closed off or left open by its key, which was protected by a wooden barrel called a fontanelle. The upper part of the key, which could be reached by the player's little finger, had a double flared wing, so that the key could be operated either left- or right-handed.

Like the recorder, the shawm could also be made double, somewhat reminiscent of the ancient Greek *aulos*; the double shawm had different numbers of finger holes on each pipe. Never terrifically popular, it phased out during the late Middle Ages.

BAGPIPE

The bagpipe is basically a reed pipe attached to a leather bag. The leather bag acted as an artificial mouth so that instead of having to circular-breathe, players only had to keep the bag full of air to get continuous sound. The bag was kept under the player's arm to keep air pressure constant.

The bagpipe came to Europe from the Middle East somewhere in the 800s. Scholars believe that it traveled up through Spain, since paintings from the same time frame show rather simple instruments in northern Europe while Spain's are much more developed. Also known as the sacphife or dudelsack (Germany), cornemuse (France), or cornamusa (Italy), the early bagpipes seem not to have used a drone, so common to modern bagpipes. But by the thirteenth century, bagpipes with two pipes appeared. One pipe was the double-reed chanter with tone holes covered and uncovered by the player's fingers to produce different notes, and the other pipe was a single-reed "drone" that had no tone holes and played a single, unending note. By the fifteenth century, the most advanced bagpipes had a chanter with seven tone holes, like that of a recorder, and two drone pipes tuned a fifth apart, which would sound more like today's instrument. Of course there was always a blowpipe on the sack, through which the player blew to keep the sack inflated.

The bagpipe was associated with shepherds from its earliest days, and it insinuated itself into European culture through liturgical dramas, specifically Christmas plays, in which shepherds play a large role. But some were also used for dance music, and others became military instruments, their music used for marching. This variety of uses is because of the variety of bagpipes developed over the Middle Ages, from simple animal bladders with only a chanter and no drone (known as a "bladder pipe" or "platerspiel"), to more complicated affairs. There were a surprising range of regional differences and preferences in sound. Not every bagpipe was as commandingly loud as modern ones. Some of the smaller bagpipes were much less obtrusive, and their sound was even a bit tinny.

HORNS/"BRASS" INSTRUMENTS

When a player's lips are pressed against the mouthpiece of a horn and make a "buzzing" sound, it is because the human lips act as the reed to vibrate the horn and produce sound. Horns, like shawms, are conical, narrower at the lip end and progressively wider. They may or may not flare out at the end in a "bell." And they vary in size from only a few inches to horns taller than a human.

CORNETTO

This instrument was a hybrid between a horn and a woodwind. Basically, it is a horn with tone holes like a recorder. Also known as the cornett (England) and zink (Germany), the cornetto was probably a cow or goat horn originally. But by the Middle Ages this instrument was made of two hollow pieces of wood glued together and covered by leather to prevent air leaks. They could be straight, or curved to resemble an actual animal horn. The wooden cornetto was used throughout the Middle Ages and hit its stride during the Renaissance as the highest voice in cornetto and sackbut consorts. (The sackbut, an early form of trombone, did not appear until the early Renaissance.)

HORN

This was originally an ox horn and was also known as a bugle, from the Latin word *buculus*—a small ox. This instrument did not come from the Middle East; it developed through both ancient Greece and Rome, and also independently in northern Europe. Early horns from animals have been found as far back as Neolithic times, but by the Middle Ages horns were made of metal and were used in hunting or warfare. Horns such as these show up on the Bayeux Tapestry, famous for showing William the Conqueror's 1066 invasion of Britain. They were also used as signal devices in more everyday settings, such as shepherds calling a flock or watchmen alerting citizens of impending danger.

As time went on, horns became longer, and longer horns were hard to hold. Eventually, some of the larger straight horns needed to be supported on a type of fork-like crutch about halfway down the instrument. Then someone had the bright idea to curve the horn, as the Romans had in former times. The English were apparently first to start the practice, and a choir-stall in Worcester Cathedral shows a man blowing a horn which curls around his body. The Burgundian Duke Philip the Bold ordered several curved horns from England in the last quarter of the

1300s. Illustrations of these long, curved horns show decorative bands at various points along its body, which indicates that they were jointed and fitted together.

One of the long, curved horns was known as a *beme* and shows up as the instrument of choice blown by angels announcing the Biblical Day of Judgment. Scholars studying depictions of these instruments believe that they probably only played a few notes, for signaling purposes.

OLIPHANT

This instrument truly had to be imported, because it was made from an elephant's tusk! The first ones were brought back from Byzantium in the tenth century. They were highly decorated and highly prized, and show up in heroic literature. "The Oliphant was the horn that Roland sounded to call his friends when the Saracens surrounded him at Roncesvalles and when defeat threatened, he strove to save from the foeman's grasp his most precious possessions, his sword and his horn."[1] Oliphants were sometimes used as a symbol, given as proof of a gift of land. This earned them the name "charter horns." The receiver was required to appear before his liege lord at a certain time of year and blow the horn three times, as a show of gratitude and fealty.

In the absence of an elephant, these instruments began to be made of precious metals such as gold. By the end of the Middle Ages, they had ceased to be a musical instrument but were handed from generation to generation as precious heirlooms. This is why many of them survive to the present day. One of the best is known as the Horn of Ulph. This was a charter horn given by King Canute to Ulph Thoroldsson, as a token of lands given. When Thoroldsson gave those lands to the Church, the horn went with them. This Oliphant is now in England's Treasure of York Minster.

TRUMPET

The Islamic military was responsible for bringing the trumpet to the attention of European Crusaders, who were seriously impressed with what they saw and heard. European armies adopted the trumpet for their own use, and the instrument shows up in paintings and miniatures all over Europe from the 1250s on. Trumpets also came through Arabic areas of Sicily around two hundred years earlier, accelerating the process of assimilation.

Trumpets came in various sizes, were made of metal, were straight conical tubes, and ended with a flared bell, as do today's trumpets. A smaller trumpet might be made of wood. It was about the length of a man's arm and was preferred by Italians, who called it a trombetta.

Larger trumpets are the kind seen in films to announce a king's entrance or the start of a jousting tournament. They had banners in the colors and personal coat of arms of the ruler hanging from the middle of the tubing. And they were indeed used for tournaments and triumphal entries in peacetime, and as signal instruments in war. The players of these instruments were greatly esteemed and paid more than other instrumentalists. Names of many trumpeters show up on payrolls of Middle Ages rulers.

During the second half of the Middle Ages, the larger trumpets began to change their shape. Possibly inspired by the example of the horns, the trumpet's awkward length began to bend. There were many experiments as to how and where that bend might take place. But eventually the "flattened loop" gained the most popularity, and is the shape of the present-day trumpet. However, the trumpet of the Middle Ages had no valves and relied completely on the overtone series for its pitches.

SLIDE TRUMPET

The slide trumpet is not a trombone! The slide was introduced as a method of changing from one set of overtones to another, before the invention of valves. The mouthpiece of this instrument fitted into the body by means of a sliding mechanism, And the performer, who could hold the instrument with one hand and still have the other hand free, could control where he wanted to slide by holding the mouthpiece in one hand and the body of the instrument with the other. By pushing and pulling the instrument, he could move from one harmonic possibility to another. This form of trumpet was better able to play in different key areas and was used throughout the Middle Ages, the Renaissance, and even into the Baroque era.

A larger version of this instrument was known as the "low slide trumpet." By the early Renaissance, in the Burgundian territory, it had developed into an instrument known as a sackbut, which was a smaller version of the modern trombone.

KEYBOARD INSTRUMENTS

For some early instruments, the word "keyboard" is a misnomer, since they used wooden sliders. Eventually, using a lever attached to a key was seen as advantageous and became the norm. Keyboards changed over time as well. Some early ones were diatonic, with only one possibility for an altered note: hard B (B-natural) or soft B (B-flat), as shown in Figure 10.5. It was not until later that fully chromatic keyboards emerged.

PORTATIVE ORGAN

Technically, the organ is both a keyboard instrument and a wind instrument. That is because air is forced through one or more pipes (each pipe being built like a one-note recorder) when a stopper is removed either by pulling a slide in and out by holding onto a "button" or pushing a key on a keyboard.

The portative organ was small and, as the name indicates, portable. It would be strapped onto a single person, who squeezed a small bellows with one hand while

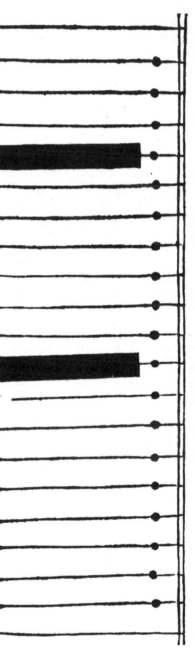

Es synd aber ander hernach kumen/die haben noch subtiler das gemacht/vnd
Boetius auch gelesen vnd nach dem andern geschlecht Cromaticū genant/das
monocordum auß geteilet .X. Du sagst mir vil von den seltzamen geschlechten
Sag mir doch was ist diatonicū genus/vnd dañ von den andern auch /so mag
ich dester baß verstan was du mir sagst Se. Diatonicū genus ist als Boetius
spricht in dem Ersten buch synet Musica an dem .xxi. capitel. So man ein iertlich
diatessaron/das wir ein quart haissen auß zwayen gantzen thonen vnnd eynem
mindern Semitonio oder auß vier schluisseln/oder vier stymen machen .X. Wye
mag ich das verston. Se. Also thu im/nym der schluissel eynen für dich/vnder
dene die dir oben für gemalet synd/welchen du wilt /vnd fang an dem selben an

Figure 10.5 An early keyboard showing only one black key per octave, giving the player a choice of a "hard" B or a "soft" one. Facsimilie of *Musica Getutscht* (1511) by Sebastian Virdung. Paris, London, Basel: Barenreiter Kassel, 1970.

working push-button slides with the other. Being a one-person instrument, it could not bear the weight of too many pipes, so it usually had about an octave to an octave and a half's worth of notes. Sometimes certain notes were missing, according to what the player intended to play. In fact, scholars believe that each player would consult with an organ builder to specify which pipes were needed and which were not.

In quite a number of paintings, the keyboard seems to be in reverse position. That is, instead of playing rising pitches from left to right, the players would be playing lowering pitches. At first this would seem to be a simple error on the part of the painter, but scholars point out that there are statistically too many of these "errors" to be an error, and so they believe that even keyboard instruments were made for both left- and right-handed people, just as the recorder was.

In some early paintings, there seems to be an "extra" pipe set off from the others. Scholars believe this to be a drone pipe that was never closed off, but played a single note continuously as long as the organ was being filled with air. In that feature, the portative organ resembles the bagpipe. Also, some early paintings show the portative organ in Church use, as an aid to keeping singers on key. By the fourteenth century, this instrument was abandoned by the Church because a single player was unable to play the complex moving lines being used. This is when the larger, positive organs entered church service, where they remain today.

For the rest of the Middle Ages, the portative organ was generally used in more personal, secular music. The one big improvement in this instrument was the invention of spring-balanced keys, which made the portative organ much more popular in secular and folk music. Keys were much easier to move with one hand than sliders were. Paintings, carvings, and stained-glass windows all show portative organs with different arrangements of pipes. Sometimes the pipes went from smallest on one end to largest on the other, and other times the smaller pipes were on the outer ends progressing to larger pipes in the middle.

POSITIVE ORGAN

This organ was too large for a single person to operate. A minimum of two were needed: one to work the slides, and one to work a set of bellows. It also had to be put (hence the name "positive"; think: "deposited") on a table or other platform in order to be played. Early positive organs had no pedals and no stops (devices for changing the tone color, or sound, produced by the instrument by selecting different kinds of pipes). These familiar features developed over the Middle Ages, and by the Renaissance the organ was more like today's instruments.

A type of organ had been known throughout the Roman Empire as a *hydraulis*, which used water pressure to force air through its pipes. But when the Romans left Europe, so did their technical knowledge for building these instruments. The instrument re-entered European life during the eighth century when an organ was sent as as a gift from Byzantium to the Frankish king, either Pepin or Charlemagne.

But this organ was powered differently. It was pneumatic; that is, a set of bellows sent air into its pipes. Over time, hydraulic organs also re-appeared in Europe, and during the Middle Ages there are accounts of both types being used. Eventually, though, pneumatic won out.

By the ninth century, Europeans were building ever-larger and more elaborate organs of their own. Germanic builders were especially adept, and even the Pope in Rome had the Vatican organ built by a "master from the diocese of Freising."[2]

Two persons were the absolute minimnum needed to play the positive organ, but they certainly were not the maximum. By 1000, an organ built in Winchester, England, had 400 pipes, seventy bellows, and two keyboards with twenty "sliders" each. These sliders were pulled to uncover the pipes, and an organ this size needed more than one player to work them. Obviously even forty sliders were not going to work on 400 pipes, so each slider operated several pipes at once. It is said that at least one of those sliders worked ten pipes at the same time, tuned to the intervals of a fifth and an octave. The seventy bellows at Winchester needed seventy people to work them. These people were behind the scenes, with their feet on blower bars and their hands on a stabilizing bar, "walking" the blowers constantly to keep enough air going to make this organ sound like the Day of Judgment!

Most church organs were not the massive affairs that Winchester had, but more and more churches used them because organs helped liturgical music stay in line. By the twelfth century, two-part organum was the norm, and some churches added a second organ so that both parts could be "helped." But the sliders were beginning to be a problem. They were very slow, and music was getting faster. So, during the thirteenth century, sliders began to be replaced with keyboards using levers (Figure 10.6). Even these were a problem, though. The friction involved made these levers very hard to move, and players could not move them with the touch of a finger—they made a fist and hit them as hard as they could!

Throughout the fourteenth and early fifteenth centuries, large organs were being built all over Europe. Around 1380, the foot keyboard developed. The reason was not only that players had run out of fingers; it was because the levers for the very lowest notes were so incredibly hard to move that players needed the full force of their foot and leg to operate them. Although organs had wider ranges, they were not necessarily chromatic. Church music still used the chant modes for most of their music, and there were quite a few keyboards with only the "white key" notes, plus a B flat, and occasionally an F sharp, and sometimes a C sharp.

Germanic builders were almost always the builders of choice. When the duchy of Burgundy became the shining light of culture near the end of the Middle Ages, their builders were sent for to build organs as far away as Spain. The different courts of Europe exchanged letters often, and if one ruler obtained a really impressive organ, another would ask who built it, and then they would ask the same builder to produce one for their own court. In the fifteenth century, organs were beginning to have unprecedented numbers of pipes. One built in Amiens, France, in 1429 had 2,500 pipes. Of course, nobody *needed* to use 2,500 pipes at

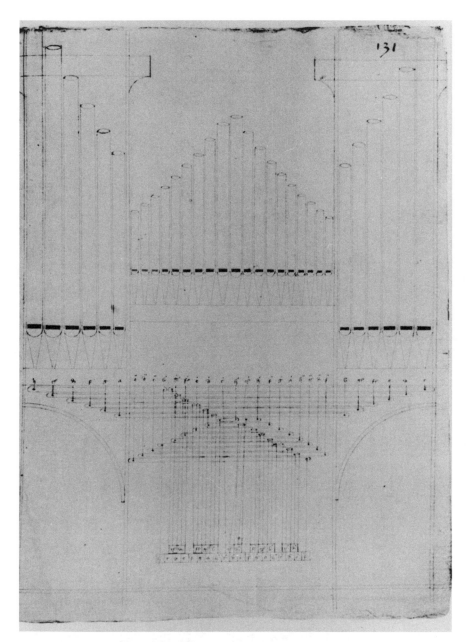

Figure 10.6 A late Middle Ages' rendition of an organ pipe and keyboard setup. Facsimile of *Les Traites* by Henri-Arnaut de Zwolle and other Anonymous contributors. Basel, Tours, London: Barenreiter Kassel, 1972.

one time. So why build so many? The reason is that organs were beginning to use different "timbres" or tone colors, which were made possible by having multiple pipes for each note, using various-sized bores or a variety of materials such as metals and woods. The player selected which kinds of pipes would sound by pulling out "stops," or slides, each of which would close or open up an entire set of pipes.

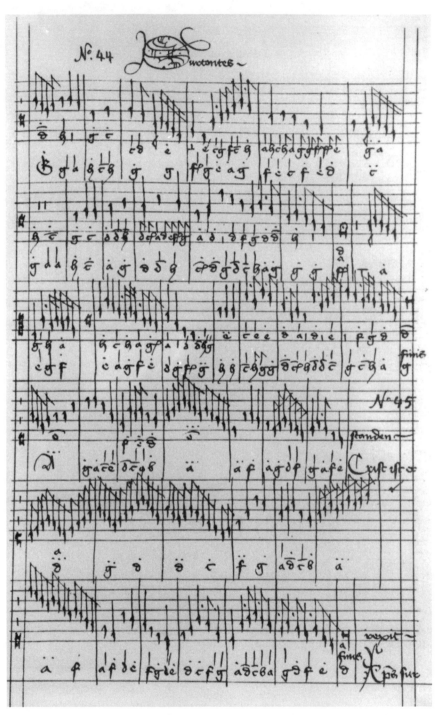

Figure 10.7 Organ notation of the Middle Ages. This specialized notation for a particular instrument is known as tablature. Facsimilie of *Das Buxheimer Orgelbuch*. Basel: Barenreiter-Verlag, 1960.

Present-day organs still employ a wide range of stops, often still in the shape of knobs to be pulled out like slides. We sometimes hear the expression "pulling out all the stops" to mean someone employing every possible dramatic effect trying to be persuasive. By the fifteenth century there were also reed stops, in which the wind, instead of being blown against an edge as in traditional organ pipes, forced a metal reed to vibrate against the base of a short tube, as in a modern clarinet or saxophone. The result was a shrill sound that people in Flanders and Germanic areas liked, but was not as popular in England and Italy.

Finally, the slides and levers used to sound the notes were replaced with balanced, spring-driven keys. Curiously, the Romans had developed this technology centuries earlier, but it was lost until at least the thirteenth century. With the new keys, players could keep up with the music without having to have the equivalent of a prize fight to produce a melody!

The large organs had their own notation system, known as tablature (Figure 10.7). This varied from place to place, but at least scholars have some idea of what was being played and how. For instance, if a tablature shows three lines, then scholars assume two keyboards and a set of foot pedals.

There are many more pictures and carvings of portative organs than of positive ones. That is because positive organs were part of the interior of a church, which was not often depicted. It was more common to show a single player of an instrument. Also, it would be hard for a single painting or carving to show the player(s) in front and the blowers in back. As a result, not a lot is known about actual performance practice on the positive organ. Only one depiction is famous for its detail: the Ghent Altarpiece, which was painted by the Van Eyck brothers during the Burgundian heyday.

HARPSICHORD

The harpsichord is so identified with the Baroque era that it seems impossible to imagine them during the Middle Ages, yet this is when they were developed. The idea came from the psaltery, and the early harpsichord has been likened to a mechanized psaltery. Like the psaltery, this instrument had strings that were plucked, but from a keyboard which worked a series of quill plectrums inside the body of the instrument (Figure 10.8). Originally the harpsichord sat on a table and it was not until later that it acquired legs and stood on its own. For its time—the early fifteenth century—the harpsichord's four-octave range was huge. And because of its larger sounding board, it was louder than the psaltery. Known as the clavicembalo or cembalo (Italy), clavecin (France), or clavicymbel (Germany), this instrument arrived in the late Middle Ages, grew throughout the Renaissance, and hit its stride in the Baroque era.

SPINET

The spinet was another keyboard instrument with plucked strings. A crow-quill was raised and plucked the desired string when a key was depressed. Though

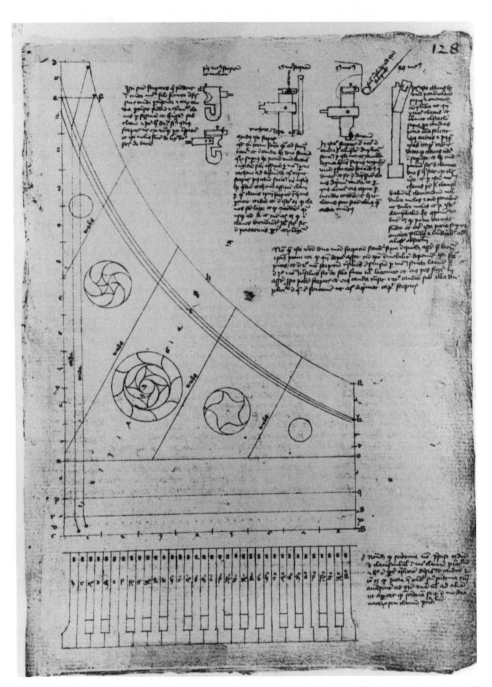

Figure 10.8 An early keyboard instrument, showing a fully chromatic keyboard and details of the key-striking mechanism. Facsimile of *Les Traites* by Henri-Arnaut de Zwolle and other Anonymous contributors. Basel, Tours, London: Barenreiter Kassel, 1972.

neither spinets nor harpsichords had much dynamic capability, they did have the advantage of volume. The spinet got its name from the Latin word for thorn: *spina*. Also known as the spinetto (Italy), schaschtbrett (Middle High German), eschiquier (French, from the word for "chessboard"), or virginal (from the Latin for rod, *virga*), the spinet was smaller than the harpsichord and had less of a range because its strings ran at right angles to the plectrums.

CLAVICYTHERIUM

This instrument also had a keyboard and plucked strings, but its strings sat upward instead of out, so that if the keyboard were on a table, the box holding the strings would be against the wall (Figure 10.9). Its workings were complicated, so it never gained great popularity, but its space-saving capabilities made it the ancestor of the modern upright piano.

CLAVICHORD

The clavichord owes its existence to the monochord. Even when the monochord had a movable bridge, it was still clumsy and time-consuming to reconfigure for each note. The answer was to add a keyboard. Now when a key was depressed, a wedge, or tangent, would swing and hit the string at the correct place. On the left side of each tangent was a piece of felt, which would deaden the entire left end of the string so that only the right side would sound. Now the monochord could play several notes on one string at the touch of a key.

The next step was to add more strings, which was possible because of the keyboard and hammer arrangement. A stained glass window from around 1440 shows an arrangement with six strings and twenty-six keys to hit them in various places to make twenty-six different notes. The clavichord's early name, *monacordys*, showed its origins, but later the Latin word for key, *clavis*, was added, and the *mono* part was dropped now that the instrument had multiple strings, so it became a clavichord. Early keyboards had only a diatonic scale with one "black" key, a B flat, as might be expected. Later, F sharp, C sharp, and eventually all the notes of the chromatic scale were added as music used more and more of the semitones.

The clavichord had advantages and disadvantages in comparison to plucked keyboard instruments. Its advantage was dynamic capabilities. By striking the keys harder or softer, a player could control how loudly or softly the sound came out. This made the clavichord a much more expressive instrument than plucked keyboard instruments. Also it could make a sort of vibrato, if the player held a key down and gently pulsed it. This was called *Bebung* (in German) and made the instrument even more expressive.

The disadvantage of the clavichord was lack of volume. It was never a loud instrument. Even if its tangents hit a double string, the sound was still weak. So the clavichord was always an intimate instrument, never incorporated into large

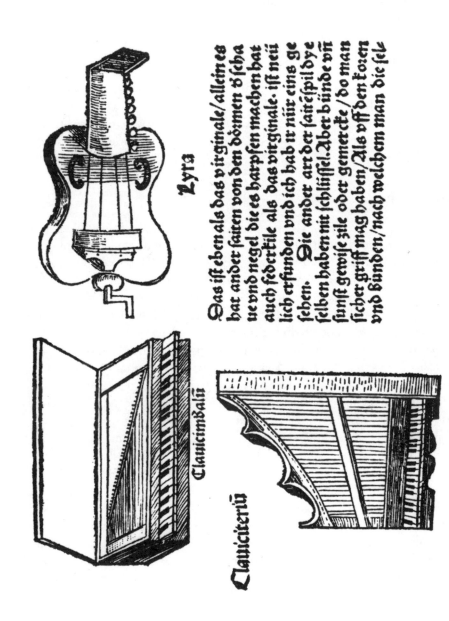

Zyra

Das ist eben als das virginale/alleines hat ander saiten von den dörmen oder ue vnd negel die es harpfen machen hat auch federtile als das virginale. ist neü lich erfunden vnd ich hab ir nür eins ge seben. Die ander art der saitespil dye selben haben mit schlüssel. Aber bünde vñ sunff gewise zile oder gemercte / do man sicher griff mag haben / Als vff den koren vnd Bunden / nach welchem man die sel

Clauicimbali

Clauiciteriū

Figure 10.9 An early harpsichord at upper left and a clavicytherium (an ancestor of the upright piano) at lower left. A hurdy-gurdy is shown at right. Facsimilie of *Musica Getuscht* (1511) by Sebastian Virdung. Paris, London, Basel: Barenreiter Kassel, 1970.

ensembles, as the harpsichord would be. It was said that the clavichord was "the only instrument on which one occupant of a double bed could play in the still watches of the night without disturbing the other."[3]

Even so, the clavichord was used throughout the Middle Ages, Renaissance, and Baroque eras and was still prized for its emotive capabilities in the Classical era by such composers as C. P. E. Bach (Johann Sebastian Bach's second son).

CHEKKER

This is one of history's mysteries. The chekker was a mechanism instead of a true instrument, and it could be used on either a clavichord or a harpsichord. It was said that using a chekker would change the sound of either instrument and "make" it into a different one, called a *dulce melos* (see the discussion of the dulcimer, under stringed instruments). All that survives of this mechanism are drawings and a description by Henri Arnaut, or Arnaut de Zwolle, a member of the Burgundian court who is not well-known but who made detailed drawings of several instruments before the invention of movable type. Scholars believe that this mechanism, said to be a "favorite of kings and princes," made a sort of early piano, almost three centuries before Cristofori is credited with having invented the latter instrument.[4]

PERCUSSION INSTRUMENTS

BELL-CHIMES

Bell-chimes, also known as cymbala, were used in late-Roman times and moved to Byzantium when the Western Empire fell. By the Middle Ages they had returned, and were very popular. Bell-chimes were various sizes of metal bells hung on a bar and hit with a hammer (Figure 10.10). Churches had been using bells for centuries to alert worshippers that it was time for Mass or to mark the Hours in monasteries. Now the tuned bells were used as a melodic device to keep choirs in tune, or as a special "color" to be played along with organs in church. By the thirteenth century, a mechanized set of bell-chimes emerged. Incorporating chimes into a clockwork allowed the bells to play a sacred tune at certain times throughout the day.

CARILLON

The carillon is a descendant of the cymbala. Taking their cue from the clockwork mechanism developed for the bell-chimes, towns—especially in Burgundian territory—began to set tuned, mechanically operated bells in their church towers. Each town wanted one better than those of its neighbors, and so carillons were built with fifty or more bells and thousands of pins on a rotating cylinder that turned at certain hours, hitting the bells and playing tunes. Church tower bells

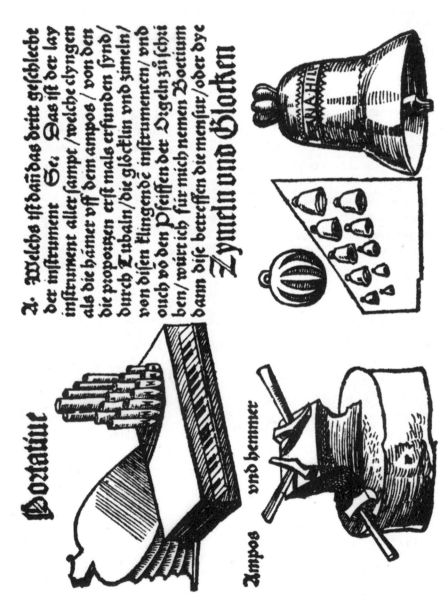

Figure 10.10 Bells, including a set of tuned bells. At upper left, a portative organ that could be played by one person. Facsimilie of *Musica Getutscht* (1511) by Sebastian Virdung. Paris, London, Basel: Barenreiter Kassel, 1970.

lead to city tower bells, which added mechanical figures appearing on the hour, and clocks of this type are still attractions in some European cities today.

KETTLEDRUM (NAKERS)

The kettledrums of the Middle Ages were not the thundering tympani of today. These drums were about the size of a human fist, were hung around the player's waist, and came west from Arab lands around the 1300s. There they had been known as *naqqara*. Called nakers (England), nacaire (France), nacara (Spain), or puke (pronounced POO-keh) (Germany), they were never played singly; there were always a pair. They were played with beaters shaped something like a tiny club. None of these have survived, so scholars have no real idea of the sound made, or whether they were tuned to the same pitch or to different pitches.

Over the Middle Ages, these drums began to be made bigger and bigger. Finally, in the fifteenth century, they culminated in big copper cauldrons with calf-skin stretched over the top (Figure 10.11). These were war drums, each pair slung over a horse's back and brought into battle along with trumpeters. Not everyone appreciated them. In 1511 musician and writer Virdung wrote about them, calling them "rumbling barrels" (*rumpelfessern*). He wrote that "the Devil himself must have invented [them] for the suppression of all sweet melodies and the whole art of music."[5]

SNARE DRUM

This drum, too, was not quite the same as the modern snare drum. It developed out of the drum used in pipe and tabor playing (see the discussion of woodwinds). On this drum, however, a long gut string was stretched across the top of the drum and rattled when the drum head was struck. That was the "snare." It did not make the metallic sound that today's snare makes, and it was smaller (about a foot in diameter), but it was a start.

OTHER DRUMS

Instead of the paired kettledrum, the *tympanum* was a single, hourglass-shaped drum played on both ends with the hands. There was also a long, cylindrical drum that was paired with the transverse flute and was, as the flute, a favorite with German and Swiss mercenary troops. This flute-drum combination eventually developed into the fife and drum corps of later ages.

TAMBOURINE

This instrument is exactly the same as today's tambourines. Then, as now, it was a one-sided drum with a bent-wood frame in which bells or small metal cymbals were set, which rang when the drum face was struck. Usually hit with the player's bare

Herpaucken Trumeln vnd dem paucklin

Dise baucken alle synd wie sye wellen / die machen vil onrűwe den Lerern frum
men alten leüten / den siechen vnd krancken / den andechtigen in den clöstern / die
zü lesen / zü studieren / vnd zü beten baßen / vnd ich glaub vnd halt es für war der
teüfel hab die erdacht vnd gemacht dann gantz kein hotlselig keit / nochgűts dar
an ist / sunder ein vertempffung / vnnd ein nyder truckung aller süßen melodeyen
vnd der gantzen Musica / Darumb ich wolgeachten kan / das ds Zympaniivil
eynander ding müß gewesen sein / das man zü dem dienst gottes gebraucht hatt /
dann yetz vnser baucken gemacht werden / vnd das wir on billich den namen de̅
tüfelischen instrument zü geben / das doch nit wirdig ist zü der Musica zü Braue

Figure 10.11 Small and large drums, and a pair of kettledrums. Facsimilie of *Musica Getutscht* (1511) by Sebastian Virdung. Paris, London, Basel: Barenreiter Kassel, 1970.

hand or shaken, tambourines were also sometimes thrown in the air and caught. Wildly popular in the Middle Ages, the tambourine inexplicably petered out during the Renaissance. It faded into the background as a folk instrument, and did not reappear until the nineteenth century, when Romantic-era composers wanted to evoke a Spanish or Arabian sound in their music.

JINGLE-RING

A variant of the tambourine, this was a hoop with metal leaves or tiny bells that jingled when the hoop was moved, but it did not have a drum head. The jingles, or "pellet bells," developed a life of their own and are known as "jingle bells" today. During the Middle Ages these bells were attached to costumes such as a court jester's, or during village festivals they could be attached to ceremonial costumes in order to chase away evil spirits.

TRIANGLE

This is another instrument which has not changed much over the years. A suspended metal rod bent into the shape of a triangle, it was struck with a straight metal rod and appeared later in the Middle Ages. Its only "improvement" was the addition of metal rings to the bottom of the triangle, which made a buzzing sound when the triangle was played.

CYMBALS

As with the kettledrum, these are not the cymbals of today that crash excitingly in marches. Cymbals of the Middle Ages were small metal plates fixed to the end of a set of tongs. Each hand held a tong set, and when the ends of the tong were pressed together, the slightly concave plates hit one another and made a lovely bell-like sound. Nowadays these would be called finger-cymbals.

Also known as zimbels (Middle High German) or cymbale (French), they began to be made in various sizes over the years. Some grew to the size of plates and had much higher domes than their smaller counterparts. Scholars believe that these various-sized cymbals were pitched instruments. At least they think so, because pairs of cymbals were tied to one another, most likely to make sure that one pitch of cymbal was not mixed with another.

JEW'S HARP

This instrument is neither Jewish nor a harp. It was already an "old" instrument by the Middle Ages, since it had been used to make music as far back as Roman times. Scholars believe that it was even old for the Romans, as Alexander the Great's troops probably brought it back from India in the fourth century B.C.! This was a small instrument with a frame that fit partially in the player's mouth. A thin

daß das/welches einer ein harpffen hat genennet/das heißt der ander eyn leyr/vñ herwiderumb/vnd der gleichen vil/Ich glaub auch/das in hundert jarn nechst vergangen alle instrumenta/so subtil/so schön/so güt/vnd so wol gestalt gemacht seind worden/Als sey Orpheus/noch Linus/noch Pan/noch Apollo/Noch keiner der poeten/hab gesehen oder gehöret/vnnd das mer ist müglich geachtet hab zü machen oder zü erdencken/Man findet auch sunst noch vil mer dotlicher instrumenta Die man auch für Musicalia achtet oder helet Als da seer Trummeln/Schelle/Jeger horn/Acker horn/Tüschellen Dütsche/vff dem basen

Auch ander mere/als pfeifflin auß den federkilen/lockpfeifflin der fogler/wachtelbeinlin/Lerchen pfeifflin/Waisen beinlin/Pfeiffen von strohelmen gemacht Pfeiffen von den safftigen rinden der böm/von den pletern der böm/das mã ge-

Figure 10.12 A collection of horns and percussion instruments. A jingle bell sits at lower left, and at the far right is a "Jew's harp." Facsimilie of *Musica Getutscht* (1511) by Sebastian Virdung. Paris, London, Basel: Barenreiter Kassel, 1970.

metal piece protruded out so that when the player struck it, the metal would vibrate (Figure 10.12). To change pitches, the player changed the shape of his mouth cavity and used harmonics to create a tune. Instruments of this type are sometimes still used in folk music.

NOTES

1. Karl Geiringer, *Instruments in the History of Western Music* (New York: Oxford University Press, 1978), pp. 58–59.

2. Ibid, p. 60.

3. Jeremy Montagu, *The World of Medieval and Renaissance Musical Instruments* (Canada: Douglas David & Charles Limited, 1976), p. 58.

4. Ibid., pp. 58–59.

5. Karl Geiringer, *Instruments in the History of Western Music* (New York: Oxford University Press, 1978), p. 88.

CHAPTER 11

DANCE MUSIC OF THE MIDDLE AGES

The brevity of this chapter reflects the lack of surviving dance music left to us from this era. While singing was esteemed and instrumental playing tolerated, dancing was roundly condemned by the Church during the Middle Ages, looked at with suspicion because of its pagan connotations. Some of the only early evidence we have that dancing was done at all comes from Church fathers scolding parish priests and their flocks for indulging in this passion. There are no "how to" books for dance during the Middle Ages, and much of the dance music was never written down.

And yet people did dance! A letter from a church elder to the priests of an entire parish complained that besides singing their psalms entirely too fast, also "caring nothing for the clerical state, they take part in dances and masques and day and night prowl around the streets and lanes of the city leading a riotous existence, singing and shouting."[1] An English church official warned that dancing and wrestling contests being held on church cemetery grounds would lead "to the scandal of the Church and the peril of souls."[2]

Most evidence for dancing comes from paintings and miniatures in manuscripts that show people obviously dancing. Some paintings show instruments being used. Pictorial evidence shows scholars which instruments were used, how people dressed, the kind of surroundings in which they were dancing, whether people paired off or danced in larger groups, and even sometimes in what sort of occasion (a wedding, perhaps) in which the dancing was done.

Dance tunes are believed to be the earliest surviving music written exclusively for instruments—that is, music without any text at all. Even so, just as people dance to songs today, there were also songs in the Middle Ages meant for people to dance to. As far as the music itself, there are about fifty surviving dance tunes from the thirteenth and fourteenth centuries. Apparently the works were written down because they were the most popular. Almost all of them are monophonic. Only a few written for keyboard are polyphonic.

CAROLE

From their scant sources, scholars have gleaned that from the twelfth to the fourteenth century, the most popular dance form was the "carole." This was a circle dance (or sometimes a line dance) with sung accompaniment. One, or all, of the dancers could do the singing, and instrumentalists could chime in and join the dance too. The carole is mentioned by medieval historian Jean Froissart (1333–1400), who wrote about young people dancing caroles and also estampies almost without pause, to the tune of a piper.

This early form of dance music evolved into the later, not-danced-to carol (see Chapter 6), and that in turn was the ancestor of our Christmas carols.

ESTAMPIE

The estampie is the dance from the Middle Ages with which people are most familiar. Estampies apparently came both with and without texts. But although some texts and some music have both survived, they have survived separately. We have music and words, but in only *one* instance do we have both, a work entitled "Kalenda Maya" (The First of May) from Raimbaut de Vaqueiras, a troubadour of the late twelfth century.

Music of the French estampie (called istampitta in Italian) had a form. Although it varied slightly in different areas of Europe, it was basically a string of short tunes called *puncta*, which followed one another without pause. Each punctum was repeated, with a first and second ending. The first ending had an *ouvert* or "open" cadence, and the second had a *clos* or "closed" cadence. After the closed ending of the first punctum, the performer played the second punctum with its open and closed endings, then the third, and so on. The number and length of puncta varied. Usually there were between four and seven of them.

Estampies were very popular in the thirteenth century and were still being danced in the fourteenth. More estampie tunes survive than other forms, possibly because of their popularity. A French chansonnier from the late thirteenth century called *Le Manuscrit du Roy* (The King's Manuscript) contains eleven dances, and eight of them are "royal estampies." There is also a *danse real*, a *danse*, and a third dance tune without an identification. They are all monophonic. Another source, the Robertsbridge Codex, is British and dates from around 1325. Three dance tunes are in this codex, but one is incomplete. Nobody knows whether these are actually British estampies, or whether they were copied from a French source. Scholars do believe that the music was intended to be played on a keyboard instrument, since it is in keyboard tablature and has two lines, one for each hand. An Italian source from the fourteenth century has fifteen dances. There are eight called *istampitta*, and they have titles consisting either of people's names or of words such as "Beginning of Joy." Four others are called *saltarelli*, one is a *trotto*, and there are two other unidentified dances. Of the estampies, some are French and some are Italian. The French ones are in a triple meter, whereas the Italians used either duple or compound meters. The Italian puncta also tended to be longer than the French.

PAIRED DANCES

The last two dances mentioned in the Robertsbridge Codex, having the titles "Tristan's Lament" and "La Manfredina," are paired dances. The first part of each piece is followed by a second work called a "Rotta." This is the first instance known of a paired set of dances, something that would become the norm during the late Renaissance and Baroque eras.

ST. VITUS'S DANCE AND TOTENTANZ

Two other dance forms became popular in the Middle Ages, but they had nothing to do with the joy of dance. The first was a kind of hysteric dancing that hit entire areas from time to time throughout Europe from the eleventh to the fifteenth century. Afflicted people would start jumping and leaping and twirling for hours or even days, leaving them exhausted, sometimes to the point of death. No music is associated with it, but its name has entered the modern lexicon as St. Vitus's dance.

The second is usually attributed to the Black Death years of 1347–1348, but it actually had begun before. The Totentanz, also known as the Dance of Death or the Danse Macabre, has been traced back as far as the thirteenth century. However, depictions of a dancing skeleton or group of dancing skeletons became more common after the plague years and continued during periodic plague outbreaks afterwards. Sometimes the skeletons are shown playing instruments, and sometimes they are shown in rotting clothes with the remnants of hair still clinging to their skulls as they enter a room full of partygoers or of a living person, as a grim reminder of the ultimate end of every human on Earth.

The Totentanz does have specific music associated with it, but it was written far after the Middle Ages was over. During the Romantic era of the nineteenth century, Danses Macabres became a musical form. The xylophone owes its inclusion into the orchestra to a composition titled *Danse Macabre* by French composer Camille Saint-Saëns that used the xylophone to represent the clacking bones of the dancing skeleton.

THE BASSE DANSE

The court of Burgundy in the late Middle Ages raised dance to a place of honor. The main dance there seems to have been the *basse danse*. No real descriptions remain of its medieval dance steps, but it seems to have been a slower processional-type dance with the dancers paired in couples. Later, in the Renaissance, the dance became faster and had music specific to it, which has survived. Scholars believe that the basse danse evolved into several later dance forms, which eventually provided sets of music known as dance suites.

NOTES

1. Nigel Wilkins, *Music in the Age of Chaucer,* 2nd edition, with Chaucer Songs (Bury St. Edmunds, UK: St. Edmundsbury Press, Ltd., 1995), p. 98.
2. Ibid.

CHAPTER 12

THE END OF THE MIDDLE AGES

Every age has an artificial line of demarcation setting it off from the age that came before. The end of the Middle Ages and beginning of the Renaissance is set at 1450. Actually, the years 1453 and 1454 were pivotal in thrusting Europe toward the Renaissance, and the three major contributors were the Peace of Lodi (1454), the end of the Hundred Years' War (1453) and the Fall of Constantinople (1453).

THE PEACE OF LODI (TREATY OF LODI OR TREATY OF VENICE)

Italian city-states were a fractious group, always at war with one another. But in 1454 three of the major offenders—Milan, Venice, and Florence—brokered a cessation of hostilities that set boundaries and confirmed rulers in areas of question. Other smaller cities signed a nonaggression pact among themselves, and all became part of the Italic League. Even the Vatican joined.

Although it was already shattered by the 1490s, this resting time had several effects: (1) the creation of "embassies" so that each area could keep an eye on the others, (2) time to develop the trade and banking interests that would bring Italy the money to fuel the Renaissance, and (3) the idea, at least, of an Italian state—even though the actual fact would be hundreds of years later.

THE END OF THE HUNDRED YEARS' WAR

For generations, France and England had dragged the rest of Europe into its seemingly eternal tug-of-war over French territory claimed by the English crown. Of course, the war had not been fought every day for a hundred years. There were dozens of treaties, and years when nothing in particular happened as well as years of great hardship and suffering. The sticking point was the area of Calais, which is the closest area between France and England. Basically, England worried that a French force gathered at Calais could attack England at any time. But the French insisted on keeping it as part of their territory. Through the war years, legendary characters such as Joan of Arc and legendary battles such as Agincourt came and went. Nobles, princes, and kings were captured and ransomed. Countries other than the two at odds sided with one or the other and provided funds or military assistance. The territory of Burgundy shifted from one side to the other. And although the balance of power swung back and forth many times, in the end, France prevailed.

When the Burgundian Dukes switched their support back to France (see Chapter 8), the balance of power shifted fatally away from England. By 1453 France had regained all of the territory held by England except one place—Calais, which remained under English control.

The effect of the end of the Hundred Years' War meant that Europe was no longer draining itself and its treasuries in useless in-fighting. Britain gave up its French ambitions and began to build itself up as a sea power instead. In France, as in Italy, the seeds of nationalism had been planted by the experience of banding together and fighting as one.

THE FALL OF CONSTANTINOPLE

While the once-powerful Byzantine Empire shrank, Eastern Islamic forces were growing. The Ottoman Empire, in particular, conquered large swaths of territory and threatened to cross the Danube into Western Europe. Unlike Arabs, who disdained firearms as dishonorable, warriors of the Ottoman Empire used all manner of firearms enthusiastically.

As early as the 1440s the Byzantine Emperors who foresaw the Ottoman danger had requested help from Western Europe in the form of a Crusade. But the only help that came was defeated before the Western army ever reached Constantinople.

By 1451, Ottoman Sultan Mehmet II (also known as Muhammed Al Fatih) had cut Constantinople off by blocking the Bosporus strait with newly constructed forts. All ships entering had to pay a heavy toll, or they would be sunk. To prove its point, a Venetian vessel that tried to sail through was sunk and its crew of thirty taken prisoner and sentenced to death. The message was brutally clear. Western Europe was to stay out.

Now desperate, the last Byzantine Emperor attempted to rejoin the Eastern and Western Churches in a last-ditch effort to save his city and the shreds of the Byzantine Empire. The move backfired, as his own people saw this as a capitulation to the Western Pope. Ottoman forces began conquering their way toward Constantinople at the beginning of the year 1453.

If things could be made any worse for the besieged city, it was by having to take care of the thousands of refugees fleeing in from the surrounding area, crowding the city and taking up precious resources. The city walls were so long that it was impossible to adequately defend them, and the Sultan's forces bombarded them mercilessly every day. But every night the citizenry came out to repair the damage. The result was a stalemate lasting months.

In April four ships from Genoa managed to fight through the Ottoman navy to get supplies to the city. Furious, the Sultan tightened controls. He called up a fleet of over sixty ships, all carrying men and supplies. The Ottomans again bombarded the walls, and also began tunneling under them. Desperate, the city sent messengers to slip through enemy lines to plead for help from the West. Though the forces from Genoa stayed to the end, no more came.

Impatient, the Sultan prepared a grand attack to begin on May 29. Two assaults failed, but a third managed to breach the walls in one small area. It was enough. Soon enemy flags were seen flying from the walls. Ottoman soldiers inside opened other gates, and the rest poured in. The killing, raping, and looting went on seemingly forever. Those who lived would live as slaves. The great Cathedral of Hagia Sophia became a mosque.

Europe, though culpable in the great city's defeat, was horrified. A Christian kingdom—even an Eastern one—had fallen to Islamic forces. There was a great flurry of calls for Crusades, after the fact, to reclaim Constantinople for the Holy Mother Church, but nothing came of them.

Those who had read the handwriting on the wall, and who could afford to leave, journeyed back to the place their ancestors had originally left—Rome (see Chapter 1), or at least to the Italian peninsula. Escapees of the carnage also flooded into Italy as refugees. They all brought as many of their possessions as possible. Many of those things were precious books and scrolls. The cynicism and lack of faith fostered by the *trecento* era (see Chapter 4) had left Italians less squeamish about reading the thoughts of pagan writers. Italy was ready to receive the "lost" knowledge of the ancient Greeks and Romans that had been preserved by the Byzantines. In fact, they welcomed the reintroduction of ancient thought.

This sudden influx of knowledge into Italy, added to the relative calm brought by the Peace of Lodi and riches brought by peacetime trade made Italy the new cultural spotlight, taking the place of France. Cultural pursuits were helped along by enriched states such as Venice hiring the excellent musicians trained by their trading partner Flanders (see Chapter 8). And the Franco-Flemish composers working in Italy added their highly evolved musical knowledge to the Italian love of melody, thus producing the music of the Renaissance.

FOR FURTHER READING

The following is by no means exhaustive. But if readers have had their curiosity sparked and would like to know more about the music of the Middle Ages, or about life in those times, it is the author's hope that these resources may be of use.

BOOKS CONCERNING MUSIC AND THE MIDDLE AGES

Bonner, Anthony (Ed. and Trans.). *Songs of the Troubadours* (New York: Schocken Books, 1972).

Geiringer, Karl. *Musical Instruments* (New York: Oxford University Press, 1945).

McKinnon, James (Ed.). *Music and Society: Antiquity and the Middle Ages from Ancient Greece to the 15th Century* (Englewood Cliffs, NJ: Prentice Hall, 1991).

Montagu, Jeremy. *The World of Medieval and Renaissance Musical Instruments* (Vancouver, Canada: Douglas David & Charles, 1976).

Nappholz, Carol Jane. *Unsung Women: The Anonymous Female Voice in Troubadour Poetry* (New York: Peter Lang Publishing, 1994).

Reese, Gustav. *Music in the Middle Ages with an Introduction on the Music of Ancient Times* (New York: W.W. Norton & Company, 1940).

Seay, Albert. *Music in the Medieval World.* 2nd edition (Englewood Cliffs, NJ: Prentice-Hall, 1975).

Weiss, Piero, and Richard Taruskin. *Music in the Western World, a History in Documents* (New York: Schirmer Books, 1984).

Wilhelm, James J. *Seven Troubadours: The Creators of Modern Verse* (University Park: The Pennsylvania State University Press, 1970).

Wilkins, Nigel. *Music in the Age of Chaucer.* 2nd edition, with Chaucer Songs (Bury St. Edmunds, UK: St. Edmundsbury Press, 1995).

Yudkin, Jeremy. *Music in Medieval Europe*. Prentice Hall History of Music Series, edited by H. Wiley Hitchcock (Englewood Cliffs, NJ: Prentice Hall, 1989).

BOOKS CONCERNING RELATED ARTS IN THE MIDDLE AGES

Happe, Peter (Ed.). *English Mystery Plays*. 2nd edition (Harmondsworth, UK: Penguin Books, 1979).

BOOKS ABOUT LIFE IN THE MIDDLE AGES

Baker, Alan. *The Knight* (Hoboken, NJ: John Wiley & Sons, 2003).

Brereton, Geoffrey (Selector/Trans./Ed.). *Froissart Chronicles*. 4th edition (Harmondsworth, UK: Penguin Books, 1981).

Cantor, Norman F. *Medieval History: The Life and Death of a Civilization* (New York: Macmillan, 1963).

Collis, Louis. *Memoirs of a Medieval Woman, the Life and Times of Margery Kempe* (New York: Harper & Row, 1964).

Gies, Joseph, and Frances Gies. *Life in a Medieval City* (Toronto: Fitzhenry & Whiteside, 1969).

Heywood, Colin. *A History of Childhood* (Cambridge, UK: Polity Press, 2001).

Lewis, Archibald R. *Nomads and Crusaders* A.D. *1000–1368* (Bloomington: Indiana University Press, 1988).

Lilley, Keith D. *Urban Life in the Middle Ages 1000–1450* (Houndsmills, UK: Palgrave, 2002).

Tuchman, Barbara W. *A Distant Mirror: The Calamitous 14th Century* (New York: Ballantine Books, 1978).

Tyler, William R. *Dijon and the Valois Dukes of Burgundy* (Norman: University of Oklahoma Press, 1971).

SOME USEFUL WEBSITES (FOR LISTENING OR SEARCHING TO BUY)

Magna Tune

www.emusic.com

www.classicsonline.com

(Also try Web pages for Performers of Middle Ages Music, listed in the Discography)

FILMS ABOUT THE MIDDLE AGES

Alexander Nevsky
Becket
El Cid
Henry V
The Lion in Winter
The Name of the Rose
The Return of Martin Guerre
The Seventh Seal
The Virgin Spring
The War Lord

PARTIAL DISCOGRAPHY
OF MIDDLE AGES MUSIC

The following are CDs and the names of groups who record music of the Middle Ages. A Web search on the name of a composer or genre of Middle Ages music will also yield results.

RECORDINGS

Canticles of Ecstasy: Hildegard von Bingen. Sequentia. Ensemble for Medieval Music with Woman's Vocal Ensemble, 1994. Co-production of BMG Music (New York) and Westdeuscher Rundfunk (Cologne). BMG Classics 05472077320-2

Carmina Burana: Medieval Songs. The Harvard University Choir with the Boston Camerata, Joel Cohen, dir. 1996. Paris: Erato 0630-14987-2

An English Ladymass: Medieval Chant and Polyphony. Anonymous IV. France: Harmonia Mundi HMU 90780

From Spain to Spain. Vox. Sausalito, CA: Read Music

La Lira D'Esperia: The Medieval Fiddle. Jordi Savali and Pedro Estevan. France: Auvidis E-8547

Love's Illusion: Music from the Montpellier Codex, 13th Century. Anonymous IV. France: Harmonia Mundi HMU 907-109

Miracles of Sant'iago: Music from the Codex Calixtinus. Anonymous IV. France: Harmonia Mundi HMU 907156

Remdih. Czech Republic: Cesky Rozhlas. Contact: Studio Macac, Tel. 00420-47-52-1-686

Le Roman de Fauvel. Ensemble Project Ars Nova with the Boston Camerata, Joel Cohen, dir. 1995. France: Erato 4509-96392-2

Songs and Dances of the Middle Ages. Sonus. Troy, NY: The Dorian Group DIS-80109.

PERFORMERS OF MIDDLE AGES MUSIC

Anonymous IV
Boston Camerata
Choir of the Monks of Saint-Pierre de Solesmes
Early Music Consort of London
Ensemble for Early Music
Ensemble Gilles Binchois
Ensemble Organum
Harmonia Mundi
Hilliard Ensemble
Jubilatores
Medieval Ensemble of London
New York Pro Musica
Piffaro
Remdih
Schola Hungarica
Sequentia
Tallis Scholars

GLOSSARY

Some definitions have been taken or adapted from *Funk & Wagnall's Standard Encyclopedia Dictionary* (Chicago: J. G. Ferguson Publishing Company, 1968).

Abbess—The Superior of a community of nuns.

Abbot—The Superior of a community of monks.

Accidental—A sharp, flat, or natural sign indicating that the following note is outside the normal key shown by the key signature.

Adversary contact—Contact as enemies; hostile contact.

Allegory—A presentation in which a moral truth is presented through fictional events and/or characters.

Annul—To declare null and void, as a marriage that has been found not to have been valid in the first place.

Apocalypse—The last days of Earth, according to the Christian Bible.

Arthurian Legends—Stories about or involving the legendary King Arthur and the Knights of the Round Table.

Ascetic—A person who leads a very self-denying life, usually for religious purposes.

Assimilation—Becoming like another thing or culture into which one is becoming absorbed.

Atonal—Lacking a central key area, in which no note is a tonic or "home" note.

Avarice/Avaricious—Greed/greedy.

Avocation—Hobby.

Axiom—A statement whose truth is taken as the basis for a system of logical argument.

Bastard—Child of unmarried parents.

Bosporus—A strait, or narrow seaway, separating Asian and European Turkey, and on whose shores Constantinople (now Istanbul) stands.

Brigand—Robber.

Cadence—A musical formula indicating the end of a phrase, movement, or entire work.

Canon—A composition in which one or more voices follows the first, using the same melody.

Canon Law—Rules of faith and life enacted by a Church council.

Canonized—Declared to be a saint, worthy of veneration by the entire Church.

Catacomb—Underground burial chamber, accessed by passageways.

Chamois—A mountain antelope of Europe and Western Asia.

Chromatic—Proceeding by semitones, or half-steps.

Clef—A symbol placed at the beginning of a musical staff to indicate the pitches associated with the specific lines and spaces.

Cleric—A member of the clergy; a churchman (but not necessarily a priest).

Coat of Arms—A marking or insignia representing a person or family.

Compound Meters—A combination of two meters, such as two groups of three beats.

Conical—Smaller at one end and larger at the other.

Convent—A religious community for women (i.e., nuns).

Culminate—Reach a high point or final result.

Cylindrical—Having the same circumference from one end to the other.

Delineation—A portrayal or description; an outline or boundary.

Diaspora—Dispersion or scattering of a group of people (culture, tribe, race).

Diatonic—Constructed of whole tones and semitones in the order tone, tone, semitone, tone, tone, tone, semitone, . . . beginning at any point in the cycle.

Dichotomy—Division into two separate parts.

Disparate—Different; separate in essence.

Ditty—A short, simple song.

Dolor—Sorrow; anguish.

Dome—A roof resembling an upturned cup.

Double Bar—A pair of vertical lines across a staff, indicating a change or ending of a work.

Duchy—An area ruled by a duke.

Duple Rhythm—Rhythm in groups of two beats.

Ecclesiastical—Pertaining to church matters.

Errant—Wandering in search of adventure.

Eucharist—A Christian ritual in which (according to Catholic faith) the body and blood of Christ are received under the appearance of bread and wine.

Eulogy—Words spoken or written in praise of another (generally at their death).

Euphemism—Substitution of one word or phrase for another more blunt, cruder one.

Excommunication—Being cut off from the sacraments, worship, privileges, or fellowship of the Christian Church.

Fad—A temporary amusement or style.

Fifth—The interval between one pitch and another pitch four diatonic scale degrees away from it, having a frequency ratio of exactly or very nearly 3:2.

Florid—Excessively ornate.

Foible—A personal weakness or failing.

Formulaic—Done according to a prescribed or exact method.

Fourth—The interval between one pitch and another pitch three diatonic scale degrees away, having a frequency ratio of exactly or very nearly 4:3.

Fret—A ridge placed across the fingerboard of a stringed instrument so that the player can raise the pitch of a string by a definite amount by pressing it above the ridge.

Giotto—Painter, architect, sculptor who worked in Florence, Italy, until his death in 1337.

Glagolitic—An early Slavic script.

Go-fer—Slang term for an employee whose duty is to "go for" whatever is needed.

Habitat—Dwelling, living place.

Half Note—A note taking half the time of a whole note; generally, two beats.

Heresy—A belief contrary to the doctrines of the religion from which it originated.

Horizontal—Parallel to the horizon; lying down.

Humors—In ancient Greek and medieval medicine, the four bodily fluids that must be in balance for good health.

Innovation—Something new.

Internecine—Destructive to both sides of a conflict as well as to the greater political whole to which the two sides belong.

Interval—The difference between two pitches. An interval of a given size corresponds to a given frequency ratio.

Intricacy—Complicated or involved.

Investiture—A ceremony to recognize a person's authority or office.

Joust—Formal combat between two knights on horseback.

Lay—(adj.) Not clergy.

Leger Line—A short horizontal line added above or below the staff lines to enable writing a note above or below the staff.

Lied—(pronounced "leed"; plural *Lieder*) German word for song.

Litany—A formalized prayer in which a leader's supplications are each met with a fixed congregational response.

Liturgy—A formalized ritual for public worship.

Lombards—A Germanic tribe in northern Italy.

Magi—Priests among the Persians and Medes; most famously, the three "Wise Men" who paid homage to the newborn baby Jesus in Bethlehem.

Magyar—Hungarian.

Manger—A trough holding feed for cattle or horses.

Martial—Pertaining to military life or war.

Millennium—1,000 years.

Misnomer—A name wrongly applied.

Mode—A set of pitches available for melodies, with certain pitches having specific roles, such as the pitch on which the melody ends or the pitch on which recited passages are sung.

Monastery—A religious community for men (monks).

Moor—A Moslem of mixed Berber and Arab ancestry, particularly in Spain.

Moslem/Islamic—A believer in the Islamic faith.

Motive (Musical)—Fragment of a melody.

Mute—Unable to speak.

Mysticism—A way of life in which the supernatural is strongly emphasized and possibly directly experienced.

Neume—In chant, one or more notes extending over a syllable or part of a syllable and written as a unit.

Obituary—Published notice of a person's death, usually with a short biography.

Octave—The interval between two pitches with a frequency ratio of 2:1.

Ornate—Elaborately decorated.

Ostrogoths—East Goths, Germanic tribe that established a kingdom in northern Italy from 493 to 555 A.D.

Paramount—Chiefly important.

Partisan—A devotee to a cause or a political party.

Passover—Commemoration of the escape of the Israelites from slavery in Egypt, during which death took every firstborn child in Egypt but "passed over" the Israelite families.

Pastry—A sweet baked article of food, usually made with a dough crust.

Pelt—Skin of an animal.

Penitent—A person performing an act of acknowledgment and sorrow for a misdeed.

Petitioner—A person making a formal request.

Pitch—A characteristic of a musical tone representing vibration frequency in cycles per second.

Portico—An open space with a roof supported by columns.

Predecessor—Something or someone already gone before.

Prefecture—An ancient Roman province or political unit modeled on such a province, governed by a prefect.

Prohibition—A decree forbidding something.

Quarter Note—A note with one-quarter the length of a whole note, generally one beat.

Ravenna—A city in North Central Italy, near the Adriatic Sea.

Rescind—To take back or repeal.

Revenue—Government income.

Ridicule—Mock or make fun of.

Rue—Regret.

Sacred—Dedicated to religious use.

Sainte-Chapelle—A Parisian church known for its stained glass windows.

Satire—Writing in which vice or folly is held up to ridicule.

Satrap—Governor of a province in ancient Persia.

Scale System—An arrangement of available pitches in ascending or descending order throughout the interval of an octave.

Scatological—Obscene.

Secular—Worldly; distinguished form spiritual.

Seemly—Appropriate, decent, fitting.

Shriven—Having had one's sins forgiven by receiving the Christian sacrament of confession or penance.

Siege—Surrounding a fortified area with the intention of capturing it, preventing the defenders from receiving food or escaping.

Sixth—An interval between one pitch and another pitch five diatonic scale degrees away, having a frequency ratio close to 5:3 or 8:5.

Slavic—Pertaining to several Eastern European peoples or their languages, derived from a common ancestor.

Smallpox—Acute, highly communicable viral disease characterized by the eruption of deep-seated pustules that result in permanent scars.

Sterling—Absolutely the best; genuine; valuable.

Stratification—Separation of social groups by class, economic means, or status.

Subservient—Subordinate.

Surmise—Guess; suppose.

Swabia—A major duchy in Germany of the Middle Ages.

Sycophant—A servile flatterer.

Syncopate—Rhythmic placing of a note so that its accent does not coincide with the metric beat.

Text—Words in a literary or musical work.

Thicket—Dense bush, thick shrubbery.

Third—An interval between one pitch and another pitch two diatonic scale degrees away, having a frequency ratio close to 6:5 or 5:4.

Tract—A short treatise.

Treatise—Formal written account of a subject.

Triad—A chord of three tones, two of which are a fifth apart and the other is a third apart from either of the other two.

Triple Rhythm—A rhythm in groups of three beats.

Unison—Two voices sounding the same pitch.

Vegetarian—A person who eats no meat or meat products.

Vernacular—The local native language.

Vertical—Upright; standing; the opposite of horizontal.

Vicissitudes—Changes of fortune.

Vikings—Scandinavian warriors who harried the coasts of Europe from the eighth to the tenth century.

Visigoths—West Goths, a Germanic tribe that invaded Rome and eventually settled into areas of present-day France and Spain.

Whole Note—A note that encompasses all the beats available within a bar; usually 4.

Zenith—The top, the pinnacle.

INDEX

About the Author

SUZANNE LORD is Associate Professor of Flute and Music History at Southern Illinois University, Carbondale. She has previously written *Music from the Age of Shakespeare* (2003).